MANAGING THE CITY: The Aims and Impacts of
Urban Policy

MANAGING THE CITY

The Aims and Impacts of Urban Policy

Edited by BRIAN ROBSON

BARNES & NOBLE BOOKS
Totowa, New Jersey

© 1987 Brian Robson

First published in the USA 1987 by
Barnes & Noble Books,
81 Adams Drive,
Totowa, New Jersey, 07512

Library of Congress Cataloging-in-Publication Data

Managing the city.

Includes index.
1. City planning — Great Britain — Congresses.
2. Urban policy — Great Britain — Congresses.
3. Urban renewal — Great Britain — Congresses. I. Robson,
Brian Turnbull.
HT169.G7M36 1987   307.7′64′0941   87-1827
ISBN 0-389-20731-4

Printed and bound in Great Britain

Contents

Introduction

Scholars and story-tellers have vied with each other over the centuries to reach the heart of 'The Matter of Britain'. Despite their endeavours, the truth about the elusive Arthur — *regis quondam regisque futuri* — escapes us. It is in its elliptical nature that the charm of the Arthurian story lies. Who would remember an obscure warrior chief from the Dark Ages were it not for the accretion of legend and the busy literary and academic industry which has grown from those tales? Clear away these luxuriant growths and we are left with very little that we can cling to. Indeed, for most of us the legend has itself become fact and the erudite books about the real site and nature of Arthur and his court — if ever he or it existed — pale into insignificance beside the mesmerising effect of the Round Table, the band of knights, the Holy Grail, and the sword Excalibur. Similarly, much of the vast amount of knowledge and research into our modern world assumes the simplicity of heroic myths. Much of that simplicity surfaces in school text books or on popular television programmes or in the distillations of teachers and lecturers. From there it becomes entrenched as popular wisdom and, as in the Arthurian legends, fact and fiction become inextricably entangled. Not least is this so in the making of urban policy.

The city — itself once thought suitable only for the myth-makers of Utopian landscapes, as Lewis Mumford suggested — has now (whether large or small, modern or ancient, developed or developing) become in the twentieth century the quarry of a wide range of practitioners in both old and new academic disciplines; it has been dissected and described through the eyes and pens of journalists, dramatists, photographers, artists, novelists, poets and, the great gurus of our age, the TV pundits. On the academic front, urban history, urban sociology, urban geography, urban studies confront us at every turn. And, of course, since the late 1960s, British policy-makers have increasingly turned their attention to the city with policies such as the Urban Programme or Urban Development Grants, or with agencies such as Urban Development Corporations, and the welter of other policies and bodies set up to tackle 'the problem of the city'. It is not an overstatement to talk of an urban oracular proliferation.

Awareness of the problems of British cities has waxed and waned among public and politicians: apathy has been interspersed with periods of panicky and fatalistic concern prompted by the intermittent upwelling of the latest riot or the newest report. The message that I hope this book purveys is that the future of cities is not necessarily as bleak as the common fatalism might suggest — that there *is* a future as well as a past to large cities. Some part, at least, of the urban problem stems from the unfavourable myths and stereotypes of the city which we carry with us as the baggage of our cultural history. The problems faced by our large old cities in coming to terms with the radically new world to which they must accommodate are indeed awesome, but there are many steps that public policy could take to make the transition less cathartic and less problematical. We need both to be more aware of the issues and hence of the unintended effects that policy decisions can have and also to develop urban policy frameworks which are more consistent and longer-term.

The contributions to the book stem from the annual meeting of the British Association for the Advancement of Science which was held at the University of Strathclyde in Glasgow in 1985. There could be no more appropriate location to consider the issues of urban decline and urban change. Glasgow is at once the worst and the best of cities. It has for long been everyone's idea of the most deprived and most run-down of the large cities of Britain; the Gorbals and 'Wine Alley' were for long archetypes, potent images of the squalor and decay which in varying degrees have become synonymous with the received wisdom about what has become of the large industrial city. The collapse of the economy, not only of the city's economy but also of the encompassing regional economy of Strathclyde, appears to have undermined any defence of the economic rationale of the city itself. If ever a policy of 'triage' was to be put into effect, Glasgow must certainly have been the prime candidate for being first in the queue at the executioner's stall. Yet today, even though the economic indicators of the city's future are little less grim, it is Glasgow's resilience in accommodating to change which is the most striking impression that its growing stream of visitors take away with them. The refurbishment of tenements; the growth of private housing in a city which had long had the most monolithic stock of council housing in its centre; the investment in new factory units in the Eastern Area; the development of the Exhibition Centre; and the unquenchable ebullience of its people: all of these have now become potent symbols of the possibilities of turning around the fortunes of cities — given resources, political will and a competence to deliver urban-oriented policy. As President of Section E at the Strathclyde meeting, I invited a number of papers on the theme of urban policy from a mixture of academics and practitioners. The following chapters are revised versions of some of these papers.

The themes which they address are ones of pressing moment to anyone concerned with the future of our cities. Some of the work on which the chapters draw derives from a major research initiative funded by the Economic and Social Research Council through its Environment and Planning Committee which I chaired for the first four years of its life. The scene is set with a broad review of the legacy of attitudes which we bring to bear on the city (Chapter 1). This suggests that, as much as anything intrinsically 'wrong' with the city, it has been public policy which has unwittingly contributed to many of the urban problems that we now face and therein lie some of the policy directions which could help to turn around the fortunes of large cities. The themes of this chapter are echoed in what follows. Paul Cheshire (Chapter 2) sets a comparative picture by placing the British urban problem in the context of other European countries, drawing on his major research programme in the EEC and suggesting not only the depth of the social and economic problems in British cities but also that such problems are not absent from the cities of mainland Europe despite its later industrial start. He sees the future role of cities as administrative centres not unlike that of major cities before industrialism. Two examples from specific British cities then follow. At one end of the spectrum, Bill Lever looks at the Glasgow case against the emerging pattern of post-industrialism (Chapter 3). He suggests the mixed success of some of the many initiatives which have been developed to tackle the economic problems of the city; with many of the problems merely having been displaced to the fringe of council estates and yet with some specific schemes which have been successfully targeted on the needy. At the other extreme, Martin Boddy looks at the supposed success story of Bristol, which is popularly seen as having made a successful accommodation to the social and economic changes of the past decade, and of the M4 Corridor of which Bristol is the western extreme (Chapter 4). His work argues convincingly that public investment has played no small part in sustaining the local economy of the area. If Bristol's supposed success is popularly — if incorrectly — associated with high technology, the chapter by John Goddard and Andy Gillespie takes up the broader regional implications of technical change (Chapter 5). They contrast the potential benefits of increasing equity which might be associated with the 'information economy' with the more likely effects that incremental change to the hierarchical development of information networks will *reinforce* the benefits of existing concentrations and will work to the detriment of northern areas.

Even if the economic rationale of the large old cities continues to look precarious, the housing and infrastructure patterns can provide rather more hopeful indicators. It is to improvements to the physical environment that local-authority approaches have traditionally turned and the following four chapters consider housing improvement, the land issue and the role of planners. Duncan Maclennan shows, in Glasgow since the middle 1970s, the way in which a well-resourced public-sector programme of rehabilitation of housing and the environment has provided the base of a new confidence on which private-sector investment has expanded within the inner city (Chapter 6). Alice Coleman takes up some of the issues of how the design of housing developments might be improved so as to avoid the vandalism and anti-social behaviour that has characterised many high-rise developments (Chapter 7). Her suggestions clearly need to be read not as alternatives but as complements to the better management of estates and the involvement of tenants. Bryan MacGregor, David Adams and A. E. Baum explore the vexed question of vacant land in cites (Chapter 8). Urban land values have proved remarkably resistant to adjusting downwards in response to lack of demand or excess supply. They argue that the commonly-used comparative methods of valuation are inappropriate to a market in which there are few sales and a declining economy and that the blockage thus created presents obstacles to the process of development in inner areas. Derek Lyddon considers the roles of planners in their new guise as both marketers of municipalities and as economic development agents (Chapter 9). He sees the traditional physical development plans and the newly-emerging economic planning process as being essentially complementary. Again, Scotland serves as a striking exemplar, with a hierarchy of national guidelines, structure and local plans, and with a central role being played by its Development Agency.

4

Finally, to look at the other side of the coin, David Grafton and N. Bolton look at 'counter-urbanisation' from the rural perspective of North Devon (Chapter 10). It has been in the small and free-standing towns and the rural areas that population growth has occurred in the last decade — not least in the South West and East Anglia. The Devon case offers both support for the idea of a 'clean break' in demographic trends during the 1970s and shows the part that local planning policies have played in attracting and accommodating to the broader processes of social economic and demographic change out of which counter-urbanisation has stemmed.

Profound social and economic changes have accompanied technical developments and the internationalisation of trade and production. Such change has been played out on a world stage, but the pangs of the transition have been most severe in the older industrial nations like Britain where change has been associated with decline rather than growth and, within them, it has been focused in the old large industrial cities. Through all of these chapters, an important undercurrent is the lessons which we might draw for the making of future policy. As a postscript to the chapters, I have therefore drawn together some of the policy suggestions made by the contributors and considered the broader issue of what kinds of policy would provide a consistent and long-term policy framework that could assist cities in the process of adjustment to such change.

I am grateful to all of the authors who first contributed to the meeting of the British Association for the Advancement of Science and then responded uncomplainingly to suggestions about the revision of their papers for publication. I am grateful too to Michael Bradford for his advice as Editor of the Series and to Peter Sowden of Croom Helm for his patience and help in ensuring the rapid publication of these essays. Glen Ransom has been a source of continuous inspiration and help.

1

The Enduring City:
a Perspective on Decline

Brian Robson

Political events in 1985 in Handsworth and elsewhere have
overtaken the mood of the urban debate. It is now difficult to
avoid writing to a theme of 'the pen or the petrol bomb?' Can and
will policy begin to listen and respond to the findings of research
or does the attention of debate only focus momentarily and fleet-
ingly on the problems of cities if prompted by riot, arson and the
threat of widespread social disorder? As part of a presidential
address to the Geography Section of the British Association for
the Advancement of Science (Robson, 1985) I outlined a
possible worst-case scenario for British towns and cities: one in
which those urban areas, overwhelmingly in the North, which are
most affected by loss of industry and population and burdened
with more than their fair share of the weaker members of society
and the physical detritus of dereliction, would be left to decay.
Within them, a few professionals, heavily guarded, would be well
paid to man minimum-standard hospitals, schools and refined
versions of the truck-shop. Other cities and towns, predominantly those in the favoured high-tech corridor, would live in a
reverse situation in which the so-called underclass would be
penned into ghettoes and allowed out to perform menial tasks.
This appalling vision of the future is neither improbable nor
impossible: as the Lozells Road burned on the night of 10
September it seemed only one more grim indicator on our
present path to such a purgatory.

Do we need to be so morbid about our cities? Apocalyptic
analysis and the search for 'solutions' are meat and drink to
academics: many of us, myself included, have danced for years
on the head of the urban pin, dissecting, describing, warning,
pontificating, arguing; but rarely praising. Politicians too enjoy

the opportunity to blame one another and to offer their own pragmatic or ideological answers to the perceived problems of the city. Most powerful, ubiquitous and ravening of all are the pundits of the media who, Pilate-like, wash their hands of blame as they gloat on the bloody images that ensure good copy: the young black in Handsworth, poised to heave his petrol bomb, glared threateningly from the pages of tabloid and serious newspaper alike; cameramen and commentators jostled to get the most frightening views of flames and damage; editorials and special articles tumbled relentlessly from the presses, stirring, moaning and advising until within a day or two other excitements and great quantities of blood were to be scented elsewhere — in child murders, spy scandals and the earthquakes in Mexico City. The same catalogue of fleeting interest could be spelled out from the events of Brixton, Toxteth and Tottenham. Such bastardised versions of Addison's idea that 'a perfect tragedy is the noblest work of mankind' everywhere scream and glower at us, encouraging in us a form of feeble fatalism in the face of events.

ANTI-URBANISM

Such sensationalism nurtures two of the deep-seated images and myths which we unconsciously accept: anti-urbanism and the myth of a golden age. Martin Wiener in his seminal book *English culture and the decline of the industrial spirit* (Wiener, 1981) reminds us that a powerful strain of Victorian anti-urbanism emanated from those whose way of life was essentially urban, a truth borne out by the modern predilection for the quaintly and ill-named country cottage which has to be provided with every modern amenity as well as two or more cars to enable families to move to the facilities of the urban areas as often as they wish. It has been fascinating over the last decade to see the speed with which developers have exploited and cultivated this image in their creation of a patina of village-ness to their housing estates of the last few years: we are insistently engulfed by a tide of developments with fanciful names — Lark Rise, Glebe Copse, Daffodil Dell — whether the tide laps in smaller towns, on the edge of cities or indeed within cities themselves. This is Greening with a vengeance. There is great power in the manipulated false consciousness of rural romanticism which we have allowed to dominate our contemporary urban society.

The more we indulge in nostalgia and longing for a world of country living that never was — except for a favoured wealthy few in reality and a mythically many in literary imagination — the worse grows our view of the city. For those whom the Bishop of Liverpool in his Dimbleby lecture castigated as 'comfortable Britain' the city has indeed become the symbol of our latter days. Riots such as those of 1980 in Bristol, of 1981 in London, Liverpool and Manchester and their subsequent echoes in Birmingham, London and Liverpool, together with all of the smaller non-reported city riots, confirm our very real dread that a bloody and despairing revolution will roll down those 'mean streets'. Apart from all the other solutions currently being peddled to avert this happening — such as a change of government, renewed investment in the infrastructure, higher taxes, lower taxes, more power for the unions, less power for the unions, import barriers, exchange controls, small businesses, self-help, self-employment — there is a growing tendency to blame 'the city' as an evil in itself. During the urban disturbances, newspaper headlines themselves ran riot: 'My hours in hate city'; 'Savage children on city streets'; 'The shame of our cities'. Both sides of the bitter war being waged over the possible breaching of London's Green Belt by the Tillingham Hall development proposals are obsessed by the same hysterical belief that there is something magical in a few square miles of ploughed land, grass and the odd copse. Both those who wish to hold the *status quo* and those who wish to share the supposed benefits of moving out of the city are convinced of the joy they will feel in breathing in the pure country air, composed as it so often is of the subtle textures of manure and the delicate acridity of burning stubble. Only time and experience will show whether an escape from the city actually frees the young from being unemployed or ensnared by the alcohol or drug culture or the old from loneliness and dementia or whether more marriages are preserved and burglaries diminished. The auguries are not good: the problems of the modern city are man-made and as such are as likely to flourish in or out of the urban context, as anybody will testify who has knowledge of the misery, the poverty and the boredom of rural life for those who belong to the less affluent groups of our contemporary society. It may well be that some perverted form of wishful thinking wants the city to die or, more precisely, wants what is seen as the worse aspects of the city to disappear. Few of those who search for Nirvana in the leafy suburbs or the supposedly quaint villages really want to be without the amenities of the large urban centres; shops, theatres, concert halls, museums, leisure centres are desirable; riotous youth, graffiti-strewn vandalised buildings, crime and violence are not; we all want the icing instead of the rather problematic cake whose preparation and cooking we have handled so inexpertly.

THE MYTH OF THE GOLDEN AGE

Such contemporary masochism goes hand-in-hand with the second element of myth and image making: a manic schizophrenia about our urban past in which we indulge our taste for misery and mayhem by perpetually re-examining the growth of our industrial cities and at the same time hankering after some mythical idea that, despite the physical squalor, life was somehow kinder, happier and more worthwhile. This reaches its apogee in those who appear to think that there was an intrinsic virtue in poor housing, long hours of work and poverty because these were the background of a working-class sub-culture which is seen through rose-coloured spectacles as being caring, warm and supportive. Endless excuses are put forward for the loss of that mythic state: the faults of planners and architects who ignored 'defensible space' and demolished the streets of terraced houses, which, in retrospect, are believed to encapsulate all virtues; capitalism and the materially minded society which it has bred is another great bogey. Armies of oral historians and eager sociologists tape the nostalgia of old people and render it up as a 'true' picture of a past where there was 'a sense of community, a system of mutual help, a sense of duty to kinsfolk and an extended family structure', where there was 'a consoling certainty that all their neighbours shared the same poverty and the same philosophy and were as uniformly helpless and resourceless as themselves' (Seabrook, 1971). Only the half-educated, wholly politicised, upwardly mobile descendants of these old people, hearing what they want to hear, could be so gullible. For every group of comrades there were the bitter jealousies of degree and kind: the neighbours who never spoke after some real or imagined slight; the children's playground rent by the handed-down taunts of adults — 'bog Irish', 'dirty gyppos', 'filthy Yids', 'sluts', and 'bastards'; the shop floor and factory torn by inter- and intra-union hostilities. The growing cities of nineteenth-century Britain are not isolated in that beloved 'other country' — the past. They are but a mirror image of our diminishing twentieth-century cities. The road to empire, power and wealth in the nineteenth century was marked by riots, bad housing, poverty, crime, violence, racialism and unpopular policing in our cities; the road to de-industrialisation has presented an inverted perspective of that social unrest in the context of decline.

Recognition of the persistent appeal and enduring quality of urban life, despite everything man does which seems to prove the contrary, should be our starting point. To paraphrase Voltaire — if there had been no city it would have been necessary to have invented it. Of course it may be said that I have in mind the dream-world of small-scale urban settlement, the vision of a Plato or a St Augustine, and I could be accused of nurturing the Tillingham view of Utopia. Academics for Barratt? Not so. I would offer no *a priori* judgement as to what is an ideal city either in size, shape or situation.

By their very nature such cities are a changing shifting mass each as ephemeral in the long-term as the earth's crust on which some of them stand. Some decline miserably like Liverpool and Detroit; some grow with style like Sydney; others, like Rio de Janeiro and Hong Kong, stretch and strain as their tower blocks watch uneasily over their miserable shanty towns. Giant cities like Mexico City live boldly with their polluted air, high altitude and teeming poverty-stricken masses, staging Olympics and world football against a background of ancient splendour and modern squalor, gambling bravely and sometimes losing against the odds of world finance and Nature. Despite the warnings of seismologists and geomorphologists Mexico City is being rebuilt on its present site, just as was San Francisco after its earthquake in 1906. From the burned-out shops of a Birmingham through the bomb-blasted dereliction of a Dresden or a Coventry to the earthquake wreck of a Tashkent, the instinct is both to stay and to start again, not to retreat to a rural arcadia whether real or romantic. And the scope for influencing the fortunes of cities in this kaleidoscope of change is not beyond our means. Who, a decade ago, would have given Glasgow a convincing urban life expectancy, placed as it was at the head of every British league table of urban decline? Yet today Glasgow has convincingly begun the process of turning itself around with dramatic improvements to its environment and new markets in inner-area housing, even in the face of continuing high unemployment. It is easy to dismiss this sort of stubborn loyalty as an instinctive and courageous response to disaster or an unwillingness to face the supposed realities of a new economic order which decrees that cities no longer have rationale. It is as convincing to argue that there is a positive liking for urban life: for the range of choice which it offers, for the sheer symbolism of large massed buildings, for the greater opportunities it offers for the development of such enterprise as is seen in the growth of the black economy.

THE MOVE FROM CITIES

The *fact* that people and activities have moved away from cities in Britain and America is not in dispute. Indeed, as Paul Cheshire shows in his comparative European research (Chapter 2), some of the symptoms of urban decline have begun to appear in continental Europe, even though the British experience is far more severe. Recent trends suggest the growth of what has unlovingly been called counter-urbanisation — the reverse swing of the process of urbanisation of the nineteenth century—which David Grafton and N. Bolton consider in the Devon context, stressing the importance of supply-side influences rather than a uniform demand-side explanation (Chapter 10). If we look at the places that were most rapidly losing population in England 1971–81 they are all London boroughs or the big cities which were the motor of the industrialisation of the country — Liverpool, Manchester, Salford, Sandwell, Nottingham, Birmingham, Sheffield, Leeds. Conversely if we look at the most rapidly growing places they make an unfamiliar catalogue — Milton Keynes, Redditch, the Wrekin, Tamworth, Forest Heath, Huntingdon — a mixture of new towns and small free-standing towns, mostly in the South. Indeed, if we relate population change to density, it is clear that (with the exception of the new towns as a rather special case) the correlation between big dense cities and population collapse is striking. Such change is not new. Its direction might be. The nineteenth century saw a similar seesawing of rank orders of towns, but that of course was in the context of growth not of decline (Robson, 1973). The question is not whether such change has occurred but whether there is something inevitable about it. Are we whistling in the dark in thinking of stemming or reversing it? Is the flight from cities a

11

'natural' or manufactured phenomenon? It is easy to show that policy *has* played some part in creating or exacerbating city decline: New Towns are a conscious creation of policy; the move to new housing, spurred by the unwarranted and regressive subsidy of those climbing the ladder of owner occupation, forces population out of the city whether they 'choose' it or not since the impulsion on developers is to build new in the peripheral areas.

Recent research which I have undertaken for the Greater Manchester Council (GMC) into private housing in the conurbation throws some light on this (Robson and Bradford, 1984). From a survey of 1,300 private owner occupiers in Greater Manchester, it is clear that households overwhelmingly moved outwards to more peripheral parts of the GMC area and were dissuaded from more central moves by their perception of dereliction, crime, poor environment and the level of local rates. Yet a significant part of this outward movement is the result of what housing is available rather than what households might wish for in an ideal world. This can be seen most convincingly in two types of house buyer: first-time buyers of new housing are particularly dependent on the advertising and marketing schemes of developers and they move to where new housing is built; in-movers to the area move disproportionately to new houses and, even though their initial search for housing ranges wide, including inner areas, they choose peripheral housing outside the city because of the location of new houses not through any innate preference for rural living. Were suitable new houses to exist in more central areas, both such sets of households would represent potential markets. Indeed, where there are examples of inner area private housing — as in the attraction of private investment associated with the successful rehabilitation of inner Glasgow (as Duncan Maclennan shows in his review of recent housing policy in Chapter 6), as in the rather special cases of the urban development corporations in London's Docklands and on the site of the Garden Festival in inner Liverpool, as in the harbour in Bristol, and as in some of the small schemes in central Manchester — there is no evidence of an absence of a market. The same is true of council tenants: many of the overspill estates scattered in similar semi-rural quasi-suburban isolation are far removed from jobs and from urban amenities; the popularity of traditional low-rise council housing recently built in inner areas can be documented across numerous large cities.

For those, on the other hand, who do move to peripheral or to rural areas, all the advertisements about the delights of country living pall when the lack of amenities and the higher-priced restricted-choice shopping becomes obvious. The indifference of farmers to landscape and their understandable hostility to encouraging open access to their land often ensures that families with young children have less green and open space to play in than they would in the many well-cared-for parks of our cities. Only the affluent can readily find the good life in country living. Unfortunately politicians of all parties, the instant opinion formers of press and TV, those academics cloistered in green site splendour or ancient colleges, continue to live in the dream-world of anti-urbanism. Among the virtues of our present beleaguered Prime Minister are that she doesn't own a farm or appear to want to own one — unlike Harold Wilson and James Callaghan, both of whom indulged in soothing Stanley Baldwin-like stances over their country acres — and that, even in apparent preparation for retirement, she chooses to stay within the city. That she can do so in comfort and security when so many people who would like to do the same cannot, is a reflection on the economic structure and financial imbalance of our society, not a criticism of the city. With money, urban living becomes not merely possible but pleasurable — even the high-rise flats so universally derided for their appalling construction and the damage they do to family life can be seen, where there is a large affluent market as in London, to offer excellent accommodation for those with the resources to ensure the upkeep of communal areas and the protection of their vulnerable areas of ambiguous privacy. The improvements to the design of public high-rise flats suggested by Alice Coleman (Chapter 7) represent moves in the same direction, but of course without addressing the issue of the poverty of the tenants.

The steady population drain from many of our own cities which seems to reflect and endorse the current hostility towards the city is all too often undertaken unwillingly because of political or economic pressure. In Manchester, no fewer than one in six out-movers made their outward move unwillingly (Hedges and Prescott-Clarke, 1983). The movement of the younger, more skilled sections of the population out of the cites shows up clearly in the census returns as does the deprived nature of the residual population. The actual appalling statistics of unemployment and crime, of decaying unrepaired housing mainly of recently-built council stock, vie with the everyday occurrences of racialism and political bigotry to fill out the picture of the city as an undesirable place to be. Yet time after time in public meetings or in house-to-house surveys in some of the worst affected areas of our decaying cites people express clear enthusiasm for staying where they are if only their living conditions and their financial prospects could be improved. Our masochistic insistence that our British cities are in such a bad way may be symptomatic of our economic and imperial decline so that we cling to being the best in something even though it may merely be by being the worst — the worst hooligans, the worst housing, the worst unemployment.

The same arguments are true of industrial and commercial activity. Is there an inevitability to the greening of employment? There is not, so far as I am aware, a convincing argument that (barring the problems arising from the cost, availability and dereliction of urban land) firms actually benefit from a non-urban location. Even high rates have recently been shown not to have an inevitable deterrent effect on businesses in cities (Crawford, Fothergill and Monk, 1985). The land question does, however, remain as one of the more vexatious issues of urban development. The continuing high cost of urban sites is a real or a convenient reason for reluctance on the part of potential investors in inner areas. Not only is there a resistance to lowering expectations of exchange value based on historic cost, but as the investigations of Adams, Baum and MacGregor show (Chapter 8), there is a suspicion that the activity of local authorities and valuers in the land market may have the effect of maintaining prices at unrealistic levels. The other aspect of the traditional role of planners in dealing with the physical framework of development which has long been controversial is the effect that planning restrictions have on the price of land (Hall *et al.*, 1973). The challenge that planners now face is in coming to terms with their *new* role as positive stimulators of economic development; a role which Derek Lyddon sees as wholly consistent with their traditional concern with the physical framework of land and site planning (Chapter 9). If this proves true and planners can indeed marry the concerns of physical planning (amongst which land values must play a more important part) with the new demands of economic development and the support of existing economic activity, then there may be brighter prospects of slowing or reversing the economic haemorrhage of large cities.

RESEARCH ON THE INNER CITY

Much of our urban decay has to be seen as the result of policy or as having been exacerbated by policy and by an inability to implement those policies which have ostensibly been aimed to help cities. Yet we have a wealth of detailed knowledge and careful research to hand to help in curing the ills that beset our cities. Recent research undertaken by teams funded by the Economic and Social Research Council (ESRC) has completed a major project in the Inner Cities Research Programme which shows how much of the urban crisis with which we are faced is of our own making (Hausner and Robson, 1985). The centrepiece of this work drew on five case studies of individual city regions, chosen to reflect the variety of experience across British cities. Two of the chapters in this book are drawn from this work: Martin Boddy writes on what is often thought of as the success story of Bristol's ability to accommodate to change (Chapter 4); and Bill Lever writes on Glasgow, the city which has experienced the longest and most profound economic contraction in Britain (Chapter 3). Yet these different contexts provide not dissimilar critiques. In both, it is clear that, while it is wider processes of change which have created the backcloth for the city's fortunes and that broader government action does much to determine the scope for economic and social renewal, there is potential for independent city-based action to help to turn and guide the prospects of the cities. Let me isolate four general conclusions from the ESRC work as a whole.

Urban collapse

First it is clear that the economic and social problems which have prompted concern about inner areas are no longer — if ever they were — simply an inner city phenomenon. Cities as a whole are now suffering a *general* contraction in their economic base and all show the associated problems of social distress and environ-mental dereliction that are concomitant to this. It does not matter greatly whether the diverse sets of indicators used by the Department of the Environment or by the various teams of researchers suggest that Brixton or Handsworth or Moss Side or Glasgow are 'worst' in the league table. It happens that the

ESRC league table showed inner Birmingham, which includes Handsworth, as heading the list of deprivation — that is neither here nor there, even though there is some perverse gratification in it. What is significant is that all of the indicators show that the gulf between big cities and other areas is massive and recurring. Even if it is in the inner areas in which the *very* worst problems are usually found, the remaining parts of our major cities do not lag far behind. Where imaginative programmes of rehabilitation have been relatively successful — as in Glasgow — the evidence shows that problems of little less severity remain within the large areas of urban council housing in the peripheral parts of our large cities. Even the so-called successful cities can only be called successful in *relative* terms. Bristol is a case in point, as Boddy so effectively shows. In the decade to 1981 employment actually fell — admittedly only by some 0.8 per cent — with losses concentrated on the city's traditional manufacturing sectors; food, drink and tobacco losing over one-third of its employment and paper, printing and publishing losing almost one-half. Even in the case of a 'successful' city like Bristol, we are now dealing with a 'success' story that is very much relative. It is simply that this 'successful' city has not done so disastrously badly as have cities elsewhere. It is clear that, looking across large cities in general, we face major potential crises. The future of cities should be high on the political agenda.

Cities and regions

Second, in the face of recession and in the absence of strong regional policy, there is a growing conflict between cities and regions. As employment has contracted and new investment grown more scarce, the competition for investment which had characterised cities or parts of cities has now extended to a competition between cities and their containing regions, each of which battle for a slice of a diminished cake. In this context one of the important findings from the Inner Cities research is that the poor who live in growing areas within declining regions do not benefit greatly from that growth; only if the disadvantaged live in growing areas within more successful regions do the poor derive much benefit from growth (Buck and Gordon, 1986). All of this suggests both that we need to develop ways of linking job and housing markets more successfully at local level and also that there is a continuing need for a regional framework of planning if we are to tackle the problems of disadvantage.

Policy inconsistency

Third, and arising from these points, it is difficult to argue that there is a consistent long-term urban policy which holds out the prospect of turning around the fortunes of cities. There are certainly some valuable programmes, many associated with DoE initiatives — such as Urban Development Grants — or with MSC training schemes. But a collection of programmes is no substitute for consistent long-term cross-departmental policy which might help the cities. This is evident in the outcomes of the different policies of the Department of the Environment and the Department of Trade and Industry: the first with a focus on aid to cities and the second with a regional focus. For Clydeside, Lever shows the way in which DTI's regional assistance to industry has resulted in resources going to areas outside the inner city and thereby running counter to the proclaimed urban bias of central policy. For Tyneside, on the other hand, Goddard's work has shown that these urban and regional assistance policies *have* resulted in similar patterns of spatial resource allocation, but that this has happened simply as the result of the fact that existing large-scale industry (which is assisted by regional policy) happens to be found in inner areas of Tyneside rather than because of a conscious attempt to use regional policy to assist urban areas. The risk we run in not having consistent conscious policy is not hard to imagine given the recency of the Handsworth, Brixton and Tottenham riots and the continuing long-term local disturbances in many cities which go unrecorded in the national press. In the absence of consistent urban policy, there is no evidence that, even with some resurgence of national prosperity, the cities will benefit from any such growth.

The Inner Cities work has explored two particular constraints to the effective development of an urban policy. First is the effect of what might be thought of as the unintended effects of non-urban policies. There are innumerable non-urban policies which cut diametrically across the intended goals of urban programmes. Boddy's work in Bristol again offers a dramatic example of this with its demonstration of the effect of procurement and other spending by the central government

Defence Department, expenditure which overwhelmingly favours the South West and which has helped to underpin the aerospace industry which is an important motor of the Bristol economy. Such spending and the multiplier effects associated with it have been an important element in sustaining the relative buoyancy of the city's labour markets. Here is a hidden regional fiscal policy whose unintended consequence is to dwarf the overt spending on needy regions and to run counter to the explicit urban programmes of other departments of government. Likewise, as a second example, central decisions to reduce spending on the creation of public service jobs have a disproportionate effect on urban areas since it has been service jobs — for example in health and in education — which have been one of the few areas of employment which has benefited poor urban residents. A third example is the conflict between giving earmarked resources for urban aid to large cities and the reductions in mainstream spending and the impact of financial penalties for overspending which have dwarfed that additional expenditure. Compared to 1981/2, the Rate Support Grant to the Urban Programme cities was reduced by some £143 million in 1984/5; yet those same cities gained only £127 million from the Urban Programme itself.

There will always be choices to be made between different sets of policy options. We need to be more alive to their potentially conflicting impacts and address the political debate about cross-departmental policy for urban areas if we are to develop an urban policy which might work towards the betterment of needy areas. We will have no urban policy unless researchers explore what are the plausible futures for our cities and unless we can develop the political will to pursue policies which make possible the realisation of feasible urban futures.

Targeting

Fourth, there is no evidence for the belief that investment in cities necessarily has trickle-down benefits to the disadvantaged residents of those cities. The workings of the job and the housing markets and the lack of integration of training, job placement, employment and development policies on the one hand, and housing and transport policies on the other, means that it is overwhelmingly not the poor who reap benefit from what growth is introduced through urban programme developments. In Birmingham, for example, only 17 per cent of the new publicly-created jobs in the Partnership area went to residents of the most disadvantaged inner areas and, nationally, some 40 per cent of inner area jobs go to commuters from outside inner areas (Spencer *et al.*, 1986; Hausner and Robson, 1985). Even earmarked assistance such as Section 11 posts, which are aimed to benefit ethnic groups, tends to be absorbed as merely another source of general revenue for education authorities. The need is clearly for a more conscious targeting of benefit to those most disadvantaged.

CHALLENGES FOR URBAN POLICY

The political challenge which we face brings me back to the issues from which I started. Given the findings of research, are we prepared to listen to the outpourings of the pen or can we merely respond to the petrol bomb? If we are to contribute to any debate on whether we need an urban policy, researchers must begin to develop scenarios of urban and regional futures. Can we develop plausible futures from the technological, economic and social changes of the present? What, for example, are the implications of technological developments in electronic communications about which John Goddard and Andy Gillespie write (Chapter 5)? They suggest that the convergence of telecommunications and microprocessors, seen in the development of telecommunication networks and switching systems, is likely to reinforce existing patterns of investment. What implications does this have for declining cities and regions? What are the likely impacts of micro-computers on transport systems? Likewise, on the social and employment fronts, can we develop medium-term worst-case scenarios associated with current patterns of employment recruitment and the changing sectoral mix of the formal economy, such as the scenario that I suggested at the outset. In thinking of future scenarios, I have in mind the possibility of developing a scenario-building study not unlike some of the work that Stone did for the National Institute for Economic and Social Research in the late 1960s (Stone, 1970, 1973). His concern was primarily technical — what are the financial costs associated with different forms of settlement systems and in what direction are we likely to be led by technical trends in construction and transport and by demographic trends? We need similar research on the basis of which we might project forward or even predict, but research which is based on a broader concern for what are the social and economic as well as the financial costs entailed by different kinds of urban and regional systems.

Then, we need more generally to decide if we have the political will to pursue any of the plausible urban futures. If so, we need to address the political seesawing of policy which comes from the adversarial base of much of our current politics and the conflicts embedded in urban and non-urban policies. The need is for cross-departmental and long-term urban policy which is more genuinely targeted to the deprived and which more effectively links housing and transport with economic development. In this, it is vital that we begin to connect the economic and the social elements of the development argument. One of the problems of policy formulation — guided not least by the compartmental structure of central government departments — is the tendency to look at economic and social issues too much in isolation. We are paralysed by our inability to solve the big macro-economic questions; but the prominence which is not unjustifiably given to tackling these economic issues leads us to the wholly unjustified beliefs that social progress will automatically follow if only we succeed in creating economic growth and that economic progress itself can be attained without addressing the social malaise which acts as a drag on its plausibility. Hence the view that regional and urban policy is an ill-affordable luxury — a hand-out to the improvident and imprudent areas and regions; as in the White Paper on regional industrial policy (Department of Trade and Industry, 1983) which argued *dismissively* that there is now only a social argument for regional policy. This is to ignore the importance of the links between social wellbeing and economic performance. How many Handsworths, Brixtons, Toxteths and Tottenhams can the economy sustain — and on what scale — before the implications of social circumstances for economic policy begin to take a firmer grip on our consciousness? The important political debate to which we need to contribute is the argument about the two-way connections between economic and social circumstances. The broader message of research is that efficiency and equity should not be seen as alternatives in considering the ways in which urban and regional policy is conceived.

REFERENCES

Buck, N. and Gordon, I. (1986) 'The beneficiaries of employment growth: an analysis of the experience of disadvantaged groups in expanding labour markets', in Hausner, V. (ed.), *Critical issues in urban economic development*, vol. 2, Oxford University Press, Oxford

Crawford, P., Fothergill, S. and Monk, S. (1985) 'The effect of business rates on the location of employment', *Final Report*, Industrial Location Research Group, Department of Land Economy, Cambridge University

Department of Trade and Industry (1983) *Regional industrial development*, Cmnd. 9111, HMSO, London

Hall, P., Thomas, R. and Drewett, R. (1973) 'Planning and urban growth: towards a verdict', in Hall, P., *et al.* (eds.), *The containment of urban England*, vol. 2, George Allen and Unwin, London, pp. 378–409

Hausner, V. and Robson, B. T. (1985) *Changing cities: an introduction to the ESRC's Inner Cities Research Programme*, Economic and Social Research Council, London

Hedges, B. and Prescott-Clarke, P. (1983) 'Migration and the inner city', *Report*, 9, Inner Cities Research Programme, Department of the Environment, London

Robson, B. T. (1973) *Urban growth: an approach*, Methuen, London
—— (1985) 'The once and future city', unpublished Presidential Address, Section E, British Association for the Advancement of Science, Annual Meeting, Strathclyde
—— and Bradford, M. G. (1984) 'Urban change in Greater Manchester: demographic and household change, 1971–1981', *Report*, Greater Manchester Council, Manchester

Seabrook, J. (1971) *City close-up*, Allen Lane, Penguin, Harmondsworth

Spencer, K. *et al.* (1986) *Crisis in the industrial heartland: a study of the West Midlands*, Oxford University Press, Oxford

Stone, P. A. (1970) *Urban development in Britain: standards, costs and resources*, Cambridge University Press, Cambridge
—— (1973) *The structure, size and costs of urban settlements*, Cambridge University Press, Cambridge

Wiener, M. J. (1981) *English culture and the decline of the industrial spirit, 1850–1980*, Cambridge University Press, London

2

Urban Policy:
Art not Science?

Paul Cheshire

There are several ways of viewing British urban policy; as 'planning'; as social policy; or as one of the two branches of 'spatial' policy — that is, policy designed to influence the incidence of activity through space. Indeed, in large measure the problem of urban policy in Britain is that it has never really been decided what its objectives are. It has not been decided whether urban policy should tackle problems of obsolete buildings and infrastructure and of dereliction, and so concern itself with physical planning objectives; or whether it is a response to the perceived social crisis in the major cities; or whether its objectives are more economic — to effect an economic revitalisation of the 'inner city' (although that phrase itself conveys a peculiarly British version of urban problems).

It has not been admitted that the aims of urban policy, nationally and often locally, are significantly political; political in the meanest sense of that word; point scoring and sweeping damaging issues under the carpet rather than seriously confronting them and resolving them. Because of this confusion and conflict between objectives, it is no surprise that the instruments of urban policy have been inadequate and ill co-ordinated.

The facts of social inequality need no rehearsing. One can, however, distinguish at least two dimensions to social inequality. There is first a purely social one. Within any community in Britain — or any larger social unit such as a region of Britain as a whole — there is a distribution of incomes and of wealth; there are rich and poor and all those in between. This is an aspect of the society in which we live, just as it is, in varying degree, of the societies in which the vast majority of the world's population lives. But there also exists, as a separately distinguishable dimension of inequality, a spatial dimension. That is most easily observable on an international level; there exist a vast number of people in Africa, for example — perhaps the bottom 50 per cent of the income distribution — who are poorer than almost anyone in Britain. Within Europe — abstracting from personal characteristics or comparing particular points on the income distribution — life chances are worse if you are born in Ireland, Greece or Southern Italy than if you are born in Germany, Denmark or South East England. Disregarding 'underbounded' regions such as Greater London or Hamburg, mean *per capita* incomes are three times as high in the richest regions of Northern Europe as they are in Calabria. Within the United Kingdom there are similar differences in life chances depending on where you are born. However, those differences, I would argue, are mainly not a result of whether you are born in the 'inner city' or its plushier suburbs — once personal characteristics such as family, education and income have been allowed for. Life chances are affected by whether you are born in Northern Ireland or, say, Merseyside on the one hand, or East Anglia or the South East on the other.

Such comparisons presume implicitly that some embracing notion of 'society' applies to the various spatial units being compared. There is a secure sense in which one can presume a British society embracing the whole of the United Kingdom and so the distinction between 'social' and 'spatial' inequality has meaning. Considering Europe as a whole as a single social system is more problematic; when it comes to differences in life chances between Ethiopia and the home counties it is possible we may regard them as really reflecting differences between different societies rather than spatial inequality within human society.

If we analyse British urban policy as a branch of that wider policy designed to affect the location of activity through space (and hence spatial inequality) what should we conclude? There exist at least two types of such policy; regional development policy and, increasingly over the last decade, those aspects of urban policy designed to channel activity to 'inner areas' or encourage development — Enterprise Zones, Local Economic Initiatives and related policies. Regional development policy has, for example in the United States or to an important extent in the EEC, been concerned with developing largely undeveloped agricultural or sparsely populated regions. A major feature of regional development policy has been large-scale infrastructure investment projects. The rules of the European Regional Fund have to be bent to allow for renovation or upgrading of existing infrastructure; hence a source of problems in applying European aid to the decaying infrastructure of Britain's old industrial cities compared to constructing new roads in Sicily or rural Scotland. In the peculiar conditions of the UK, the major concerns of regional development policy have been different. Given the early date of industrialisation in Britain, the problem since regional policy was established has mainly been that of declining industrial regions. Whilst there has certainly been a focus on attracting new mobile investment, the provision of new social capital has not been a major item of concern. Indeed the first clear statement of the case for regional policy in the report of the Barlow Commission gave the underuse of social capital in declining regions as a reason for intervention in the distribution of population.

MECHANISMS OF SPATIAL ADJUSTMENT

At a simple level, I would claim we understand enough about spatial adjustment mechanisms and the workings of regional economies both to operate such policy and, less surely, to assess its effectiveness. Through a series of studies on the workings of regional and local labour markets (Cheshire, 1973 and 1979; Metcalf and Richardson, 1976; Evans and Richardson, 1981; Burridge and Gordon, 1981; Gordon and Lamont 1982; and Gordon, 1985) there has developed a core of quite hard knowledge.

For example, in determining variations in unemployment rates once differences in personal characteristics have been standardised, the degree of self-containment of a labour market is crucial. If in- and out-commuting averages more than about 25 per cent of the employed labour force, then local employment creation or job loss has no observable impact on local unemployment. Between larger/more self-contained units (the two characteristics — size and self-containment — are associated but not identical), adjustment occurs via migration and differential rates of job creation/elimination. Local employment creation thus tends to have an impact on the local residents, but because migration flows respond to differential job opportunities there may still be little effect on local unemployment. Instead, net migration flows tend to respond and one can think of equilibrium unemployment differentials between regions determined by the costs of adjustment between them and differential movements in demand for and supply of labour. In turn these adjustment costs primarily reflect migration costs, including the human and social costs implicit in migration.

Thus unemployment differentials between regions may be regarded as reflecting differentials in regional demand for labour; but they may equally be taken as reflecting the cost of adjustment between regions. By extension, the same may be true of income differences for individuals of identical characteristics although income differentials (and to a more limited extent unemployment differentials) also reflect structural differences. The implications are also that one should not measure the 'success' of regional policy in terms of unemployment reduction alone, but in terms of differential employment change *compared to that which would have occurred in the absence of policy intervention*. This is because it seems as reasonable to assume there is a welfare gain if someone is not forced to migrate as if they cease to be unemployed. The causes of regional differentials — differential changes in demand combined with cost of spatial adjustment — themselves provide the mechanism which allows regional policy to be effective; the cost of spatial adjustment between independent self-contained regions are such that the influences of policy intervention are contained within the largest regions.

This, however, is at a restricted level of analysis. It suggests that if a dam is built or a factory opened, the immediate and direct effects of that proportion of spending that is within the region (there will also be inputs purchased from other regions) will be contained within the region rather than benefiting residents of other regions. It does not, however, tell us about the complicated processes of regional growth and decline; why some regions of Europe such as the south west or eastern-central France, southern Germany or East Anglia are growing rapidly and others, such as North West England and southern Belgium, are declining, and yet others, such as Calabria and parts of Ireland, more or less stagnate.

THE SWITCH TO URBAN POLICY

Within the UK, regional policy has increasingly been run down over the last ten years or so and the emphasis has switched to urban policy. The reasons for this shift are complex. Underlying it is a major change that is transforming our patterns of living. There is a general pattern of decentralisation. This goes further than the suburbanisation of earlier periods since it is not just a process of residential decentralisation (along with employment activities related to residential population such as construction or retailing) but of the decentralisation of wide sections of employment as well. This pattern of ex-urbanisation is not peculiar to Britain although some of its particular manifestations are. The process of ex-urbanisation was first documented in the US (see, for example, Leven, 1978). Britain was probably the first European country affected, but progressively other North European countries have felt the impact, with those that were more and earlier industrialised being affected sooner and more intensely (see Hall and Hay, 1980; and Van den Berg *et al.*, 1982). Now there are indications that even countries in Southern Europe such as Greece are experiencing a slow-down in their rates of urbanisation.

This shift to urban policy has been closely associated with the incidence of this process of decentralisation. Urban policy designed as a reaction to metropolitan stagnation and urban decline was developed first in the US in the early and mid-1960s. By the late 1960s or early 1970s Britain was following this lead. The Educational Priority Areas Scheme in the UK dates from 1967; the Housing Act of 1969 introduced the first area-based housing improvement schemes. Only later did countries such as France (1975 to 1981), Germany (1974 to 1979), Belgium (1973/4), Ireland (1975) or Italy (1978), introduce policies designed to combat that syndrome of problems often associated with population loss and now referred to as 'urban decline'. Indeed Greece — where all major cites are still growing, albeit at falling rates — has no such policies and Italy, despite a major national debate in 1984, stopped short of introducing measures beyond those earlier introduced to provide for more general conservation in historic city centres. The Italian response, reflecting the continuing North/South differentiation in urban and economic experience, has been to avoid a systematic national framework for urban policy and to rely on a pragmatic city-by-city approach.

Another sharply divided country, Belgium, although intensely affected by problems of urban decline in the French-speaking south, has similarly failed to develop a systematic national policy.

There does not seem to be any immediate reason why population decentralisation, which necessarily tends to imply population loss in large cities (although that relationship is mediated via differential rates of natural change of population), is socially or economically undesirable. In the second half of the 1970s, cities such as Antwerp, Copenhagen, Düsseldorf or Frankfurt were losing population at rates faster than Dortmund, Lille, Birmingham or Manchester. Yet it does not seem reasonable to argue that they had greater urban problems; the indications are very much to the contrary.

The problems seem to arise when population loss is in a wider context of industrial decline and net job loss. The very existence of many major cities in Europe, and the form of more, was largely a product of the industrial revolution and the growth of the manufacturing sector. Before the Industrial Revolution major cities existed but as administrative, commercial and cultural centres. The prototype city of the first half of the nineteenth century was Manchester, however, which increased from a population of 100,000 or so at the beginning of the century to over 1 million by mid-century. It was the creature and creation of the Industrial Revolution. In it, the new forms of production and the new ways of living existed in symbiosis.

Now the manufacturing sector is relocating, and employment in it is declining both absolutely and relative to the service sector. It is only to be expected, therefore, that industrial cities are experiencing not only population loss but serious urban problems. These problems can conceptually be viewed as the adjustment costs in terms of spatial patterns of living, socio-economic adjustment and the built environment of industrial restructuring. These sorts of urban problems are the latter day version of the rural poverty, deprivation and depopulation of the eighteenth and nineteenth centuries. The urban riots in British cities of the early 1980s were in some sense the equivalents of the rural unrest of the early decades of the nineteenth century. All these problems of adjustment are intensified by economic recession since the mechanisms of spatial adjustment — migration and job creation — are impeded and resources are not available to accommodate the problems.

However, as was argued earlier, in the face of these forces and these problems, the objectives of urban policy have never been just the adaptation of regional policy to urban ends. There has been a proliferation of initiatives apparently designed to shift resources into distressed local areas within the declining major cities. This has paid relatively little regard to whether the areas of distress are small sections of major urban areas in comparatively prosperous regions — such as in inner London; or relatively larger areas of cities in declining regions. The mechanisms of spatial adjustment may ensure that regionally specific expenditure mainly benefits the inhabitants of the broader region. However, in the context of small areas, within urban regions, these same mechanisms virtually ensure the reverse. London boroughs, for example, have on average about 25 to 30 per cent in- and out-commuting. As the most rigorous and detailed analysis by Gordon and Lamont (1982) concluded: 'For a sub-labour market area open to commuting, the effects of local job creation rapidly diminish and, for an area 75% open (averaging in and out flows) appear to disappear altogether.'

As has been shown elsewhere (Cheshire, 1979), even if spatial patterns of job search were entirely random (which is unlikely since job hunters are likely to have some information about the availability of jobs within the radius of their search area), then the knock-on effects between linked and interacting local sub-markets would lead to an equalisation of unemployment rates for people of given characteristics. The labour markets of large cities embody just such characteristics. They are composed of a set of strongly interacting sub-markets. Thus unemployment differentials persist between self-contained local labour markets (such as urban regions or regions) because of costs of adjustment, but not between sub-markets within them because of the virtual absence of adjustment costs.

SOCIAL SEGREGATION WITHIN LARGE CITIES

Why then does one observe a sharp differential in unemployment rates across different areas of large cities? The most important reason is social segregation (there are others too, including the fact that what we observe is seldom an equilibrium). In reality the characteristics of the population vary considerably from one neighbourhood to another. A study by the Department of

Environment (1983) illustrates a problem associated with this. They used eight census indicators for local authority districts as a means of measuring the extent of urban problems. Many smaller and medium-sized cities are approximately defined by a single district; for these smaller cities that district contains a more or less complete representation of the socio-economic groups who live within the city. The functional reality of London, however, is far larger than the Greater London area and that area is composed of 32 separate districts. The districts of London thus often contain a very biased sample of the population of London as a whole. Since London is a very large city, there are within it very many poor people, unskilled workers, unemployed people, ethnic minorities, inadequate houses (all of which are used as indicators of urban problems). Because of social segregation these are concentrated in particular districts. Not surprisingly, therefore, the DoE analysis showed that on certain indicators, London boroughs did very badly; two were in the worst 20 districts in the country on unemployment and, perhaps not surprisingly given the cost of housing in London, 14 of the 'worst' districts in the country in terms of crowding were in London (basic economic analysis suggests that as space costs rise households adjust by consuming less space compared to other goods, thus measures of 'crowding' increase). Equally, however, 18 London boroughs scored amongst the best in the country on all measures. Although two London boroughs had amongst the worst unemployment in the country, very small parts of London were being compared with complete provincial cities. The unemployment rate, even for the Greater London area (still considerably smaller than the interrelated functional urban region of London), is below the level for the UK as a whole; to claim that unemployment in London is a problem on the scale of that of Glasgow, Sunderland, Liverpool or Manchester because there are, in London, more unemployed people than in any of those cities, makes as little sense as to claim that unemployment is a worse problem in Japan than it is in Belgium because there are more unemployed people in Japan.

Nor is residential segregation unique to Britain. It can be observed in all major cities of Western Europe and North America and elsewhere too. What is a peculiarly British (and North American) characteristic, however, is the particular pattern of residential segregation. In Britain the poor, by and large, live in the older high-density housing of the inner area and in the large local authority estates that have replaced that housing *in situ*. In the countries of continental Europe, especially in France and Italy, the reverse tends to be true. The rich tend to live in the historic cores (that mainly predated industrialisation); the poor live in low-quality private and public housing on the periphery or in surrounding satellite industrial communities.

The comparison between Nancy, Liverpool, Glasgow and Bologna shown in Table 2.1 is instructive on this point. If we look at the distribution of three different socio-economic groups between the built-up core and the surrounding commuting hinterland (these data relate to the Functional Urban Regions defined by Hall and Hay, 1980, on as consistent a basis as possible for the whole of Europe) we can see the very different pattern. The relative size of core and hinterland is not constant across urban regions so the absolute values have to be interpreted with care. But we can see that in Bologna professional workers were strongly concentrated on a residential basis in the core, but that their relative de-centralisation was more rapid during the 1970s than was that of manual workers. In Liverpool

Table 2.1: Occupational spatial segregation in European cities

		Employed male residents of the core as percentage of those of the hinterland			Ratio of core: hinterland unemployment[1]	
		1971	1981	Change	1975/6	1982/3
Bologna	a	216	145	−71	0.53	0.91
	b	262	165	−97		
	c	99	74	−25		
Glasgow	a	29	42	+13	1.39	0.72
	b	67	33	−33		
	c	68	34	−34		
Liverpool	a	40	32	−8	0.99	0.85
	b	46	38	−8		
	c	63	54	−9		
Nancy	a	181	−	−	0.87	0.99
	b	175	−	−		
	c	86	−	−		

Notes:
a = Professional and other higher white collar employers and employees.
b = Supervisory and lower white collar workers.
c = Manual excluding agricultural workers.
1 = Index of core unemployment (1980 = 100) as a ratio to index of hinterland.

30

and Glasgow, in contrast, there was a relative concentration of manual workers in the core (although in both cities there was a lower absolute ratio of resident employed population in the core compared to the hinterland); in Glasgow, however, professional workers became relatively more concentrated in the core during the 1970s compared to manual workers, in Liverpool there was some slight manifestation of a similar change. The data for Nancy for 1981 were not available at the time of this analysis, but the pattern for 1971 is similar to that of Bologna with a strong relative concentration of professional and white collar workers in the core compared to the hinterland.

This different pattern of residential segregation, reflecting different patterns and dates of industrialisation, different cultural values and different historical experiences of development, gives rise to quite different perceptions as to the nature of urban problems and, in consequence, policy responses. The British perceive an inner-city crisis and respond with small-scale spatial intervention in central areas. Bologna is, by Italian standards and even by those of Europe, a prosperous city. In Italy urban problems are perceived largely as problems of the old urban centres of the Mezzogiorno — of Naples, Cagliari or Palermo — and attention was hardly turned to the few declining centres of the north such as Genova or Turin. In France, however, Nancy is a comparatively declining city, but the urban dimensions of the problem of the declining Lorraine region is seen as being a problem of the small industrial 'satellite' cities in the hinterland of Nancy and beyond. The historic city of Nancy does not strike the British visitor as exhibiting problems. Thus the French view the 'urban crisis' as a crisis of small industrial cities mainly located in the north east of the country; the British view it as a problem of the inner areas of the large nineteenth-century cities spawned by the industrial revolution. There is much in common in the underlying causes of urban problems in both countries — the historic decline of old nineteenth-century/ early twentieth-century industries, economic and spatial restructuring and worldwide economic recession — but the urban manifestation and hence the perception and the policy response are very different across the countries of the EEC and, as is too often the case, the contrast is strongest between France and the UK.

There is a further consequence of residential segregation. Different groups exhibit a different incidence of unemployment.

The over 55s, the under 25s, the unskilled, the unqualified, the less educated and the disabled, all have a high propensity to be unemployed. Moreover, these characteristics are correlated with each other; a person who is poor is also more likely to be less skilled and/or less fit, less educated and unemployed. Rising unemployment generally affects these groups proportionately more. In Britain, patterns of residential segregation are such that poor people (who have a higher propensity to suffer unemployment) tend to be concentrated in inner areas, in low-quality housing. In France, as is exemplified by the case of Nancy, more or less the reverse pattern of residential segregation is common. The 'inner city' problem in Britain is thus significantly a spatial manifestation of social segregation interacting with economic restructuring and regional and national economic failure. The inner city is the social and environmental wreckage exposed by the receding tide of industry and economic success.

The changing pattern of social segregation noted above is reflected in the changing spatial incidence of unemployment. The data are extremely difficult to assemble so only a very limited number of observations is available where there are time series data for both relative core: hinterland unemployment and the socio-economic structure of employed residents on a consistent basis. However, for the three cities for which such data have been assembled (Cheshire, Hay and Carbonaro, 1985), the two patterns coincide. In Bologna where there has been relative decentralisation of less unemployment-prone groups, core unemployment has risen relative to hinterland; in Glasgow, where less unemployment-prone groups have become relatively more centralised, core unemployment has fallen relative to that in the hinterland. In Liverpool, where there was some slight relative centralisation of the less unemployment-prone groups, core unemployment shows a slight relative fall.

EXAMPLES OF SUCCESSFUL URBAN POLICY

Differences in unemployment rates and their changes across different areas of an urban region thus mainly reflect patterns of social segregation. The many local labour markets within a single urban region interact too strongly for local job creation, produced by the simple transfer of resources, to have much effect on the unemployment rates of local residents. We may conclude, therefore, that in as far as urban policy is the application of regional policy on a smaller scale it is neither science nor art nor even witchcraft. It is perhaps political makeshift. Urban policy is not just this, however. There are examples in Europe of apparently successful urban policy in the context of the severest urban problems. Glasgow, indeed, appears to be a good example. So far as one can observe, the city *is* 'miles better'; and this in a context of a depressed regional and national economy. In the more successful economic context of Germany, the Action Programme for the Ruhr seems to have been another example of effective urban policy.

What, if anything, do these policies have in common? They appear to have had clear objectives and an integrating administrative structure. Their various interventions — in local economies, in the urban environment and with respect to manpower and social policies — have, as a result, been co-ordinated. The GEAR initiative in Glasgow brought together all the agencies involved and, after a settling down period, seems to have produced agreed objectives which were supported by local residents. Because all agencies were brought together, their actions and those of the various tiers of government were co-ordinated to achieve those objectives. This is a view which is given additional support by Lever in Chapter 3. Moreover, because of the different administrative system in Scotland, urban policy interests were clearly represented at ministerial level. This is in strong contrast to England where separate agencies appeared too often to pursue conflicting objectives and central and local government were themselves too frequently in conflict. Sometimes, as in London's Dockland until the creation of the London Dockland Corporation, the objectives even as between the various representatives of local government have been in conflict. Moreover, the division of responsibilities between ministries in England and Wales meant less effective representation of urban policy interests at national level. Likewise in the Ruhr cities, the existence of a strong regional tier of government provided proper co-ordination between different agencies and access to both regional and federal funds. In both Glasgow and the Ruhr cities, urban policy was conceived of as a co-ordinated push for urban revitalisation employing a wide range of instruments for multiple objectives. Urban policy operated via local economic initiatives it is true, but also via co-ordinated land, housing, planning and environmental policies. Nor were economic policies confined just to investment incentives or the provision of industrial premises. They extended to manpower and advisory services, land recycling and to social policies too.

This is, of course, far too brief a summary to be other than greatly simplified, but the point to be made is that to date examples of more successful urban policy seem to be pragmatic and common-sense based rather than scientific. They have not been constructed on a fundamental analysis of the causes of urban problems and the workings of an urban system. Rather, using some insights derived from such analysis coupled with principles of good policy implementation, clear objectives and an empirical approach to seeing what worked, they have developed as they have gone. Their success has been based on integrated administrative structures. They have, in other words, been art not applied science.

JUSTIFICATIONS FOR URBAN POLICY

Why, it may be asked, should we have any urban policy? Some have argued that the world has changed so that people no longer need or want cities. Modern transport and communications have rendered cities economically and socially obsolete. If people wish to live in small settlements or in the ex-urban 'countryside' why should policy interfere? This is a view which should not be dismissed unconsidered. It does not seem either likely or desirable that we could re-create the high-density industrial urban areas of the past with their labour-intensive manufacturing industry. Manufacturing, as a source of employment, is inevitably going to decline in Britain for some time yet and there is no prospect of attracting such industry as prospers, with its associated pollution and congestion, back to the centres of large urban areas. That does not, however, mean that cities are dead as employment centres. In many US cities, employment growth in service industries has exceeded employment loss in manufacturing in the last 15 years (Leven, 1985).

The reasons for urban policy are several. There are economic reasons concerned both with equity and efficiency. The problems of adjustment that industrial and spatial restructuring impose produce substantial costs and, in Britain, those costs are concentrated in large urban areas. Moreover, because of externalities in the urban economy, there are no reasons for supposing that change is economically optimal either at the neighbourhood or wider urban region level. Indeed there are *a priori* arguments which suggest that decentralisation and neighbourhood decay will go further than is optimal if market forces are left to themselves. There are also important urban public goods which urban policy can and should provide and whose provision in turn affects the extent of urban problems.

There are also non-economic reasons for policy intervention. In EEC countries, urban areas represent concentrations of social distress and social problems. This is even becoming true in Italy where the effects of the Common Agricultural Policy have been to increase the displacement of workers from agriculture via capital labour substitution, to increase the incomes of those that remain in the countryside, but to reduce the real incomes of the poorer sections of the urban population via higher food prices. Large-scale green field investment projects have tended to reinforce this effect. Only in Greece, Spain and Portugal, do urban areas still appear as apparent nodes of opportunity although there are of course still significant pockets of rural poverty in all EEC countries. For administrative reasons alone, therefore, it may be efficient to have a social policy administered on the basis of particular areas within major cities because that is the most effective way of reaching a high proportion of those 'at risk'. There are also strong political reasons — some good, some (such as the loss of electors) less so. There may also be cultural reasons for urban policy.

I would claim that we have no rigorous scientific understanding of how a particular urban region changes and develops through time nor how precisely it interacts with other urban regions and wider economic and social forces. Nor do we even have hard insight into the detailed workings of urban areas at the local level; of how cultural values or economic forces interact with urban design and social forces for example, in such a way as to be able to predict the detailed impact on a neighbourhood of a particular development. We do have hard insight into detailed aspects of urban change, however, and probably enough accumulation of knowledge and experience to predict that particular changes will not produce one set of possible changes, but could lead to some other set of possible changes.

One feature of change for which there seems to be growing hard evidence is a link between population loss or gain from cities and tenure change in housing. There has been a growth in owner occupation relative to rental housing stock across all EEC countries since 1971. If we look at rates of population loss or gain from urban cores during that period there is a strong statistical relationship between the differential growth of owner occupied housing stock in the city core relative to the surrounding region, on the one hand, and population loss on the other. In cities such as Copenhagen, Belfast or Manchester, where the growth in owner occupied housing stock in the core has been small (or negative) and in the surrounding region strong, there has been a rapid rate of population loss from the core. In cities such as Palermo, Bari or Strasbourg, where owner occupied housing stock has increased as fast or faster in the urban core than in the surrounding region, there has been population gain in the core. With observations for 17 urban regions across six EEC countries, the correlation ($R^2 = 0.48$) was statistically significant. There are several reasons underlying the changes in housing tenure. Policy decisions are themselves important; subsidisation of owner occupation and unfavourable treatment of private rental housing. A plausible (but not the only possible) interpretation of the evidence is that the fact of this transfer has meant that, where opportunities for owner occupation have not been available in city cores, people have chosen to move out of cities to the surrounding region. This, in turn, has increased social segregation.

There are many other reasons for urban population loss and, as has already been remarked, such loss is not necessarily undesirable. For a century and a half the most often cited urban problems were, after all, congestion and overcrowding. Above all, the reason for population loss seems to be that because of changes in transport and communications, both industry and population have become more footloose. Instead of being tied to railway access points and ports, industry can now locate anywhere within reasonable distance of the motorway network. As a result the always present penalties associated with urban areas, of high land and labour costs and congestion costs, can be increasingly avoided; particularly as those economies of agglomeration and access to business services, formerly the preserve of major urban areas, become more widely available as a result of changing communication costs and decentralisation of business services. Couple this with the fact that containerisation means that 'trans-shipment' points are now anywhere a container can be unpacked, and there are powerful forces for decentralisation of employment. People, too, as employment decentralises and real costs of transport have fallen, can exercise residential preferences with less significant constraints than ever before.

FUTURE URBAN PROSPECTS

This does not, however, mean that cities have no future. Key types of activity are still bound to major cities; these are a wide range of high-level administrative and service activities that depend on face-to-face contact and supporting business services that only major urban areas provide. Similarly, a wide range of consumer services and cultural and recreational activities are, and will continue to be, urban because they depend on large concentrations of people and/or on face-to-face interaction. The experience of going to a concert or a play is different from that of listening to a record or watching television. In addition, these and similar activities seem to have a high income elasticity of demand and to be relatively labour intensive. Employment in urban service activities has grown relative to manufacturing and is likely to continue to do so.

Similarly, residential preferences are not homogeneous. Whilst some prefer the 'amenity' of low-density green living, others prefer urban amenities. The balance of such preferences appears in part to reflect demographic factors and education. Younger people and single-person and adult-only households appear to be more attracted by urban amenities. Urban amenities seem to have a higher relative value in some cultures — particularly in the countries of continental Europe as compared to the UK or US. In addition, the loss of population from urban cores releases space, thereby both lowering the price of space in urban areas relative to ex-urban areas and allowing lower-density urban living; and it lowers the congestion costs associated with urban living. Traffic jams in Glasgow are now relatively minor. In growing cities of poorer regions such as Athens or Naples, congestion is endemic and a major social and economic problem.

Thus cites have a future role. European cities that have suffered from the worst problems of urban decline since the 1960s, appear to be those that were amongst the dominant manufacturing centres of the nineteenth and early twentieth centuries. Those that have been most successful are typically cities, such as Augsburg, Strasbourg or Norwich, which were major regional but not heavy industrial centres. The future role of cities is not as dense concentrations of manufacturing and associated employment, but as something much closer to that of the major cities before the Industrial Revolution; as administrative centres, as cultural centres in the broadest sense of the term, and as the providers of higher-level urban services and urban amenities. Unlike the period before the Industrial Revolution, however, the population is now not tied to the countryside by low productivity peasant agriculture; and low cost/high speed communications and travel allow a much wider choice of where to live and where to work than ever before. To thrive, therefore, cities must compete as attractive locations to live and as advantageous places to locate economic activity. Thus, in the past, whilst the demand for the output of a city's manufacturing base may have been seen as the source of its growth, in the future such growth will depend as much or more on its urban services and amenities and its ability, on this basis, to attract residents (with their incomes), activities and even tourists. Equally, however, since people are no longer tied to the countryside by agricultural employment, if cities are attractive, a high degree of urbanisation can be economically and socially supported.

Thus successful urban policy has to extend far beyond the simple transplantation of resources to inner areas (which, as we have seen, is likely to be ineffective on its own). It has to extend to questions of the attractiveness of the urban environment; to the provision of services and to the upgrading of the urban infrastructure and the provision of housing and services that will attract all groups.

REFERENCES

van den Berg, L., *et al.*, (1982) *Urban Europe: a study of growth and decline*, Pergamon, Oxford

Burridge, P. and Gordon, I. (1981) 'Unemployment in the British Metropolitan Labour Areas', *Oxford Economic Papers*, **33**

Cheshire, P. C. (1973) *Regional unemployment differences*, Regional Papers II, NIESR/CUP, London

—— (1979) 'Inner areas as spatial labour markets: a critique of the Inner Area Studies', *Urban Studies*, **16**, pp. 29–43

—— Hay, D. and Carbonaro, G. (1985) 'Regional policy and urban problems: the Community's role in tackling urban decline and problems of growth', unpublished report to the Commission of the

European Communities, Joint Centre for Land Development Studies, University of Reading

Department of the Environment (1983) *Urban Deprivation*, Information Note 2, Inner Cities Directorate, London

Evans, A. W. and Richardson, R. (1981) 'Urban unemployment: interpretation and additional evidence', *Scottish Journal of Political Economy*, **28**, pp. 107–24

Gordon, I. (1985) 'The cyclical sensitivity of regional employment and unemployment differentials', *Regional Studies*, 19, pp. 95–110

—— and Lamont, D. (1982) 'A model of labour market interdependencies in the London Region', *Environment and Planning A*, **14**, pp. 237–64

Hall, P. and Hay, D. (1980) *Growth centres in the European urban system*, Heinemann Educational, London

Leven, C. L. (1978) *The mature metropolis*, D. C. Heath, Lexington

—— (1985) 'Urban revival', Washington University, St Louis, mimeo

Metcalf, D. and Richardson, R. (1976) 'Unemployment in London', in Worswick, G. D. N. (ed.), *The concept and measurement of unemployment*. Allen & Unwin, London

3

Glasgow: Policy for the Post-industrial City

W. F. Lever

The Western nations are increasingly being described as 'post-industrial' in character. Just as the late eighteenth and early nineteenth centuries saw a radical transformation not just of Britain's economy but of its society, changes of a similar magnitude have accelerated in post-war Britain as the country moves towards post-industrialism. Observers have described a society typifying post-industrialism as having certain characteristics: the pity is that British cities, not least Glasgow, are acquiring only some, and not always the most beneficial, of these characteristics.

The first, and perhaps visually the most obvious, of the characteristics of post-industrial economies and societies is the decline of the old industrial base, the so-called 'smokestack' industries (Bell, 1973). Industries such as coal-mining, steel-production, shipbuilding and heavy engineering are in decline, both in terms of output, and, as *per capita* output grows, even more in terms of employment. In some cases this decline represents a real reduction in demand: in other cases more of the demand is met by imports. Alongside this decline is that experienced in the consumer goods industries, not always thought of as smokestack industries, with massive import penetration in industries such as cars, domestic goods and electrical equipment. Psychologically the decline of these industries has been even more damaging, for they were the growth industries of the 1960s and played a large role in regional policy designed to help the depressed regions of Britain recover employment and investment. Few people expected coal-mining, steel or heavy engineering to offer large-scale employment growth in the 1960s, but the consumer goods industries were the providers of thousands of jobs not only in the affluent South but on Merseyside and Clydeside. If any industrial sectors are likely to expand in the post-industrial era, then they are likely to be highly dependent upon the new technologies and concerned with new products and/or processes. This assumption, within the definition of a post-industrial economy, is based on the Schumpeterian idea that growth is dependent upon innovation. Products will be created and during the initial production stage their manufacturers will enjoy a competitive advantage: as demand for the products expands, mass production becomes the dominant form of processing and the locus of production typically moves away from the major cities and from the developed economies towards more peripheral sites and to countries with lower labour costs. Thus, as the manufacture of a wide range of goods from ships to hi-fi equipment increasingly moves to the newly industrialising countries, post-industrial economies will depend, for manufacturing jobs, on innovation and high technology.

The second characteristic of post-industrial society is the growth of the service economy (Gershuny, 1977, 1978). Rising income leads people to demand a wider range of services, some of which are provided privately and some of which are provided by the public sector, and to demand higher-quality services. At the same time, industry and business is also demanding more service support as its products and processes become more sophisticated. This distinction between personal services, demanded by individuals and households, and producer services, demanded by industry, has become increasingly important as the enhancement of producer services, such as research and development, data processing, financial services, design and marketing, is seen as helping industry to expand, whereas the growth of public sector personal services such as education, health and welfare, and private sector personal services such as leisure, is seen as wealth consuming. Nevertheless, many of the new job creations are in the personal service sector associated with such developments as tourism and entertainment, and the 'quality of life' arguments for the success of industrial developments in some regions such as the South West and East Anglia appear to show that the new industries are attracted not just by the quality of the local producer services, but also by the availability of high-quality personal services such as education, entertainment and retailing.

The third element in the post-industrial society is the growth of real income. Higher levels of productivity tend to be equated with higher *per capita* income and this is paralleled by an assumption of greater equality in income distribution. This would in part be achieved by greater work-sharing and an overall reduction in the average working week. This, in its turn, leads to the fourth characteristic of post-industrial society, namely, more leisure time. This would occur as a consequence of work-sharing and as the need for manual labour was reduced by mechanisation. A fifth and final characteristic of post-industrial society is greater participation and democracy and great equality in the standards of living. This will occur for a number of reasons. The decline of smokestack industries will reduce inequalities in environmental standards; rising real incomes will reduce inequalities in housing conditions; the shift from factory-based manufacturing to services and high technology industry should offer greater equality in working conditions; and more sophisticated information technology (such as computerised voting) should offer the chance to achieve higher levels of participation in decision-making.

In this prophetic vision of a post-industrial society there is much that is good and little that is objectionable. Those who look to the transitional stage in which many cities such as Glasgow now find themselves can discern, however, only some elements of the post-industrial society. Just as the first industrial revolution was not achieved without severe problems of over-rapid urbanisation and rural abandonment, the transition to post-industrialism is creating its own acute problems. The decline of manufacturing industry is releasing large quantities of labour, much of it typically male, semi-skilled and manual, whilst the expanding sectors are recruiting very different types of labour — usually female and/or those leaving full-time education. Thus the rate of registered unemployment has risen much more quickly than the change in total employment would suggest. Second, the location of employment within the urban system is also changing. The major cities, once the most rapidly growing elements in the industrial system, throughout the 1970s were found to be the worst locations for manufacturing, with higher costs and lower profits. The small towns, offering pleasant environments and more docile labour forces, proved much more attractive not only to the new manufacturing industries but to some of the rapidly growing service industries. Within the larger cities, the 'inner city' problem identified so confidently on the basis of the 1971 Census of Population and located in the inner city areas so positively in the 1978 Inner Urban Areas Act, is now a more spatially diffused phenomenon. The peripheral public sector housing estates have worse problems than the old inner city areas. Built contemporaneously with the greenfield industrial estates of the 1950s and 1960s, the collapse of the consumer goods industries on those estates has left their resident workforces isolated, jobless and immobile. The older inner city areas have received much more investment, the housing stock is better, public transport works reasonably well and many of the new jobs are located not far away in the central city business and entertainment areas.

The prediction of more leisure *has* been realised, but in its least beneficial form with rapidly rising unemployment rates. Assumptions about work-sharing have not been borne out, either because the skills required were not possessed by the workless or because tax and insurance provisions have made it more advantageous for employers to use their existing workforces more intensively through overtime rather than to take on additional workers. There have, contrary to predictions, been increasing disparities in household incomes, and these disparities have not been reduced by compensation within the tax system. Lastly, the prediction of increased democracy and participation is hardly borne out by the facts, as voting patterns show an increasing polarisation between North and South, between the cities and elsewhere. Increasing participation may be emerging as 'the community' is increasingly asked to provide employment and demand in areas where the formal economy has proved incapable of using all the local labour supply. Discussion continues on the viability of community business, but suspicions remain that it may well be a case of achieving the right ends (greater participation, enhanced community services) for the wrong reasons (rising unemployment, withdrawal of public sector expenditure on local authority services).

The reality of the post-industrial city is proving, at this point in the transition, to be rather less attractive than its prophets would have had us believe.

GLASGOW — A CITY IN TRANSITION

The economy of Glasgow has changed greatly since 1950. The

old industrial base, founded on an iron industry and local coal serving the needs of metal-using industries such as shipbuilding and heavy engineering, has declined. New industries, developed during the 1960s, required different locations, predominantly greenfield sites, and employed different types of labour. Services grew in importance and they too employed different groups of workers. Over the same period the urban fabric was greatly transformed. The city development plan issued in 1960 promised a massive programme of housing renewal involving almost half of the city's housing stock. At the time, the implications of these proposals for commerce and industry were not realised, but studies (e.g. Bull, 1981) have demonstrated the dislocative effect of renewal on this scale. Administratively too the conurbation was restructured in the mid-1970s.

The city is no stranger to change. Glasgow, having developed as an ecclesiastical, market and university town, found itself a role as a major commercial centre when the trans-Atlantic colonies grew up. To this day there are streets in the city's commercial quarter with names such as Virginia, Tobago and Jamaica, and the tobacco and cotton industries still survive in and around the city (Gordon, 1983). A further transition occurred when Britain began to lose its North American colonies and the existence of local coal and iron ore provided the basis for Glasgow's manufacturing growth. During the nineteenth century the urban population grew as large numbers of settlers from the rural Highlands and Ireland arrived looking for work. This very rapid growth in population was accommodated only by providing mass housing of very low standard at very high densities, and this by 1950 had left Glasgow with the worst housing stock in Europe (Gibb, 1984).

Thus the changes which have occurred in Glasgow since 1950 come as no surprise to the city, but their speed and intensity are new. So too is the role of the public sector in initiating so much of the change. Glasgow still holds an unenviable position in the league tables of economic, social and environmental health. It is perhaps because of the severity of these problems that Glasgow, and indeed the whole of the conurbation, has come to be regarded as something of a laboratory for urban policy, and the city is now involved in a number of comparative research projects which seek to assess the effectiveness of the wide range of policies practised in the city, to learn from other cities, and to offer its experience to other cities with similar problems

(Hausner and Robson, 1985).

This chapter concentrates upon the economic problems of the city and the policies which have been devised to confront them. The economic problems, however, can only really be understood within the context of the environmental and social problems which parallel them. Although the concepts of 'multiple deprivation' and 'intergenerational transmission of poverty' were fashionable in the 1970s (linking failing local economies with poor housing and inadequate local services leading to poor educational and health standards which generated a subsequent workforce particularly vulnerable to unemployment and underemployment), the Inner Area Studies (Department of the Environment, 1977) and other linked research exercises stressed the *economic* basis of much of this problem. For this reason we concentrate on problems and policies for Clydeside's economy, although well aware of the links between the failing economic base and the environmental and social problems.

In terms of employment three quite clear trends have emerged in the economy of Clydeside since the 1950s (Lever and Mather, 1986). First, there has been a substantial drop in total employment from 850,000 in 1951 to 685,000 in 1981 and an estimated 640,000 in 1984. The rate of job loss steepened from 400 per year in the 1950s, to 4,500 per year in the 1960s and to 25,000 per year in the 1970s and early 1980s. The second trend has been the growing suburbanisation of employment. Decline in Glasgow has been continuous throughout the period since 1951; but the outer conurbation which is a heterogeneous mixture of suburban dormitories, New Towns and old industrial towns, experienced increasing employment at least until the mid-1970s. Thus the share of the conurbation's total employment located in Glasgow fell from 66.8 per cent in 1951 to 57.2 per cent in 1978, but thereafter there has been a rise to 58.2 per cent in 1981 and an estimated 58.5 per cent currently. Before this slight reversal in trend is seen as a major endorsement of the inner city policies currently implemented in Glasgow, it should however be pointed out that the change since 1978 is more a result of the growth of business failures in the urban periphery than a major upturn in the fortunes of the inner city. The third major trend, entirely consistent with the development of a post-industrial economy, is the switch from manufacturing to services. Total employment in manufacturing fell from 58 per cent of all employment in 1961 to 37 per cent in 1981. It is no exaggeration to say that in those 20 years Clydeside moved from being an industrial city to a service centre. Manufacturing employment fell from about 400,000 in 1961 to 180,000 in 1981, whilst service employment rose from 300,000 to 430,000 over the same period. Examining this change over a 20 year period tends to conceal just how much of the change has occurred since 1978. Sectors such as metal manufacture, cars, textiles, chemicals and metal goods manufacture all lost 35-40 per cent of their total employment in this three-year period. Over the same period the only sectors to increase their employment levels were finance, personal services and administration.

Explanations of this decline in the economic base are numerous. The standardisation technique 'shift-share' analysis shows that it is not sufficient to blame the conurbation's poor performance on an adverse industrial structure, or on over-dependence upon sectors which have declined nationally (Lever, Danson and Malcolm, 1980). Even when the industrial structure is taken into account, the conurbation in 1981 had about 70,000 jobs fewer than would have been expected on the basis of its employment structure in 1971 and national trends in the period 1971–81; and these missing jobs were very significantly concentrated in Glasgow. Shift-share analysts usually develop this argument by examining the nature of the competitive failure of local industry, but it should be pointed out that many of Glasgow's missing jobs are not in the competitive private sector but in the public sector and reflect the scaling-down of provision of employment in health, education and social welfare as the resident population of the city fell.

Explanations of the city's economic decline have suggested that it is disadvantaged by concentrating upon the labour-intensive elements in manufacturing industry so that it has been particularly vulnerable in periods of high wage inflation, and it has correspondingly low levels of investment per worker compared with national trends (Lever, 1982). The rate of new-firm formation has also been low compared with national and even rest-of-Scotland rates, and it has been suggested that the old industrial structure based on steel, large heavy engineering firms and shipbuilding, did not provide a climate which led to entrepreneurship. The high point of regional policy in the 1960s brought many branch plants to the Clydeside conurbation although significantly few came to Glasgow itself. Concern was expressed at the development of a regional 'branch plant economy' and to an extent these fears were justified in the late 1970s when the employment performance of non-locally-owned plants was much worse than that of locally-owned plants. For example, between 1978 and 1981 foreign-owned plants in the conurbation lost 43 per cent of their employment compared with a figure of 25 per cent for locally-owned plants (Firn, 1978; Hood and Young, 1982).

The inevitable consequence of this manufacturing employment decline, and the shift to services, has been rising unemployment. In 1971 the male unemployment rate in Glasgow was 16.1 per cent: by 1981 it was 24.6 per cent. The comparable figures for the rest of the conurbation were 10.7 per cent and 23.0 per cent, respectively. Even more striking than the overall rise in unemployment are the very marked spatial differentials: by 1981, the suburban dormitories of Eastwood, and Bearsden and Milngavie, had male unemployment rates of about 5 per cent; whilst the rate in the two New Towns was about 12 per cent; that in the old industrial towns such as Motherwell, Coatbridge and Clydebank was about 20 per cent; and Glasgow's was almost 25 per cent. A more detailed spatial analysis of male unemployment using 1971 and 1981 Census of Population data shows graphically how, within Glasgow, the worst areas of unemployment have shifted from the inner city to the peripheral housing estates. It remains unclear whether this is because employment prospects in the inner city have improved relative to those on the peripheral housing estates or whether policies of urban renewal and public sector housing management have concentrated the unemployed on the peripheral estates. By 1984 male unemployment rates in some wards were as high as 40 per cent; elsewhere rates of 3 or 4 per cent might be found. With such contrasts, area-based strategies have proved a frequent instrument for economic regeneration and job creation (McGregor and Mather, 1986).

POLICY ASSESSMENT

The multiplicity of policies and agencies developed for the economic regeneration of Clydeside has inevitably attracted a great deal of interest. Attempts at monitoring or evaluating these polices have encountered a number of problems which have had to be tackled in a fairly pragmatic way, for much of the analysis is quite new. Prior to the growth of urban policy in the late 1970s, most spatially discriminant policies for employment creation and maintenance were operated at the regional level, and therefore much of the evaluation of these policies adopted a regional framework. There are a number of reasons, however, why we cannot use such methodologies for evaluating the success or failure of urban policies. First, many of the areas designated to receive additional assistance with investment, labour costs and planning approvals are so small in extent as to make it highly likely that the benefits will spill over into the surrounding areas. Where Enterprise Zones, Partnership or Programme Authorities, or Joint Economic Initiatives are defined, they are targeted on the areas of greatest need, but (unlike the regions in receipt of regional aid prior to 1984) their size means that the employment and income benefits will go in many cases to populations resident outside the defined areas. For example, much of the eastern quadrant of Glasgow extending from the edge of the Central Business District to the edge of the city's administrative jurisdiction is covered by the Glasgow East Area Renewal programme. A survey at the start of GEAR in 1978 showed that 75 per cent of the jobs within the area were held by workers resident outside the area, and of the employed resident workforce 75 per cent held jobs located outside the area. By 1985 the number of jobs inside the GEAR area exceeded the area's total employed workforce *plus* the local registered unemployed; yet in Parkhead, at the core of the GEAR area, male unemployment was 40 per cent.

A second problem in estimating the effects of urban policy on employment is the lack of a long time series of data. Estimates of regional policy impacts have been able to use time series data from the 1950s onwards to compare 'policy on' and 'policy off' periods (Moore and Rhodes, 1973; Diamond and Spence, 1983) but the brevity of the period of urban policy since 1978 precludes this approach.

It is possible to identify five major problems in evaluating urban policy in Clydeside and elsewhere. First, wherever intervention in a local economy occurs there is the need to measure what would have happened without such intervention. Policies which achieve only what would have happened anyway suffer from the problem of *deadweight*. For example, when the Manpower Services Commission evaluated the Enterprise Allowance Scheme (Manpower Services Commission, 1984) it estimated that of every 100 jobs created, 72 would have been created without the incentive. This has the effect of quadrupling the estimated cost per job of the scheme.

Second, whenever a firm or an area is assisted, there is a risk that other firms or other areas not so assisted will decline as a consequence. This problem, known as *displacement*, is well illustrated in the case of the Enterprise Zones (EZ). The effect of the rates relief in EZs, the most powerful attractive force, has largely been to draw in firms from outside the EZ rather than to assist in new creations. For example, in the Clydebank Enterprise Zone, of the first 1,764 jobs, 1,165 were in pre-existing firms making short-distance moves into the area; in the Lower Swansea Valley EZ the proportion was even higher. Evaluation of such schemes is even more complicated when one attempts to measure closures outside the area caused by subsidised competition from inside the EZ (a net loss to the system) and to measure businesses moving into the EZ which otherwise would have closed without the benefit of the subsidy (a net gain to the system).

The third problem is that of employment *duration*. During the 1960s when the economy was more buoyant it was hoped that intervention to create jobs would be a temporary phenomenon, and that with the next upswing in the economy the assisted regions would become self-sustaining without the need for continuing subsidy. In the more depressed climate of the 1980s, many of the jobs created do not appear to be commercially viable and will require continuing subsidy. Where jobs are created with a one-off injection of financial or other assistance, part of the evaluation must take into account how long the job will survive. Many of the jobs created under Urban Programme projects are funded for three years only, whereafter it is hoped that they will be self-supporting or taken on by Local Authorities' mainstream funding. With Local Authority finance now sharply cut back, there is little likelihood of this occurring and the employment may therefore end. For example, by late 1984 the three London boroughs of Hackney, Islington and Lambeth had 600 jobs funded under the Urban Programme, all of which were approaching the end of their funding. Strathclyde Region, in operating an employment subsidy scheme using European Social Fund money, attempted to assess the permanence of these jobs and found that, of the first 7,000 created, 90 per cent survived more than six months and 5,750 had been in existence more than 18 months.

Evaluative studies of urban policy must also confront the issue of the *distributional* impact of job creation. Most of the emphasis is placed upon job creation, but very little upon the allocation of the jobs and whether additional steps are taken to target these jobs to the most disadvantaged groups. Much of the targeting that does occur within urban policy is in the field of training, where a large number of schemes have been directed at youth unemployment (including the expanding Youth Training Scheme), at the long-term unemployed, at ethnic minorities and at females (Lever, 1985). Targeting can take three forms: area based, firm or sector based, and individual based. The last is clearly more specific and more accurately targeted, although there are few successful examples. The Strathclyde Employment Grant Scheme, however, does differentiate between disadvantaged groups, providing a 30 per cent wage subsidy to jobs filled by school-leaver unemployed and long-term unemployed, and a 60 per cent wage subsidy to jobs filled by the disabled.

Lastly, policy evaluation which takes the form of cost-per-job estimates of specific policies has disregarded the problem of 'piggy-backing', that is of a job being created with assistance from more than one source, but without all the separate costs being aggregated.

POLICY FOR THE POST-INDUSTRIAL CITY

We have distinguished between old and new policies in Clydeside. The old policies were devised before 1978 when the national economy was fairly robust and the assumption that there would be a return to 'reasonable' levels of unemployment prevailed. The 'new' policies were developed to deal with the problems of the long-term unemployed, very high rates of school-leaver unemployment, and the creation of enterprises which were unlikely to be economically viable in the long run.

Old policies

Regional policy, based largely on capital investment grants, has been a major part of government strategy for bringing jobs to areas of high unemployment. However, as the areas eligible for assistance under this scheme expanded, potential investors were able to become more selective in their choice of location within the assisted areas. This in turn permitted them to avoid inner-city areas which were felt to be risky and unattractive. Analysis of recent grants made under regional policy show it to be anti-urban in its effect. Although, as we have shown, unemployment rates are consistently higher in Glasgow than elsewhere in the conurbation, it receives less grant aid. Thus Glasgow, which has 55 per cent of the conurbation's manufacturing, received only 31 per cent of the assistance offered under the Regional Development Grant (RDG) system between 1979 and 1983. This imbalance is not merely a reflection of the differential industrial structures of the two areas: sector by sector almost without exception the grant per worker was higher in the outer conurbation. We estimate that some 3,000 jobs were either created in the conurbation or maintained by RDG between 1977 and 1983, but in the context of 140,000 unemployed, this expenditure, some £100m in all, has had an impact of no more than 0.02 percentage points on the unemployment rate. Regional Selective Assistance (RSA) brought £36m to Clydeside in 1979–83 and in this case Glasgow's share was even less: only 22 per cent. RSA, however, in terms of cost per job does appear to be rather better value, with 16,600 jobs either created or maintained. The third element in conventional regional policy is the scheme of assistance under the Office and Service Industries Support Scheme. This, at least, does address itself to the trends of the post-industrial city with its growing service sector rather than its declining industrial sector. However, expenditure on OSIS amounted to only £7m compared with £136m under RDG and RSA. This supported some 900 jobs of which the bulk were in Glasgow.

Despite the reservations expressed about the vulnerability of a 'branch plant economy', the attraction of inward investment to Clydeside has remained a continuing element in the industrial strategy. By 1973 almost 60 per cent of the Clydeside conurbation's employment in manufacturing was in companies whose ultimate locus of ownership lay outside Scotland. Local authorities used various powers to promote their attractiveness, and studies from the 1960s showed that firms did tend to be impressed by the enthusiasm of local authorities in the area. However, compared with the rest of Scotland, the performance of the west central Scotland conurbation in attracting incoming firms was poor. Within the conurbation, Glasgow was particularly hard hit as it tried to compete with the New Towns and attractive semi-rural sites on the periphery. Using a 'fair shares'

51

type of analysis, Glasgow gained some 18,000 jobs in incoming firms, but might have expected 52,000 jobs in the post-war period. Of the 'missing' 34,000, Cumbernauld and East Kilbride accounted for almost a half. By the mid-1970s two trends were clear. First, the national and international recession meant that there was much less mobile industry within Britain and international investment was increasingly likely to go to low-cost labour areas such as the newly industrialising countries. Second, the fact that all local authorities had the power to undertake promotion and to attempt to attract inward investment was proving confusing to potential investors, especially those abroad, and in consequence might well be proving counter-productive. The answer, within Scotland, was relatively simple: to hand the whole business over to the Scottish Development Agency. The SDA after 1978 operated a 'one-door approach' and in 1981 this was formalised into Locate In Scotland. LIS operates with an annual budget of £2m through offices in New York, San Francisco, Chicago, Houston and Tokyo. In 1981–4, LIS drew some 9,000 jobs to Scotland and existing foreign companies expanded by 11,000 jobs. LIS does provide a quick and effective service, although it has been criticised for being too reactive and lacking defined targets. Unlike conventional regional policy which has tended to support the old industrial base, LIS has shown a marked concentration upon electronics and mechanical engineering. The major problem with LIS, at least from the perspective of the local authorities which it has replaced, is its spatial effect within Scotland. LIS, in general, markets Scotland as a whole rather than particular locations within Scotland and tends to respond to the preferences of its client firms which tend to favour locations such as the New Towns and not the inner city. However it can be argued that these unattractive locations are no worse off than they were when their local authorities undertook their marketing, and in aggregate we would judge LIS to have been more successful since 1981 in attracting investment than the local authorities would have been.

One of the elements of the post-industrial city is the survival of small high technology firms in a type of 'continuous-creation' process. Partly because of the assumed competitive advantage implicit in a continuous process of new-firm creation, and partly because of the poor recent employment performance of large plants, whether branch plants or not, assistance to small businesses has been a consistent element within the policies of most large cities. The Clydeside conurbation does have a large stock of small businesses, although its new-firm formation rate is low and the long period of urban redevelopment has had a serious effect on this section of the economic base. Small firm promotion, environmental improvement, and the provision of small industrial premises in the urban core have been the main elements in the inner city revitalisation programme. Small firm development in Clydeside has an unusually wide range of support agencies with differing forms of advisory and financial support from national programmes of the Department of Industry, through the SDA, through local authorities and increasingly through specialist agencies linking the private and public sectors.

This diversity does raise the potential problem of overlap and confusion, although co-operation between the agencies seems to have kept this to a minimum by their adopting interlocking rather than overlapping functions. For example, the Small Business Division of the SDA provides only specialist technical and investment advice, leaving the provision of general advice on setting up in business Glasgow Opportunity, the local Enterprise Trust. The diversity of agencies has achieved a high level of penetration with approximately 70 per cent of small businesses aware of the SDA's programme and around 30 percent aware of local authority schemes. It has become clear, however, that the mere provision of finance is insufficient and that much better survival rates are achieved where financial help is linked to management advice, and in some cases jointly provided business services.

The fourth policy, which dates from before 1978, is the provision of infrastructure, particularly industrial and commercial premises. District councils have tended to see one of their most important roles as the providers of industrial floorspace, partly one suspects because of a greater sense of trust in bricks and mortar, which would survive the closure of a tenant firm, than in finance or advice which would not. The SDA, which inherited the role of Scotland's major industrial landlord from the Scottish Industrial Estates, now finds itself with an embarrassingly large stock of large vacant premises, mostly of the 1950s and 1960s, for which there is little demand, and which pose difficult problems of conversion. The market for small premises, however, is much more buoyant, especially when these come with on-site business advice and common service as in Glasgow's schemes.

New policies

We briefly list six new policies which, whilst far from being a comprehensive list of urban policies in Clydeside, each exemplifies one of the emergent characteristics of the post-industrial society.

First, analysis has demonstrated that Glasgow is a labour-intensive city, yet the emphasis in regional policy has been on capital subsidy. Whilst this is intended to have the effect of enhancing competitiveness, its effect on employment may be small or even negative in the long run. A labour subsidy programme has rarely been a part of national policy (with the exception of the old Regional Employment Premium), but Strathclyde Region's Employment Grant Scheme, in part using the European Social Fund, is aimed at getting employers to create additional jobs by providing a wage subsidy. More than half the jobs are in manufacturing and monitoring indicates that the jobs are reasonably durable. By the end of 1985, some 8,500 jobs should have been created although the scheme is (hopefully temporarily) in abeyance. The particular merit of the scheme is its capacity for targeting on specific disadvantaged groups within the jobless. Thus the level of subsidy distinguishes between long-term adult unemployed, school-leaver and youth unemployed, and disabled. This makes it one of the few policies which pay attention not only to job creation, but also to job allocation.

A second scheme which identifies a target group within the unemployed is the Enterprise Allowance Scheme, albeit that this is not strictly speaking *urban* policy. EAS provides capital and assistance to workers who have been unemployed for more than 13 weeks and have £1,000 of their own to invest. With some exceptions, the businesses are not vetted. The urban significance of EAS is that it operates out of selected MSC offices and in Clydeside these comprise two in the old traditional inner city (Partick and Shawlands) and two located in old industrial towns selected for special SDA initiatives (Motherwell and Clydebank). In this light it is not surprising that there has been comment that the rate of uptake of EAS from the peripheral housing estates in Glasgow has been low. Allowing for deadweight effects, EAS costs £2,700 per job, which makes it very cost effective, compared with regional policy's RDG figure of £39,000, and if 60 per cent of the EAS jobs last for more than two years the figure falls to around £700 per job.

With the increasing severity of the national recession, and its growing duration, it has become apparent to policy-makers that public sector agencies working alone to exert pressure unilaterally on the private sector to create jobs are unlikely to be adequate. In consequence, new alliances have emerged to create jobs. Community Businesses have emerged linking public sector finance and advice with community initiatives and needs. In theory they operate under community ownership and control, they target employment creation upon particular localities, they may create collective profits which should be ploughed back into the community and they should harmonise community development and economic regeneration. In practice there appear to be difficulties in reconciling their community and business objectives, and their contribution to employment creation (about 600 jobs in 25 CBs in Clydeside by 1984) is marginal. However, the creation of Strathclyde Community Business to provide finance and advice and a major new initiative by the region in 1985 should increase the scale of activity considerably. The second alliance, between local authorities and the private sector, has taken the form of the Enterprise Trusts which are locally-based consortia of local authorities, the SDA, and private sector finance and expertise assembled to assist new business start-ups. The largest in the conurbation, Glasgow Opportunity, has about 80 operating projects with 300 jobs and more in the pipeline: there are other smaller ones in Monklands, Motherwell and Cumbernauld. So promising is this form of agency that the SDA has now chosen the ET format to manage its most recently declared area-based initiative in Greenock/Port Glasgow.

Using public policy to facilitate the development of the private sector by removing restrictions and taxes has been a recurrent theme of the present government. Applied at the urban scale, this philosophy has generated the Enterprise Zones, the most successful of which is located at Clydebank, west of Glasgow. In the Clydebank EZ, £23m of public sector money has been used (£14m on factory construction, £3 on environmental schemes) to lever a further £18m of private sector money into an unemployment blackspot created by the closure of the Singer sewing-machine plant. By late 1984 there were 1,750 jobs in the EZ of which 1,250 had existed prior to the declaration of the EZ, the majority of them outside the designated area, and 500 in new firm creations. Analysing the complete effect of EZs is not easy, as the consultants found, for it is difficult to assess plant closures outside the EZ due to subsidised competition, and to assess the extent to which the subsidy preserved jobs which would otherwise have been lost. Survey analysis shows the prime attraction of the EZs to be relief from rates, and much of the Clydebank EZ's success is attributable to the groundwork done by the SDA's Taskforce in preparing and promoting the site. We estimate a *net* increase of some 1,000 jobs to date at an average cost of £30,000, but short-distance movement into the EZ has caused resentment in surrounding Districts, not least Glasgow.

The very sharp spatial differentials in unemployment within the conurbation have inevitably forced the agencies concerned to declare areas of special treatment. This initiative owes much to the SDA's overview of the needs of the conurbation as a whole. The earliest area-based initiative was the comprehensive renewal strategy developed for Glasgow's East End (GEAR) after the cancellation of Scotland's sixth New Town at Stonehouse. Total public sector costs by 1984 amounted to over £200m, but with 3,300 jobs created, private sector housing returning to the area and a significant rise in environmental standards, the scheme must be considered a success. The second model of area-based project, termed by some the 'fire brigade' approach and exemplified by the Clydebank Taskforce of the SDA, followed GEAR. Subsequent SDA designated schemes have chosen areas of potential, rather than areas of economic disaster, and include Motherwell and Coatbridge. The apparent success of concentrating investment and effort by the SDA into quite small areas within the conurbation has inevitably provoked imitation by the local authority sector. Strathclyde has an extensive programme of areas of priority treatment, defined on a range of welfare criteria, and Glasgow has defined a number of areas — first in the inner city, such as Maryhill and Govan, and more recently in the peripheral areas — to receive assistance. Such schemes to date do seem to have achieved 'critical mass' with environmental improvement and some success in job creation, but inevitably their success leads to increased pressure from similar, but undesignated, areas to receive the same treatment.

The last feature of the post-industrial city which now seems to play a part in the development of urban policy is the growth of leisure-related activities as employment creators. A slogan of 'Come to Glasgow for your Holiday' might have been unthinkable a decade ago, but a series of developments makes the concept more viable. A programme of major hotel-building within the city over the past five years reflects a changing planning policy and the success of attempts to woo major hotel chains to the city. The opening of the Burrell Gallery, which incidentally publicised Glasgow's other museums and galleries more effectively, the projected Garden Festival, and the planned development of the St Enoch and Buchanan Street sites with further facilities, have all served to broaden Glasgow's range of interests to visitors. On the business front, the opening of the Scottish Exhibition Centre will not only draw revenue to the city but hopefully convince businessmen of the advantages of location within the city. Finally, it would be difficult to subject the 'Glasgow's Miles Better' campaign to econometric analysis, but there is a belief that it had considerable economic impact on the city.

THE FUTURE

If one has to look to the future of urban policy as the conurbations move towards post-industrialism, some conclusions emerge. First, it is impossible to predict the economic health of the cities without knowing what shape the national economy will be in. With alternative economic models predicting national unemployment at anywhere between 1.7m and 4.5m by 1989, the amount and the spatial distribution of urban unemployment might vary widely: these figures, for example, would give Glasgow an estimated unemployment rate of anywhere between 11 per cent and 32 per cent by 1989. Second, the 1960s and 1970s were the period of what became known as the urban-rural shift, as the large city economies collapsed and the small urban places prospered: the 1980s have offered enough evidence to suggest that a reversal of this trend is due and the term 'Urban Renaissance', heard in the streets of Pittsburgh and Boston, may become a European expression. Third, whereas regional policy always had to be defended on economic grounds — freeing up the labour supply, relieving congestion and avoiding spiralling land prices — in the current climate urban policy cannot be so defended. It is as much social policy as economic policy: it is about giving people hope, self-respect and a decent environment as much as a high income or secure employment. The price of failure, as the 1981 urban riots showed, may be higher than the country can afford.

ACKNOWLEDGEMENT

The research on which this chapter draws was funded by the Economic and Social Research Council.

REFERENCES

Bell, D. (1973) *The coming of post industrial society: a venture in social forecasting*, Basic Books, New York

Bull, P. (1981) 'Redevelopment schemes and manufacturing activity in Glasgow', *Environment and Planning*, **13**, pp. 991–1000

Department of the Environment (1977) *Inner Area Studies: Liverpool, Birmingham and Lambeth: summary of consultants' final reports*, HMSO, London

Diamond, D. and Spence, N. (1983) *Regional policy evaluation: a methodological review and the Scottish example*, Gower, Farnborough

Firn, J. R. (1978) 'External control and regional policy', in Brown, G. (ed.), *The Red Paper on Scotland*, EUSPS, Edinburgh

Gershuny, J. I. (1977) 'Post industrial society: the myth of the service economy', *Futures*, **9**, pp. 103–14

—— (1978) *After industrial society: the emerging self service economy*, Macmillan, London

Gibb, A. (1984) *Glasgow: the making of a city*, Croom Helm, London

Gordon, G. (1983) 'Industrial development, c1750–1980' in Whittington, G. and Whyte, I. D. (eds.), *An historical geography of Scotland*, Academic Press, London, pp. 165–90

Hausner, V. and Robson, B. (1985) *Changing cities*, ESRC, London

Holtermann, S. (1975) 'Areas of urban deprivation in Great Britain: an analysis of 1971 Census data', *Social Trends*, **6**, pp. 33–47

Hood, N. and Young, S. (1982) *Multinationals in retreat: the Scottish experience*, Edinburgh University Press, Edinburgh

Lever, W. F. (1982) 'Urban scale as a determinant of employment growth or decline', in Collins, L. (ed.), *Industrial decline and regeneration*, Edinburgh University Press, Edinburgh

—— (1985) 'Targeted economic development', unpublished paper, Society of Local Authority Chief Executives Conference on Strengthening Local Economic Development, November 1985, London

——, Danson, M. and Malcolm, J. F. (1980) 'The inner city employment problem in Great Britain, 1952–76', *Urban Studies*, **17**, pp. 193–219

—— and Mather, F. (1986) 'The changing structure of business and employment in the conurbation', in Lever, W. F. and Moore, C. (eds.), *The city in transition: policies and agencies for the economic regeneration of Clydeside*, Oxford University Press, Oxford

McGregor, A. and Mather, F. (1986) 'Developments in Glasgow's labour market', in Lever, W. F. and Moore, C. (eds.), *The city in transition: policies and agencies for the economic regeneration of Clydeside*, Oxford University Press, Oxford

Manpower Services Commission (1984) *Community Programme postal follow-up survey*, Employment Division, MSC, London

Moore, B. and Rhodes, J. (1973) 'Evaluating the effects of British regional economic policy', *Economic Journal*, **82**, pp. 87–110

4

High Technology Industry, Regional Development and Defence Manufacturing: a Case Study in the UK Sunbelt

Martin Boddy

Hopes of economic renaissance in the UK have frequently been pinned on the broad swathe of country from Cambridge to London, and along the M4 from Berkshire to Swindon and Bristol — Britain's 'Sunrise Belt'. This part of southern England has escaped the worst of the recession and rising unemployment, and has raised hopes of future growth based above all around a new wave of electronics and high technology activities. With companies like ICL established at Maidenhead, Digital at Reading, Intel and Logica at Swindon and Hewlett Packard and Inmos at Bristol, parallels have been drawn with California's Silicon Valley. Until recently, however, there has been little in the way of hard analysis to set against image and optimism. Detailed study of one particular locality, the Bristol area, allows a more critical look at this high-tech growth image and some of the underlying processes. It identifies in particular the key role of defence-related R&D and manufacturing to the Bristol locality, leading to a more general discussion of the spatial impacts of defence manufacturing in the UK.

Bristol itself, 120 miles west of London and with a population of around a million in the continuous built-up area, is the largest urban area along the M4. Its unemployment has risen, as elsewhere. By January 1985 it was up to 11.6 per cent. This was, however, significantly lower than the national figure of 13.7 per cent and compares very favourably with other major urban areas such as Glasgow (17.7 per cent), Newcastle (18.5 per cent) and Birmingham (16.4 per cent). The city would appear to have survived relatively well. By 1981, Bristol was, according to the *Sunday Times* (26 August 1981), 'well on the way to becoming the high technology centre of Britain . . . set to become Britain's

Silicon Valley of the 1980s'. Kenneth Baker, when a junior minister in the Department of the Environment, described the city in 1985 as 'the shining buckle on Britain's high-tech belt'. Reinforcing this image, Hewlett Packard now manufacture computer peripherals on the city's northern fringe and are establishing their first R&D facility outside the USA alongside it. Dupont are soon to start producing electronic components for the UK market and Inmos, the microchip company originally set up with government backing, has its R&D centre in the city. Other companies manufacture electronic capital equipment, and a range of computer-related companies including Digital, ICL, GEAC and Systime, have taken premises on the up-market AZTEC West industrial estate on the M4/M5 interchange at the city's expanding northern fringe. On the face of it, this seems to bear out the image of high-tech expansion and the Silicon Valley parallels; but is the image more than skin-deep?

More systematic analysis reveals a rather different and more complex picture. One problem is the lack of a very precise definition of 'high technology' industry. The popular image is of electronics, microchip industries, computer-related activities and possibly 'bio-technology', together with R&D activity and a high level of scientific and technical employment, although the label has been used very loosely. For practical purposes we can use a grouping of official Census of Employment categories, on which researchers are reaching some consensus as a pragmatic definition of what constitutes 'high technology'. Excluding aerospace for the moment, high technology (mainly electronic components, computers and electronic capital goods) in fact accounted for under 1 per cent of employment locally in 1981, compared with 2 per cent nationally (Table 4.1). This represented only 2,500 jobs in the Bristol region. The *rate* of expansion over the decade to 1981 was rapid, but represented fairly modest growth, around 1,700, in *absolute* terms. These figures, the latest official statistics currently available, are obviously dated. Survey evidence, however, suggests that around 1,000 jobs had been added in new and existing firms by mid-1985, making 3,500 in all — Bristol's Economic Development Office puts the figure somewhat higher at around 6,000, but this was based on a looser definition of 'high technology' and a more generous definition of the Bristol region. To put growth of high technology employment in perspective, however, employment in Food, Drink and Tobacco, locally fell

Table 4.1: High technology employment as a proportion of total employment and change in high technology employment, 1971–81

	Share of total employment		Change 1971–81	
	Bristol	Great Britain	Bristol	Great Britain
	%	%	%	%
Non-aerospace high tech[a]	0.77	1.99	+151	−9.3
Aerospace	7.26	0.88	−7.6	−12.3
All high tech	8.03	2.87	−1.8	−10.0

Note: a. Includes: Pharmaceutical chemicals and preparations; Scientific & industrial instruments and systems; Radio & electronic components; Broadcasting equipment; Electronic computers; Radio, radar & electronic capital goods.
Source: Annual Census of Employment.

by 9,000 over the decade to 1981 and over 7,000 jobs were lost in Paper, Printing and Packaging, with further losses since then. Furthermore, the major *growth* in employment locally has been concentrated above all in the service sector with Miscellaneous Services expanding by a massive 10,500 jobs in the decade to 1981 and Financial Services by 9,500 (Figure 4.1).

There *are* examples of companies, locally, which are at the forefront of their technologies, with a significant R&D content and which are expanding rapidly. Others concerned with computing equipment and related activity, however, are essentially regional sales and service outlets. And the locality has failed to attract large-scale employment in mass manufacture electronics companies, including Japanese and American investment. This has typically gone to the assisted areas of South Wales and Scotland. Job gain, locally, has moreover generally fallen short of enthusiastically inflated claims: Hewlett Packard, initially expecting to employ 1,300 by the mid-1980s rising to 6,000, actually employed around 300 by mid-1985 and expected to increase this to 500 by the end of 1986.

Engineering Industry Training Board returns allow us to look more widely at the national context (EITB, 1985a). In terms of absolute numbers, electronics employment is particularly concentrated, first, in the older conurbations including Greater London, Manchester and the West Midlands and, second, in newer growth areas, the south-east counties — Hampshire,

Figure 4.1: Employment change in the Bristol region, 1971–81

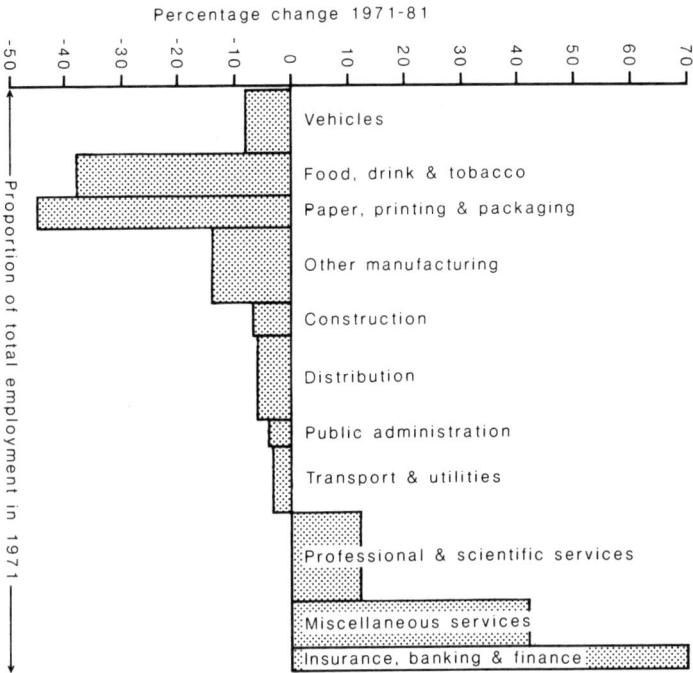

Percentage change 1971-81

Proportion of total employment in 1971

Vehicles

Food, drink & tobacco

Paper, printing & packaging

Other manufacturing

Construction

Distribution

Public administration

Transport & utilities

Professional & scientific services

Miscellaneous services

Insurance, banking & finance

Berkshire, Herts and Essex — and Strathclyde in central Scotland (Figure 4.2). There is no evidence, on these figures at least, of an 'M4 corridor', or indeed an 'M11 effect' extending up to Cambridge. Avon County, with only 2,472 electronics jobs in 1984, was ranked 34th out of the 61 counties and Scottish regions (Table 4.2). The major increases between 1978 and 1984 were polarised geographically, between Berkshire on the one hand, and Lothian and Gwent on the other (Figure 4.3). So although the *eastern* end of the 'M4 Corridor', specifically Berkshire, stands out, Avon was one of a number of counties experiencing much more modest growth.

Non-aerospace high technology employment, on the available evidence, is therefore significantly less important locally than nationally. Electronics employment is modest compared to both

Figure 4.2: Employment in electronics by county, 1984

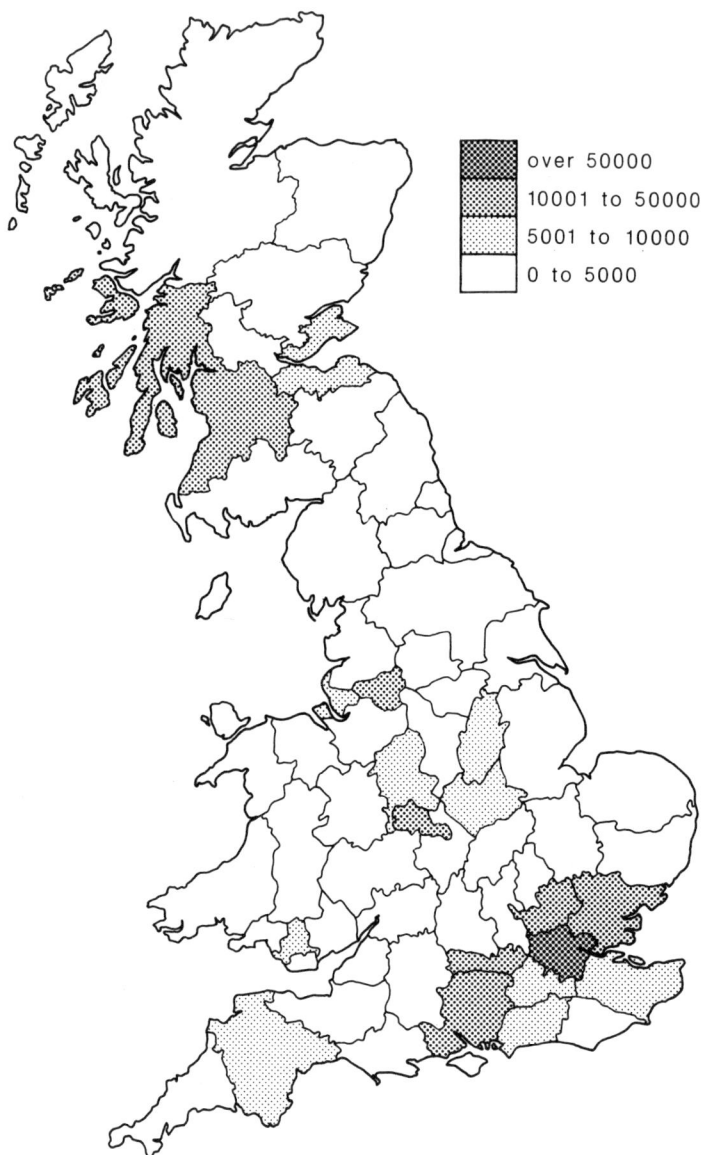

over 50000
10001 to 50000
5001 to 10000
0 to 5000

Figure 4.3: Change in electronics employment by county, 1978–84

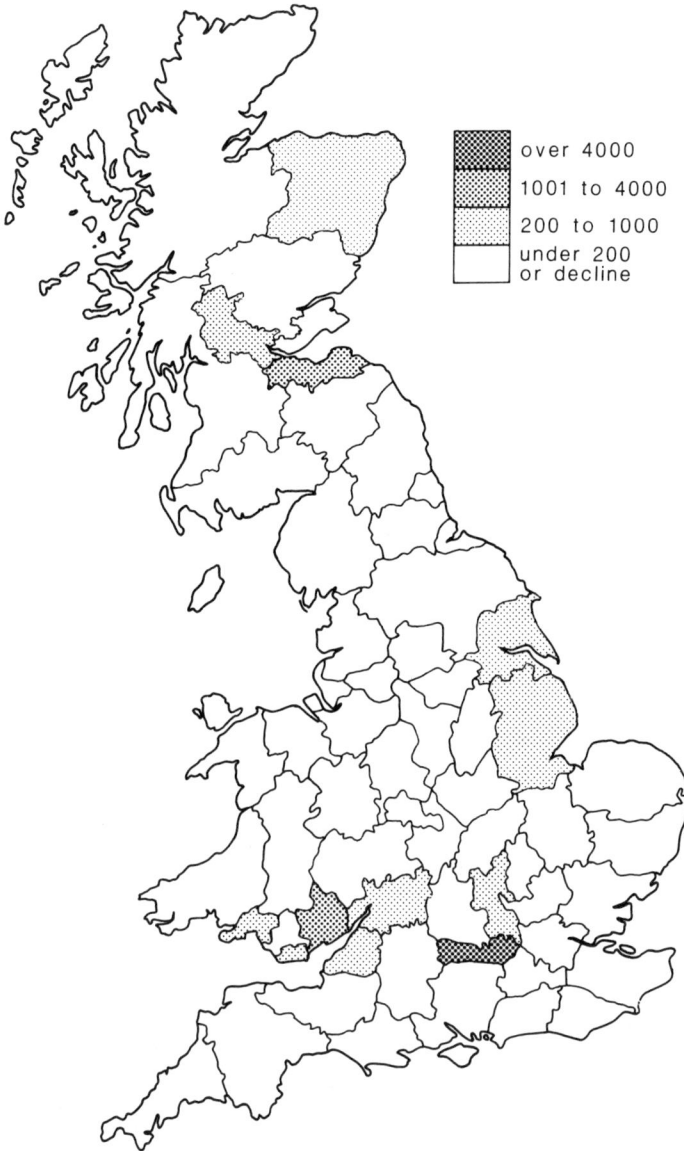

over 4000
1001 to 4000
200 to 1000
under 200
or decline

Table 4.2: Electronics employment by county, 1984

County	Employment	Number of establishments	County	Employment	Number of establishments
1 Greater London	55,438	348	31 East Sussex	3,471	32
2 Hampshire	19,247	100	32 Northampton	3,188	26
3 Berkshire	17,996	114	33 Norfolk	2,479	21
4 West Midlands	16,127	73	34 Avon	2,472	36
5 Essex	15,286	67	35 Dorset	2,414	38
6 Greater Manchester	15,125	94	36 Derbyshire	2,323	19
7 Hertfordshire	14,470	133	37 Suffolk	2,031	29
8 Strathclyde	14,210	81	38 West Glamorgan	1,996	6
9 Kent	9,170	55	39 Cleveland	1,848	11
10 Lothian	8,636	44	40 Cheshire	1,825	29
11 Surrey	8,127	64	41 Lincolnshire	1,691	7
12 Fife	7,823	27	42 Cumbria	1,645	10
13 Staffordshire	7,615	25	43 Northumberland	1,289	4
14 West Sussex	7,548	51	44 Somerset	1,282	12
15 Merseyside	6,618	22	45 Shropshire	1,245	15

No.	County			No.	County		
16	Devon	6,063	35	46	South Glamorgan	1,212	11
17	Mid Glamorgan	5,538	16	47	Borders	1,192	8
18	Nottinghamshire	5,488	20	48	Hereford & Worcester	976	15
19	Leicestershire	5,349	39	49	Gwynedd	913	5
20	West Yorkshire	4,885	67	50	Humberside	720	8
21	Buckinghamshire	4,766	64	51	Clwyd	639	14
22	Gloucestershire	4,731	32	52	Isle of Wight	601	8
23	Tyne & Wear	4,729	34	53	Grampian	601	17
24	Gwent	4,551	28	54	Oxfordshire	552	13
25	Durham	4,200	13	55	South Yorkshire	549	10
26	Bedfordshire	4,012	32	56	North Yorkshire	534	7
27	Cambridgeshire	3,924	42	57	Cornwall	477	13
28	Tayside	3,876	11	58	Warwickshire	417	7
29	Wiltshire	3,809	36	59	Highlands	226	8
30	Lancashire	3,632	20	60	Powys & Dyfed	172	5
				61	Central, Dumfries & Galloway, Orkney and Shetland	87	4

Total Electronics Industry in Great Britain	334,056	2,235

Source. EITB (1985a).

the older conurbations and newer growth areas including Berkshire, Hampshire and central Scotland. High technology employment is relatively modest, locally, both in absolute terms and in the context of employment growth and decline in other major sectors.

AEROSPACE IN THE BRISTOL REGION

Technologically advanced activity and employment is in fact dominated locally by aerospace, which accounted directly for nearly 22,000 jobs in 1981. This represented over 7 per cent of total employment compared with under 1 per cent in the country as a whole. Job loss locally has been much less severe than in other manufacturing sectors — only 9 per cent in the decade to 1981. This contrasts with the experience of many other localities where manufacturing employment in established sectors has collapsed across the board. In the context of the locality as a whole, aerospace has in a sense shored up manufacturing employment, maintaining a core of technologically advanced activity in the face of generalised manufacturing decline.

Employment is mainly concentrated in three major establishments. British Aerospace Dynamics is involved in large-scale R&D and the production of electronics-based systems, computers and sub-assemblies for guided weapons, space and communications equipment and related product areas. Employees classed as scientists and technologists account for nearly a third of total employment in the company. British Aerospace Aircraft and Rolls Royce Aero Engines are also involved in technologically advanced R&D and production, although primarily engineering and materials, rather than electronics based. BAe Aircraft, largely responsible for the UK contribution to Concorde in the 1960s and early 1970s, now does work on the BAe 146 'Hush Jet', overhauls American F111 fighter bombers, is lead site for the UK contribution to the European Airbus project and is taking an increasing role in Airbus production. R&D and production at Rolls Royce, largely responsible for Concorde's Olympus engine, has more recently concentrated on military engines including the RB199 for the Tornado and Pegasus for the Harrier 'jump jet'. Aerospace thus includes a major concentration of specifically electronics-based R&D and production at the leading edge of a range of technologies, as well as advanced engineering and materials-based activity. It also includes a major concentration, across these activities, of scientific and technological expertise.[1]

The local impacts of aerospace have, moreover, been multiplied both by subcontracting to and purchasing from local firms and by the effects of wages and salaries spent in the local economy, although linkages as a whole are not particularly localised (Lovering, 1985a; Boddy and Lovering, 1986). Significantly, it has generated a pool and tradition of production labour with electrical and electronics skills, and technical and professional staff. This has been particularly important to firms such as Hewlett Packard who saw this as a positive attraction of the Bristol locality, and also to smaller electronics and specialist engineering companies established locally. Thus aerospace has been important both to companies directly linked to the industry as, for example, engineering subcontractors or design consultants and, indirectly, to others which have drawn on the skills and expertise of the local labour market.

Again, using Engineering Industry Training Board figures (EITB, 1985b), we can look at the national context. In terms of the geographical distribution of aerospace employment, Avon stands out, along with Lancashire, Greater Manchester, Derbyshire, the West Midlands and Hertfordshire (Figure 4.4). The adjoining counties of Gloucestershire and Somerset are also prominent. In regional terms, the South East accounts for over a quarter of aerospace employment. The South West, however, with only 8 per cent of all engineering employment nationally, accounts for another quarter. This regional concentration in the South West obviously reflects in part the importance of British Aerospace, Rolls Royce and other, smaller companies in Bristol itself. These, however, are at the geographical core of a wider belt of defence-related activity, particularly in aerospace, including the much-fought-over Westland Helicopters at Weston super Mare and Yeovil to the south, Smiths Industries and Dowty at Cheltenham and Gloucester to the north, and a range of smaller establishments across the region. Not surprisingly, all these companies loom large in the latest Ministry of Defence list of major contractors for defence equipment (Table 4.3). Unlike the picture for non-aerospace high technology, Avon and adjoining counties are indeed prominent at the national scale in terms of aerospace employment. This contrasts with the growing concentration of electronics employment at the eastern end of

Figure 4.4: Employment in aerospace by county, 1978–84

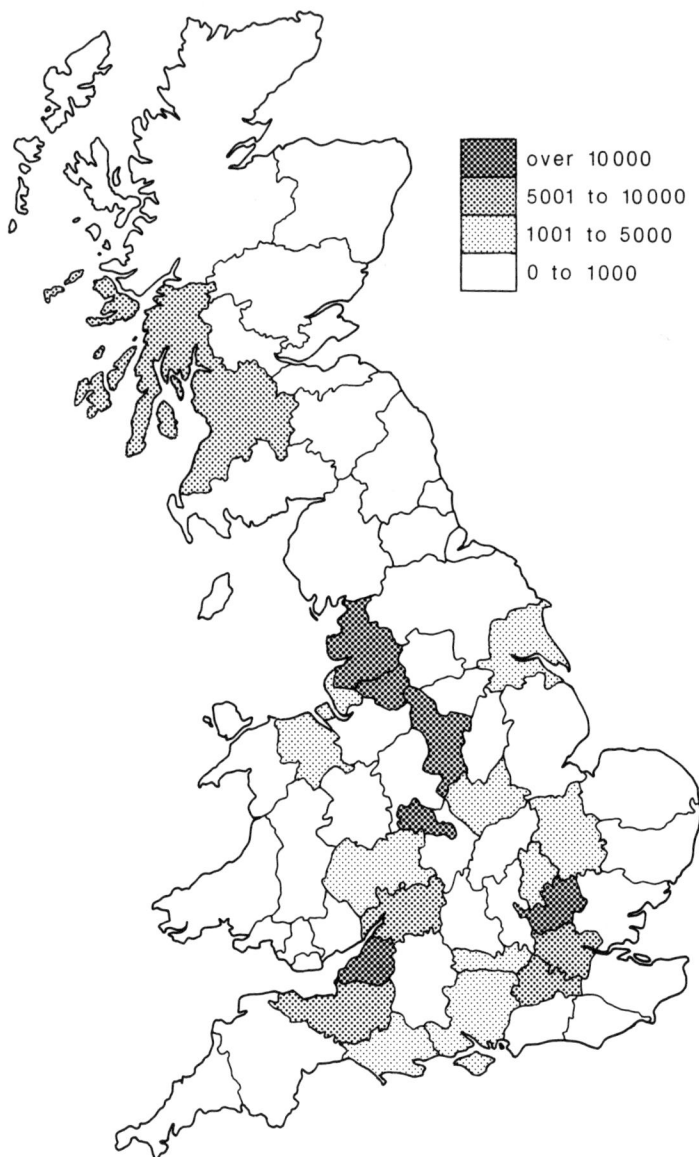

over 10 000
5001 to 10 000
1001 to 5000
0 to 1000

Table 4.3: UK-based MoD contractors paid £25 million or more by the MoD in 1983/4

Over £100 million	
British Aerospace plc (Aircraft)[a]	Racal Electronics plc[b]
British Aerospace plc (Dynamics)[a]	Rolls Royce Ltd[a]
British Shipbuilders	Royal Ordnance Factories[b]
Ferranti plc	Thorn-EMI plc[b]
The General Electric Co plc[b]	Westland plc[a]
The Plessey Co Ltd[b]	

£50–100 million	
Austin Rover Group Ltd	Philips Electronic &
Dowty Group plc[a]	Associated Industries Ltd
Hunting Associated Industries plc	

£25–50 million	
General Motors Ltd	Short Bros Ltd
Lucas Industries plc	Smiths Industries plc[a]
Marshall of Cambridge (Engineering) Ltd	United Scientific Holdings plc
Pilkington Bros plc	Vickers plc

Notes:
a. Firm with major presence in South West (employing 3,000 plus).
b. Firm with smaller presence in South West (employing under 3,000).
Source: HMSO (1985), and local information.

the 'M4 Corridor', in Berkshire in particular, emphasising the differences in the nature of 'high technology' growth along the Corridor and its different origins. Elsewhere nationally, there are significant overlaps between electronics and aerospace employment, particularly in Hertfordshire, the West Midlands and Greater Manchester and, to some extent Berkshire and Hampshire. There are also, however, significant contrasts with Lancashire and Derbyshire prominent in terms of aerospace, as well as the south-west counties.

Also significant is the skill composition of aerospace employment. The industry's workforce is highly skilled. The proportion of scientists and technologists is more than twice as high as in engineering as a whole. More than one half are scientists, technologists, technicians or craftsmen compared with a third in engineering as a whole (EITB, 1985b). Moreover, while aerospace employment overall declined marginally, by around 9 per cent, from 1978 to 1984, the number of scientists and technologists grew by 34 per cent. Regional figures indicate that the proportion of scientists, technologists and technicians is

71

marginally higher in the South West than in the country as a whole.

The Bristol region is therefore a major focus for technologically advanced activity. However, overwhelmingly this is related to the continued prosperity and development of the long-established aerospace sector, rather than the recent growth of computer-related activity and microchip companies central to the popular image of 'high tech'. This distinction is not meant to imply that aerospace is in any sense less technologically advanced than more recent arrivals — in many senses the reverse is the case. It is important, however, to differentiate the two. The development of the aerospace sector and its local expression has its specific history underlain by specific processes. It is these which differentiate it in many respects from non-aerospace high technology, and which are outlined in the section which follows.

DEFENCE SPENDING AND THE AEROSPACE INDUSTRY

Aerospace was established in the Bristol area with the early days of aviation and was consolidated by re-armament and subsequent post-war reconstruction. Its continued development and importance locally reflects a complex history of corporate restructuring and decision-making (Lovering, 1985a, 1985b). These have combined to maintain Bristol's position in what remained essentially an expanding industry, building on existing capacity and on the skills and expertise of the established workforce locally. Particularly important were the early establishment of guided weapons development on which the growth of British Aerospace Dynamics was based; the allocation in the 1960s of much of the UK work on Concorde to Bristol — the airframe to what is now BAe and the engine to Rolls Royce (then Bristol Siddeley); the market success of specific locally-based projects, including guided weapons such as Seawolf, and the RB199 and Pegasus engines; and BAe Aircraft Group's recently expanded European Airbus role. As this suggests, many factors are bound up in the sector's growth and development. Fundamental, however, has been the role of defence markets, both domestic and overseas, and the specific relationship this has involved between government and the defence manufacturers. Defence equipment nationally accounted for over 70 per cent of British Aerospace sales in 1983 and 60 per cent in the case of

Rolls Royce (*Financial Times*, 4 June 1985). UK government contracts accounted for nearly two-thirds of defence sales in the case of British Aerospace and over half for Rolls Royce, the rest going to export markets. Locally, moreover, given the particular mix of activities and products, the sector is particularly biased towards defence as opposed to civil projects — somewhat less so in the case of British Aerospace Aircraft Group.

UK and overseas government spending on defence equipment have thus been a major and sustained source of demand for the sector locally. Moreover, the profitability and development of the industry have been underpinned by the particular relationship developed between the UK government and the defence industries. Projects typically extend over several years, with a succession of new versions and developments. Manufacture brings related work on support, maintenance and spares. R&D costs are often largely financed by the government. Contracts themselves have commonly been awarded on a negotiated rather than open tender basis often on a 'cost plus profit' rather than fixed price basis. Finally, export sales, largely of products developed under contract to the UK Ministry of Defence, are heavily backed by the government in financial and marketing terms. This includes export credit guarantees, soft loans and reciprocal trade agreements negotiated at government level, and ministerial involvement in sales missions. These links between government and the defence industry are symptomatic of the intimate relationship, historically developed, between the British nation-state and the defence industry. This relationship reflects a combination of economic concerns, domestic politics and geo-political issues, and strategic factors (Lovering, 1985a, 1985b). The Westland affair in late 1985 and early 1986, for example, touched on a number of these.

High technology industry in the Bristol area relates therefore above all to the aerospace industry. The aerospace sector locally has been heavily underpinned by government defence spending and the particular structure of government-industry relations developed around this — relations in terms of R&D support, the nature of the tendering and contracting system and support for export sales. It is not simply the market demand for defence products which has been crucial, but rather the nature of that market and of the government-defence industry relationship. This in turn has helped to develop and maintain the major export capacity of the industry.

Table 4.4: US Department of Defense share of output by industry, 1979–87

SIC Code	Title	1979	Defence share of output 1983	1987	Defence output growth 1982/87
		%	%	%	%
3795	Tanks and tank components	78.1	93.8	95.0	47.2
3483	Ammunition	95.1	90.9	93.2	55.6
3489	Ordnance	85.1	79.7	81.2	35.3
3761	Complete missiles	71.0	67.5	79.4	64.4
3731	Shipbuilding and repair	47.9	61.7	62.1	24.1
3662	Radio and TV communication	44.8	58.0	62.5	54.2
3724, 64	Aircraft and missile engines	42.3	53.5	56.1	32.9
3728, 69	Aircraft and missile equipment	43.4	41.2	44.2	34.9
3721	Aircraft	35.0	40.4	46.1	58.7
383	Optical instruments	21.6	28.0	30.7	38.0
3811	Engineering instruments	23.5	27.7	33.6	59.9
3767–9	Electronic components	12.0	17.0	19.8	49.3
3674	Semiconductors	9.5	12.5	12.5	51.4
3361	Aluminum foundries (castings)	7.9	9.1	11.2	58.5
3334	Aluminum production	5.8	7.5	9.0	51.4
3469	Metal stampings	5.8	7.3	9.1	60.3
3671–3	Electron tubes	8.3	7.3	11.5	105.3
3573	Computers	3.6	7.1	12.7	141.0
345	Screw machine products	5.6	6.9	8.6	57.5
3462	Iron and steel forgings	7.9	6.9	7.6	31.4
3541	Machine tools – cutting	6.1	6.2	7.5	54.4
3544–5	Special dies and tools	4.9	6.0	7.5	45.4
3499	Fabricated metal products	5.0	5.6	6.8	53.4
281	Chemicals	5.5	5.6	7.1	53.3
3312	Blast furnace steel mills	4.5	5.6	6.7	45.6
3313	Electrometallurgical products	4.9	5.4	6.3	26.7
3542	Machine tools forming	5.0	4.8	6.3	70.0
332	Iron and steel foundries	3.9	4.5	5.2	45.1

Source: D. Henry (1983), 'Defense spending: a growth market for industry', *US Industrial Outlook*, XXXIX–XLVII, reproduced in Markusen (1985).

The case of Bristol has emphasised the role of defence-related manufacturing in relation to aerospace in particular. Other work in the UK and the USA has drawn attention to the importance of the defence sector to high technology and electronics more generally. Hall *et al.* (1985) have suggested the key role of defence contracting, the nature of the contracting system and the clustering of contractors in proximity to Government Research

Establishments to the growth of electronics and high technology activity in Berkshire and the Thames Valley noted earlier. Similarly, for the US, Markusen (1985), drawing on more detailed information than is available in the UK, provides evidence of the importance of defence expenditure across a range of 'high technology' sectors (Table 4.4). The general picture which she paints is probably very similar for the UK.

THE REGIONAL IMPACT OF DEFENCE SPENDING

As the Bristol case study illustrates, defence spending can have a major impact on specific localities. This raises the more general question of the relative importance of defence spending to different parts of the country. Relatively neglected until recently, this issue has been receiving increasing attention both in the UK (Short, 1981; Law, 1983; Lovering, 1985a; Boddy and Lovering, 1986) and in a number of other countries including the USA, Canada and the Federal Republic of Germany (Markusen, 1985; Todd and Simpson, 1985; Kunzmann, 1985).

The UK spends more both in absolute terms and *per capita* than any other NATO country apart from the USA (HMSO, 1985). In 1984 defence spending represented 5.3 per cent of GDP in the UK, compared with 6.9 per cent in the USA — significantly higher, for example, than France (4.1 per cent) and Germany (3.3 per cent). We can get some idea of the importance of defence equipment expenditure at the more general, regional, level in the UK from information obtained by Short (1981), although the latest period for which any precise information is available is the mid-1970s. From this, it is obvious that the largest share of defence equipment expenditure in absolute terms goes to the South East (Table 4.5). We can get a better idea, however, of the relative importance of defence spending to economic activity in the different regions by relating it to regional manufacturing output. On this basis, it is clear that the South West in fact benefits disproportionately from defence equipment expenditure. Defence contracts were equivalent to 10 per cent of manufacturing output in the South West compared with 8 per cent in the South East, 4 per cent in Scotland and only 1.5 per cent in Wales. On the basis of these figures, defence equipment expenditure is, therefore, higher relative to overall manufacturing output in the South West than in any other region,

Table 4.5: Defence procurement and regional assistance by region. 1974//75–1977//78[a]

Standard region	Net manufacturing output £m	Regional[b] assistance £m	Defence procurement £m	Procurement as a percentage of output	Regional assistance as a percentage of output
North	10,478	476	573	5.5	4.5
Yorkshire and Humberside	15,393	89	245	1.6	0.6
East Midlands	12,047	10[c]	744	6.2	0.1
East Anglia	4,673	–	264	5.7	–
South East	46,726	–	3,674	7.9	–
South West	9,078	26	889	9.8	0.3
West Midlands	20,531	2	599	2.9	–
North West	23,920	250	949	4.0	1.1
Wales	7,448	239	112	1.5	3.2
Scotland	14,225	424	549	3.9	3.0
Great Britain	164,519	1,516	8,598	5.2	0.9

a = Sum of totals for financial years 1974/75 to 1977//78 in current terms.
b = Regional Development Grant plus selective regional assistance.
c = Includes assistance not split between East and West Midlands.
Sources: *Regional Studies*, CSO, Net manufacturing output and regional assistance, Short (1981), defence procurement.

including the South East — the economy of the South West region is in a sense more 'defence dependent' than any other region. This is particularly true of the Bristol locality, given its major share of regional defence manufacturing. These figures exclude export sales which would boost the importance of defence-related manufacturing relative to overall manufacturing output across all regions. Given the importance of exports to the major Bristol companies, the inclusion of exports would probably increase even more the particular importance of defence-related activity to the South West.

Estimates of the employment consequences of defence manufacturing in the UK as a whole have varied. Pite (1980) estimated that, in 1979, defence contracts nationally supported 219,000 jobs directly and a further 270,000 indirectly, through the purchase of materials and components. Dunne and Smith (1984) estimated that in 1981 there were 600,000 employed by MoD contracts in 1981, while the government itself estimated that in 1984 there were 125,000 jobs directly related to MoD contracts in the UK and a further 188,000 indirectly (HMSO, 1984). It was estimated in the following year that overseas defence sales in 1985/6 would sustain around 130,000 jobs nationally (HMSO, 1985). A crude estimate of the regional employment impact of defence manufacturing in the South West is possible if we assume that the region's share of total defence has remained at just over the 10 per cent level of the mid-1970s. This calculation suggests that between 70–90,000 jobs are supported by MoD contracts in the South West, somewhat lower at around 50,000 according to the government estimate. On the same basis, a further 20,000 jobs are supported by defence exports.

There is, then, a major regional bias in the pattern of government spending on defence equipment and the spatial distribution of defence manufacturing. This favours, in particular, the South East and South West regions, with less prosperous parts of the country losing out — Wales, Yorkshire and Humberside, and Scotland being the most conspicuous examples. In terms of regional economic impacts, it is instructive to compare the pattern of defence equipment expenditure with that of explicit regional policy expenditure (Table 4.5). The pattern of defence equipment expenditure clearly runs directly counter to that of regional assistance. Moreover, in terms of crude monetary value, defence equipment expenditure in the more prosperous regions, the South West and South East in particular, more than outweighs regional assistance in every other region. Taking the two together, defence equipment expenditure plus regional assistance are equivalent to over 10 per cent of manufacturing output in the South West and 8 per cent in the South East, compared with only 2 per cent in Yorkshire and Humberside, 5 per cent in both Wales and the North West, and 7 per cent in Scotland — only the North suffers no actual deficit in these terms compared with the South West. Regional assistance for the country as a whole came to only £1,500 million in the mid-1970s compared with defence equipment expenditure of over £3,500 million in the South East alone and nearly £900 million in the South West.

These crude comparisons are not meant to imply that defence equipment expenditure and regional assistance are directly comparable in terms of economic and employment impacts. Nor is defence equipment expenditure in any simple sense a form of 'subsidy' to particular regions. Defence equipment expenditure does however sustain technologically advanced R&D, and manufacturing, with a bias towards scientific, technical and skilled employment, and with major export markets. It does so in part by providing a major and sustained source of demand, but more specifically by the particular relationship between the government and the defence manufacturers outlined earlier. Explicit regional policy, on the other hand, relates to a much broader range of industrial sectors and a wide spread of activities including for example speculative factory provision and infra-structure work, the economic impacts of which are at best indirect and hard to evaluate. So, while defence equipment expenditure is not in any simple sense equivalent to explicit regional assistance, and it would be difficult without much greater information to assess their relative economic and employment effects with any accuracy, the regional impacts of defence-related manufacturing are clearly of major importance. Defence spending represents in effect an unofficial regional policy. It is a policy which is distinctive, however, in that it favours the more economically prosperous parts of the country and runs directly counter to the government's official regional development policy.

CONCLUSIONS AND OBSERVATIONS

A few general conclusions are worth highlighting from this analysis of high technology industry in the Bristol region and the more general discussion of defence equipment expenditure which followed from it. First, the relationship between defence spending and national economic performance has received considerable attention, at least in academic debates. The more specific question of spin-off or the lack of it from defence-related R&D and manufacture has been part of the national debate on strategies to promote high technology industry and product innovation — the recent appointment of 'ferrets' in Government Research Establishments to help identify commercially exploitable products is an illustration of this. However, in Britain little attention has been paid to the spatial economic and employment impacts of defence spending. There has been some concern over the employment effects of the rundown of naval dockyards or shipbuilding in the peripheral regions or the threatened closure of particular facilities. These have largely, however, been isolated instances, generating essentially locally-based lobbying activity. Yet, as we have seen, the spatial bias in defence equipment expenditure runs directly contrary to explicit regional policy. Many factors obviously underlie the geographical pattern of defence spending including questions of cost, efficiency, the maintenance of capacity, and strategic considerations, as well as the undoubted inertia of the Ministry of Defence. It is not clear, however, that the possibilities for developing an explicitly spatial policy dimension alongside these other factors have been explored by government. Yet it is evident from the scale and existing pattern of expenditure that such consideration is essential. Defence equipment expenditure is heavily implicated in patterns of regional economic perfor-mance and of the developing high technology sector in particular. Its impacts should, therefore, be explicitly considered in policy terms. Lack of up-to-date information on the spatial incidence of defence equipment expenditure is itself a symptom of this neglect. It should also be remembered that this analysis has looked only at expenditure on equipment, currently around 46 per cent of the total defence budget. Other aspects of defence expenditure, while different in terms of economic and employment impacts, also have markedly uneven spatial effects. Indeed, the MoD, prompted mainly by the concern for cost saving of the then Secretary of State, Michael Heseltine, has in fact been reviewing the heavy concentration of military establishments in the South East and South West regions and evaluating the possibility of shifting selected installations northwards (*Sunday Times*, 27 October 1985). This suggests that, even under Conservative government, there could be possibilities for marginal change.

Second, the case of defence spending emphasises the need to look more closely at the spatial economic and employment impacts of the full range of government policies and expenditures. This is vital if we are to understand the diverging economic performance of different localities and to develop more effective urban and regional policies. As a recent *Times'* leader observed, 'much public policy seems to be made by people who are geographically blind . . . The regional policy which ought most to concern government is that which falls squarely within its own compass — the local incidence of its own expenditures' (*The Times*, 23 October 1985). Again, lack of information is the first and most immediate obstacle. Ideally, the government's annual spending plans including the programmes of the individual departments should be broken down by region. This should be linked to a commentary on the likely regional economic and employment impacts of this pattern of expenditure.

Third, while Britain has failed to develop any coherent national strategy for technological innovation, promotion of high technology has, in a relatively *ad hoc* fashion, been a goal of urban and regional policy. The current fashion for 'science parks' and the self-promotion of many localities as sites for high technology industry illustrate this. Hall and Markusen have suggested the need for a more systematic R&D-based research strategy focused around universities, the 'selective development of high-technology growth in older industrial regions . . . "anchor sectors" for the rejuvenation of their regions' (Hall and Markusen, 1985, 150). What the Bristol case study, and other work in the UK and the USA, suggests is that any systematic attempt to develop a spatially explicit strategy of high technology development will be heavily constrained and shaped by the structure and spatial pattern of defence-related R&D and manufacture. Particularly important in this is the specific nature of the relationship between the British nation-state and the defence industry.

Finally, it would be wrong to conclude that this, and similar analyses of the spatial pattern of defence spending, necessarily imply the development of a regional policy based on the regional reallocation of MoD contracts and expenditure. There might, as already suggested, be some scope for such shifts. There are, however, economic as well as political arguments why a naive policy of this type could be undesirable. At the national level, the volume and structure of defence spending obviously reflects political and strategic objectives. Options currently on the agenda across the political spectrum include varying degrees of arms reduction, nuclear arms freeze or reduction, and non-nuclear defence strategies. And purely on economic grounds, there is considerable evidence to suggest that, at the national level, defence spending depresses economic growth and inhibits technological innovation (Dunne and Smith, 1984; Smith, 1985). Historical and econometric evidence suggests, moreover, that disarmament, and conversion from defence to civil markets, can be achieved provided it is accompanied by a clear political programme for conversion to civil products, that civilian demand is expanded to compensate for the reduction in military expenditure, and policies are implemented to transfer resources to civilian use (Dunne and Smith, 1984). Given this scenario, cuts in defence spending can be economically beneficial. The same arguments can be applied at the regional level. Strategies which simply reallocated existing defence spending might be less effective than more general strategies for the development of high technology incorporating defence conversion. This is backed up by the fact that while defence manufacturing can, as in Bristol, have a marked localised impact, the dynamic regional economic impacts may be more limited than is the case with civil manufacturing. The defence sector may represent an enclave, with significant but relatively limited spillover effects (Lovering, 1985b; Boddy and Lovering, 1986; Schnieder and Patton, 1985). Defence conversion would, in any case, have to be a part of any move to reallocate defence contracts away from localities in the South East and South West, if the gain to the more peripheral regions was not to be bought at the direct expense of these core areas. Depending, then, on the political and strategic scenario and the balance between this and economic arguments, different policy trajectories are possible in terms of regional development. In this sense, the kind of analysis presented here is only a starting point. It is, however, an essential starting point if we are to rethink the relationship between high technology and regional economic development.

ACKNOWLEDGEMENTS

This chapter arises out of work carried as part of the Economic and Social Research Council, 'Inner City in Context' research initiative, Bristol Project (Grant number DO 320005). I would like to acknowledge the contributions to this work of Frankie Ashton, Keith Bassett, Tom Davies and, in particular, John Lovering. For a full account, see Boddy, Lovering and Bassett (1986).

NOTE

1. It is worth remembering in addition the role of government finance and support for *civil* aerospace projects to the Bristol locality, in particular Concorde and, most recently, the European Airbus. Concorde for example may not have been a major success in sales terms, but it brought a massive injection of government money into the Bristol area for development and production. Government spending on Concorde totalled nearly £1,300 million in the 1970s alone. Support for specific projects such as Concorde and the Airbus, moreover, comes on top of general R&D spending and sectoral assistance to aerospace, plus government support for domestic and export sales of civil aircraft.

REFERENCES

Boddy, M. and Lovering, J. (1986) 'High technology industry in the Bristol sub-region: the aerospace/defence nexus', *Regional Studies*, **20**, pp. 217–31

Boddy, M., Lovering, J. and Bassett, K. (1986) *Sunbelt City? A study of economic change in Britain's M4 growth corridor*, Oxford University Press, Oxford

Dunne, J.P. and Smith, R.P. (1984) 'The economic consequences of reduced UK military expenditure', *Cambridge Journal of Applied Economics*, **8**, pp. 297–310

Engineering Industry Training Board (1985a) *Does the M4 Corridor exist?*, EITB, London

—— (1985b) *The aerospace equipment manufacturing and repairing industry*, EITB, London

Hall, P. and Markusen, A. (1985) 'High technology and regional-urban policy', in Hall, P. and Markusen, A. (eds.), *Silicon landscapes*,

Allen and Unwin, London, pp. 144–52
—— Breheny, M.J., Cheshire, P.C. and Hart, D. (1985) 'The genesis of high technology industry in the M4 corridor', End of Award Report, Economic and Social Research Council, London
HMSO (1984) *Statement on the Defence Estimates 1984*, Cmnd. 9227, HMSO, London
—— (1985) *Statement on the Defence Estimates 1985*, Cmnd. 9430, HMSO, London
Kunzmann, K.R. (1985) 'Military production and regional development in the Federal Republic of Germany', *Built Environment*, **11**, pp. 181–92
Law, C.M. (1983) 'The defence sector in regional development', *Geoforum*, **14**, pp. 169–84
Lovering, J. (1985a) 'Defence expenditure and the regions: the case of Bristol', *Built Environment*, **11**, pp. 193–206
—— (1985b) 'The development of the aerospace industry in Bristol 1910–1984', *Project Working Paper*, **7**, ESRC Inner City in Context, Bristol Project, School for Advanced Urban Studies, University of Bristol
Markusen, A. (1985) 'The military remapping of the United States', *Built Environment*, **11**, 171–80
Pite, C. (1980) 'Employment and Defence', *Statistical News*, **51**, pp. 15–20
Schnieder, J. and Patton, W. (1985) 'Urban and regional effects of military spending: a case study of Vallejo, California and Mare Island Shipyard', *Built Environment*, **11**, pp. 207–18
Short, J. (1981) 'Defence spending in the UK regions', *Regional Studies*, **15**, pp. 101–10
Smith, R.P. (1985) 'The significance of defence expenditure in the US and UK national economies', *Built Environment*, **11**, pp. 163–70
Todd, D. and Simpson, J. (1985) 'Aerospace, the state and the regions: a Canadian perspective', *Political Geography Quarterly*, **4**, pp. 111–30

5

Advanced Telecommunications and Regional Economic Development

J.B. Goddard and A.E. Gillespie

Even the casual observer will be aware of the rapid technical changes in telecommunications which have recently been brought about by the widespread adoption of micro-electronics. The economic and spatial implications of these technical changes arise because of their impact on the ease and cost of information transfer between locations. As more and more economic activity becomes concerned with the generation, processing and exchange of information, technical developments which effect this activity are of potentially far-reaching significance. As we have observed elsewhere, telecommunications are the electronic highways of the future which will influence the geography of economic opportunity in the emerging 'information economy', as much as did railways in earlier periods of profound structural change in the 'industrial economy' (Goddard et al., 1985).

The chapter is divided into three parts. It begins with a review of the emerging 'information economy' and considers the implications for regional development. It then outlines developments in the telecommunications technology itself — in networks and services and the way that these are regulated and the likely consequence in terms of the geography of the information economy. The paper concludes with a discussion of specific examples of policy initiatives that can be pursued to exploit the opportunities and to counter the many threats.

ISSUES CONCERNING THE INFORMATION ECONOMY

Although the focus of the chapter is on the geographical impact of advances in telecommunications technology, it is important to begin by showing that these advances are embedded within, and are helping to facilitate the development of, a much broader and more fundamental shift in the nature of the economic base of our society.

A number of commentators have postulated models of structural economic change which suggest that advanced economies will evolve into service-based economies or, in the terminology of Daniel Bell (1973), into 'post industrial' economies. Bell contrasts industrial and post-industrial society by focusing on their main dynamics. In industrial society, in which manufacturing is the dominant sector, he suggests that the key 'strategic resource' is finance capital; in the emerging post-industrial society, however, he argues that a very different strategic resource comes into play, that of 'knowledge', the embodied and disembodied products of the education and research systems. Knowledge thus becomes the cornerstone upon which any post-industrial society is going to depend for its prosperity and future economic development.

Just as in industrial society finance capital had to be transformed in order to become of economic benefit, so in post-industrial society knowledge has to be harnessed if it is to be of benefit. Essentially, knowledge has to be expressed in the form of *information*, information which can be exchanged, processed, transferred, manipulated and *applied*, in a multitude of ways and amongst a multitude of users. It is this application of information which is transforming the economic base of society. For this reason, we prefer to use the term information economy rather than post-industrial society to capture the essential characteristics of the changes that are taking place.

The changes raise a number of important distributional issues relating to the nature of the society that is being created — essentially, who gains and who loses in the information economy? The answer is equivocal, depending very much on the role of and control over technology; how it is used, who it is used by, and to what ends. In the most rosy scenario, the information economy would be both more equitable in distributional terms, and at the same time more efficient. For if access to information becomes the key to economic success, then the new technologies could help to ensure that information is more widely disseminated, and the benefits to be derived from its use more broadly spread. At the same time as having these positive distributional benefits, decision-making based on more perfect information would enable markets to operate more efficiently.

If we look at the way the information economy is developing in practice, however, this attractive scenario appears decidedly unrealistic. In reality, the information economy might turn out to be neither equitable nor efficient, because of the way the new technologies are being applied in practice as opposed to how they could potentially be used.

First, the information economy may become less equitable, as a result of the key strategic resources, knowledge and information, becoming marketable commodities to far greater extents than they are at present. Increasingly, information which has been conventionally regarded as public, in terms of access, is becoming private — something that can be obtained only at a price. This process of the *'commodification of information'* is being greatly facilitated and extended by the possibilities opened up by the new technologies — for example, when the information available at a single point in a public access library becomes available on a private on-line data base service to all with the technology and the economic resources to gain access via the telecommunications network.

Second, the information economy may turn out to be less efficient (in the sense of the neo-classical assumptions concerning the optimal allocation of resources arising from the process of competition) because of the way the new information technologies are being applied so as to benefit particularly the largest corporations, who are extending their control over global markets. The essential communications infrastructure for the information economy — high speed, digital telecommunications — is being created by and for the *transnational corporations*. Rather than encouraging greater efficiency through more competition, then, the new technologies are facilitating the development of oligopolistic rivalry amongst the biggest companies.

These sorts of developments have prompted one commentator to argue that: 'A major challenge for social policy will be to find methods to ensure that developments in the IT Sector do not exacerbate class divisions in society and that the benefits are spread across all sectors of society' (Melody, 1985). Such issues should also be of the greatest interest to those concerned with urban and regional policies. Our thesis is that developments in the information economy, and in the use of the new technologies that articulate that economy, are likely, without policy intervention, to exacerbate geographical divisions and to make worse geographical disparities in economic wellbeing. In the interests of equity *and* efficiency, it is important to ensure that the benefits that the information economy can potentially bring are shared between the different cities and regions which make up our society.

THE EXISTING GEOGRAPHY OF THE INFORMATION ECONOMY

How can the information economy be measured, and how may its geography be delimited? A methodological problem here is that the information economy cuts across conventional methods of classifying activities, such as the well-worn distinction between manufacturing and service activities. One solution, devised by Porat, is to define the information economy according to the types of job that people do, that is on an occupational basis, based on the notion of an 'information worker', someone whose job is primarily concerned with the generation, or manipulation, or transformation, or processing of information (Porat, 1977). When classified in this way, the information sector is seen to have grown rapidly in employment terms in all advanced Western countries (OECD, 1981 and 1985).

Using this methodology and applying it to occupational data from the 1981 Census of Population, 45 per cent of Great Britain's employed workforce can be classified as information workers (see Hepworth *et al.*, 1986, for a fuller description of the methodology and presentation of the results). How does this proportion of information workers vary regionally?

The first feature of the geography of the information economy, which is summarised in Table 5.1, is that of the eleven regions only London and the South East region have an above-average share of information workers. In London, fully 58 per cent of all jobs can be classified as 'informational'. At the other end of the information economy spectrum, the traditional 'assisted area' regions of Scotland, Wales and the North are seen to have the lowest shares of information employment, with the North being the lowest of all at 39 per cent. So the geography of the information economy is not unfamiliar to us. It does, however, provide us with a different interpretative framework for understanding familiar patterns of geographical inequality.

Table 5.1: Information occupations as percentages of total regional employment, 1981

London	57.8
South East	47.3
Great Britain	45.0
North West	43.8
South West	43.7
West Midlands	42.0
East Anglia	41.5
East Midlands	40.9
Yorkshire and Humberside	40.3
Scotland	40.0
Wales	39.4
North	38.8

Source: Hepworth, Green and Gillespie (1986).

In spite of this clear 'spatial division of information labour' (Hepworth *et al.*, 1986), in which London and the South East constitute the 'core' and the rest of Britain constitutes the periphery, it needs to be stressed that information employment is important in *all* regions of the country — as we have seen, even in the depressed Northern region of England with its manual employment traditions, nearly four jobs in ten are deemed to be primarily informational. This is essentially because the information economy is not narrowly based — it pervades all sectors of conventionally-defined economic activity.

This can be clearly seen in Table 5.2, which shows the percentage of jobs within each of eight sectors (using a classifi-

Table 5.2: Information occupations as percentages of employment within each industry, 1981

	GB	London	North
Agriculture	7	13	4
Manufacturing and Construction	37	48	30
Distributive Services	53	62	45
Retail Services	43	49	37
Non-profit Services	46	52	44
Producer Services	85	87	82
Consumer Services	37	45	31
Public Admin.	53	64	59
Total	45	58	39

Source: Hepworth, Green and Gillespie (1986).

cation which follows Singlemann, 1979) that can be classified as information jobs. While some service sectors have very high proportions of information employment (reaching 85 per cent in Producer Services), even in the mining, manufacturing and construction industry sector some 37 per cent of total employment can be classified as primarily informational. While in the North of England this proportion drops to 30 per cent, this 'base-load' of information work existing even in a heavily branch-plant dominated economy, coupled with the powerful counter-balancing role of public sector (i.e. non-profit) services and public administration, ensures that information employment is important the length and breadth of the country — even if its geography is an uneven one.

Essentially, the existing geography of the information economy reveals the structure of regional dependency in Britain. Many of the information jobs located in London and the South East control economic activities in other parts of the world as well as other parts of Britain. Comparisons of the size and nature of different regions' information employment bases are consequently indicative of regional interdependencies. The spatial division of information labour which exists in Britain suggests a structure of core-periphery interdependencies which are far from neutral or symetrical.

The Northern region of England, for example, is not in any sense an independent regional economy. A total of 80 per cent of its manufacturing employment is 'externally controlled', in the sense of being headquartered from outside the region (Smith, 1979). This helps explain the relatively small size of the information component of the region's manufacturing employment which we noted above; many of the information functions associated with the branch production units have been separated out and located elsewhere.

The *nature* of the region's information economy, as well as the relative size of its labour force, will also reflect the high degree of external control. In particular, many of the information flows and exchanges will be taking place *within* the large multi-site companies as part of their internal corporate control relationships. As far as small or indigenous firms in the North are concerned, this domination by intra-corporate information networks will not produce a 'regional information environment' which is conducive to innovation. Nor, as we will see in the following section, is this structure likely to be improved by developments in advanced telecommunications, which in many instances are serving to further the interests of the large multi-site users at the expense of small single-site users.

TECHNICAL AND REGULATORY CHANGES IN TELECOMMUNICATIONS

The essential key to understanding what is happening in the information economy is the convergence of computing and telecommunications. Prior to the recent advances in microelectronics, POTS (the plain old telephone service) was concerned only with voice communications, with sound being transmitted in analogue form, in waves or pulses. When computers were utilised it became necessary to transport digital data over telephone lines, and modems had to be introduced to cope with the digital/analogue interface. However, it has long been recognised that the most efficient way to transmit information is in digital form, and telephone companies are increasingly converting to this form of transmission for both data and voice. Moreover, a public telephone network is not only concerned with transmission. Another key element is switching — the connection of one subscriber to another. This is done by the local telephone exchange which bundles calls together and transmits them through the long-distance trunk network to destination local exchanges where they are rerouted to the destination number. Once calls are in a digital form this switching can be done electronically rather than mechanically.

Most telephone services are moving towards fully digital services or what is known as ISDN (Integrated Services Digital Networks). With such a system the telephone becomes in effect a computer terminal giving access to a worldwide network. With ISDN the charging structure is most likely to be related to volume of digital information transmitted and may bear very little relationship to distance. This is because computer control is used to optimise the use of the network resulting in the routing of calls via the least loaded routes. With such a tariff structure and service available, the forces for geographical agglomeration will be limited. However, ISDN will not arrive overnight, but through a series of incremental modernisations. This incremental process of change will be a major factor *reinforcing* existing concentrations of economic activity and areas of economic advantage rather than leading to a major dispersal as some commentators have suggested.

There is a further reason why existing patterns of economic activity will be reinforced, and this is the way in which the telecommunications industry is currently regulated. The advent of digitalisation clearly presents a major economic opportunity for all sorts of business activity, in terms of new terminal equipment and new services; technological change has clearly broken forever the notion that telecommunications is a 'natural monopoly'. Nevertheless, because of the social as well as the economic importance of telecommunications, governments find it necessary to regulate the industry. The extent of monopoly or the nature of the regulation of the telecommunications industry is a final consideration that has important implications for the location of economic activity.

These key points can be summarised by reference to the diagram of the structure of the telecommunications network linking two workplaces (Figure 5.1). Within the workplace there is the local area network (LAN) managed by a computer linking the various terminal devices together, with the private branch exchange (PBX) providing the same role for voice. The two networks link, one via a modem, to the local exchange which gives access to the long-distance network. The exchange also provides a range of value-added network services and manages mobile radio.

An important feature of the diagram is the service bypass and facility bypass. Because many exchanges are non-digital, the series of digital/analogue/digital interfaces encourages companies with large volumes of data to bypass the exchanges by renting telephone lines which plug directly into the long-distance network where high-speed transmission is available (the service bypass). The telecommunications operators provide a number of special data services to permit this. There are also facility bypasses which use microwave or satellite links to 'miss out' the local switched network and gain access to the trunk network. The most radical development is the total bypass which avoids the public network altogether and directly connects large users. One such example is the New York 'teleport', in which high-capacity optical fibres run through Manhattan to collection points in Staten Island and New Jersey for onward satellite transmission to the whole world. The teleport concept will enable not only the largest global corporation to bypass the public networks but will

Figure 5.1: Telecommunications networks and services

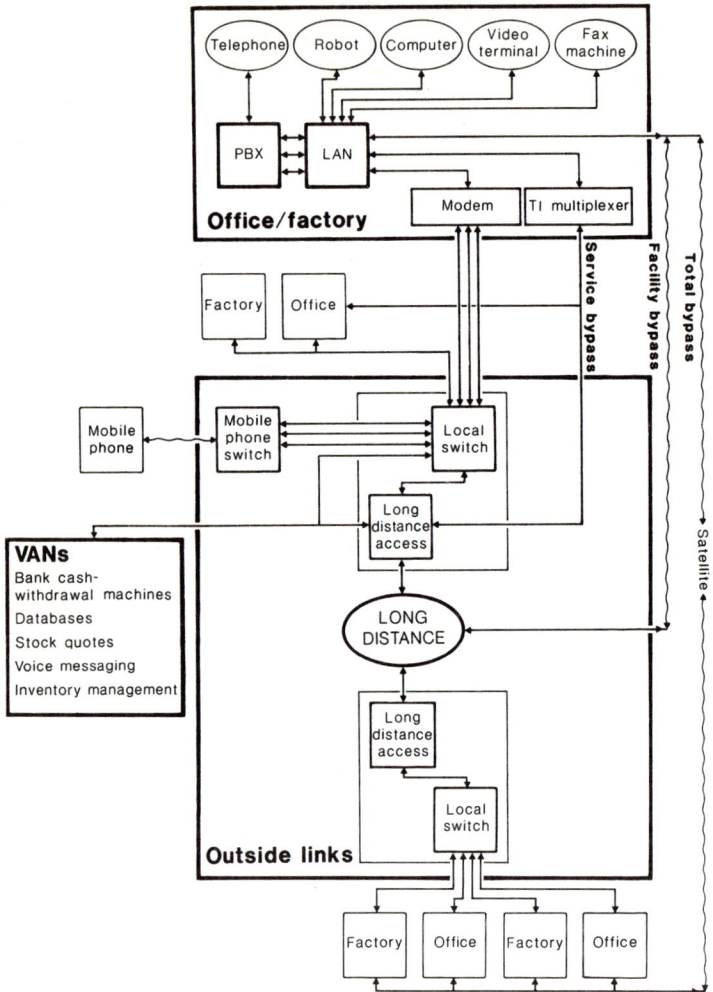

Source: *The Economist*, 23 November 1985.

also provide bypass services for local areas with a high-density of smaller users linked to a teleport by high-speed fibre optic cables. In the UK, a teleport is being developed in the London Docklands providing global telecommunications facilities to the rapidly growing number of financial service companies.

IMPLICATIONS OF RECENT DEVELOPMENTS

What are the local implications of these developments in networks, switching, services and telecommunications regulations?

Transmission networks

As far as transmission is concerned the most dramatic reduction in costs is occurring in long-distance transmission where fibre optic cables are replacing the older copper cables, dramatically increasing the volume of data or voice that can be transmitted. However, the installation of such cables is only justified when the volume of use is high — which means on the trunk routes and in the high-density central business districts. Lower density residential areas or rural and peripheral regions, it is argued, do not justify this type of investment. This argument suggests that new transmission systems will favour existing concentrations of economic activity.

The impact of new fibre optic networks will not be directly visible to the end user until the entire network is digitalised. However, to speed up the availability of the advantages of rapid transmission rates to business users, telecommunications administrations have created a number of special overlay networks such as PSS (Packet Switch Stream) in Britain or TRANSPAC in France (Figure 5.2). The critical point about such networks in terms of urban and regional development is that they are limited coverage networks. Subscribers in exchanges outside nodes on the network do not have access to the facility. They either have to lease private lines (or local bypasses) into PSS exchanges in Britain or make do with the basic telephone network with all the problems of digital/analogue interfaces. Another form of overlay network is that associated with mobile radio and here again coverage is seldom geographically complete.

Satellite bypasses are one of the ways around the constraints imposed by terrestrial networks, but this is generally only an option available to the largest corporations. Such organisations are able to operate on a global scale and able to control production from a central location without recourse to the traditional national and regional hierarchy of cities and intermediate

Figure 5.2: The pattern of introduction of packet-switched standards in the UK

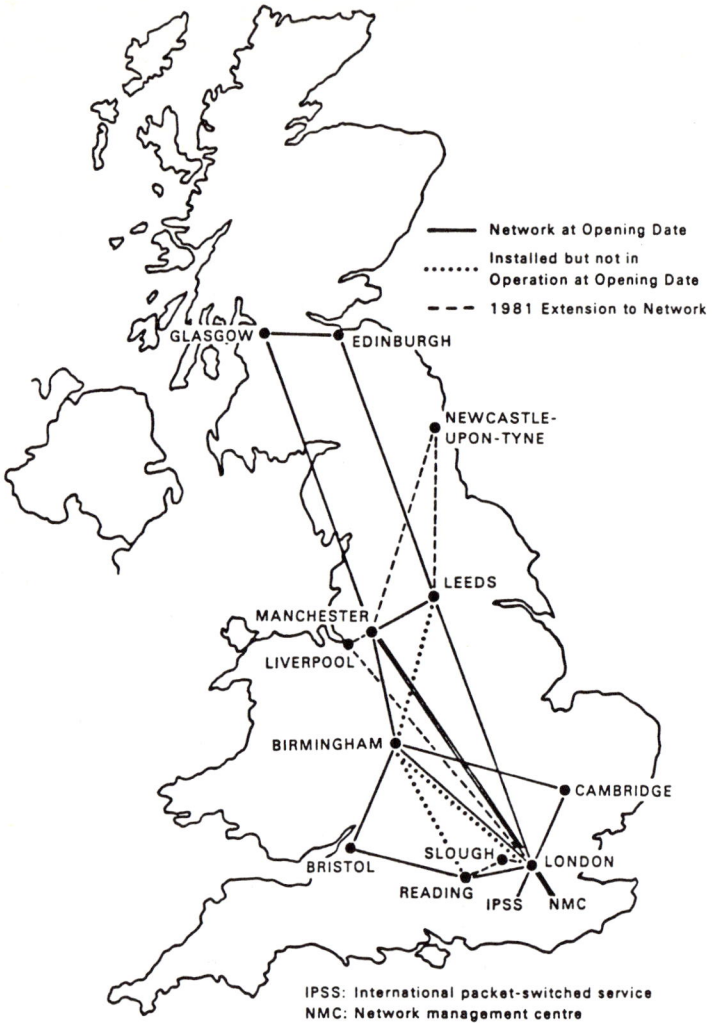

Source: British Telecom.

offices. The hierarchical network of terrestrial telecommunications has generally reinforced the existing business hierarchy and intermediate level cities; the evolution of the bypass could undermine this structure. More generally it could be suggested that the development of specialised data networks and the use of leased lines which is preceding the full-scale introduction of ISDN is likely to mean that the benefits of reduction of costs in telecommunication are accruing principally to the largest business users and not the small and medium sized enterprise which Development Agencies are pinning their hopes on to regenerate the economies of declining or less developed regions.

Switching

The keynote in switching is the introduction of fully electronic exchanges to replace the old electro-mechanical 'step by step' exchanges. The new digital exchanges are essentially computers; the important point for the end user is that they make possible a wide range of enhanced services which will be described shortly. In terms of urban and regional development it is important to appreciate that the modernisation of switching as well as the network is occurring on an incremental basis. Areas which have in the recent past received investment in the intermediate semi-electronic exchanges will have to wait until this equipment is fully amortised before receiving the fully electronic facilities. Those areas with the new capacity will then be able to gain a comparative advantage because of the earlier availability of enhanced services. Although the time lags in the progress of exchange modernisation may be limited, these lags may provide important 'windows of opportunity' for enterprises located in the favoured areas. If the introduction of international subscriber trunk dialing is anything to go by, these favoured areas will be the largest cities and not the low-density rural areas and peripheral regions (as is demonstrated by Clark, 1978). In Britain a pilot form of ISDN is being installed on a limited basis, but it only connects the largest cities.

Services

A wide range of new services is being provided over telephone networks. In Britain the longest established is Prestel. This is a general information service with 320,000 pages of information available from 43,000 terminals. The information is made available by a wide range of information providers. Prestel also operates closed user groups for particular industries such as the travel trade, providers of home banking and the agriculture industry. British Telecom also provides a range of other services like RITA, a real time integrated ticketing administration for the theatre trade.

The critical spatial question concerns the degree of universality of these new services. In Britain, Prestel was initially only available in a limited area although its coverage is now extended to 94 per cent of the country at a local call rate. In addition to such public services a wide range of private value added network

Table 5.3: Registrations under the VANS general licence as at 18 October 1985

Companies: 164	
Services (some companies provide more than one service):	
Automatic ticket reservation and issuing	12
Conference calls	10
Customers data bases	54
Deferred transmission	50
Long-term archiving	27
Mailbox	71
Multi address routing	49
Protocol conversion between incompatible computers and terminals	71
Secure delivery services	24
Speed and code conversion between incompatible terminals	43
Telephone answering using voice retrieval systems	89
Telesoftware storage and retrieval	24
Text editing	29
User management packages, e.g. accounting, statistics, etc.	46
Viewdata	49
Word processor/facsimile interfacing	40
Total:	**688**
Location of companies	
London and Home Counties	125
South West	15
W Midlands	4
E Midlands	3
Yorks and Humberside	3
N East	–
N West	9
Scotland	4
Wales	–
N Ireland	1
Total	**164**

Source: OFTEL News.

services is also being introduced in Britain, but particularly by companies in London and the South East (Table 5.3). Such activities not only generate employment directly, they also provide better services for local companies. Moreover, as the costs of transmission fall, companies in the core regions will be able to sell telecommunications services into less favoured regions, undermining the markets for information services provided in traditional ways by existing business service firms — for example, accountancy and legal services.

Regulation

Value Added Network Services (VANS) provided by private companies are a new feature of the competitive telecommunications environment introduced into the United Kingdom alongside the privatisation of British Telecom (BT). These private services are nevertheless only a minor part of the changes that have occurred and which have important spatial implications. Market considerations also have important implications for the development of the network itself. Here the key issue is the extent of cross-subsidisation that exists between the high-cost low-density rural and domestic services at the extremity of the network and the much more profitable trunk network. There is much debate about the extent of this cross-subsidisation, but in Britain there are indications in the recent higher rates of increase for local as compared with long distance calls that British Telecom as a commercial organisation will inevitably seek to maximise profits for its shareholders. Furthermore, on its trunk routes, particularly within the core regions of Britain, BT is faced with some competition from the only other licensed carrier, Mercury (Figure 5.3). Outside these limited areas BT is a monopoly provider. Although it is charged in its licence with providing a national service, this only applies to basic telephony and telex, and not to more advanced services. While BT attempts to provide advanced services everywhere, there is every likelihood that it will come under increasing pressures to withdraw or not to provide services in regions in which there is limited demand. Much will depend on the extent to which the 'watchdog' which has been established to regulate the virtual monopoly, OFTEL, forces BT to give due weight to regional considerations in its operation. However, the most serious threat

Figure 5.3: Mercury's planned and possible routes through the North of England to Scotland

Source: Economist Informatics/CURDS, 1985.

Figure 5.4: Interconnections between global computing and telecommunications companies

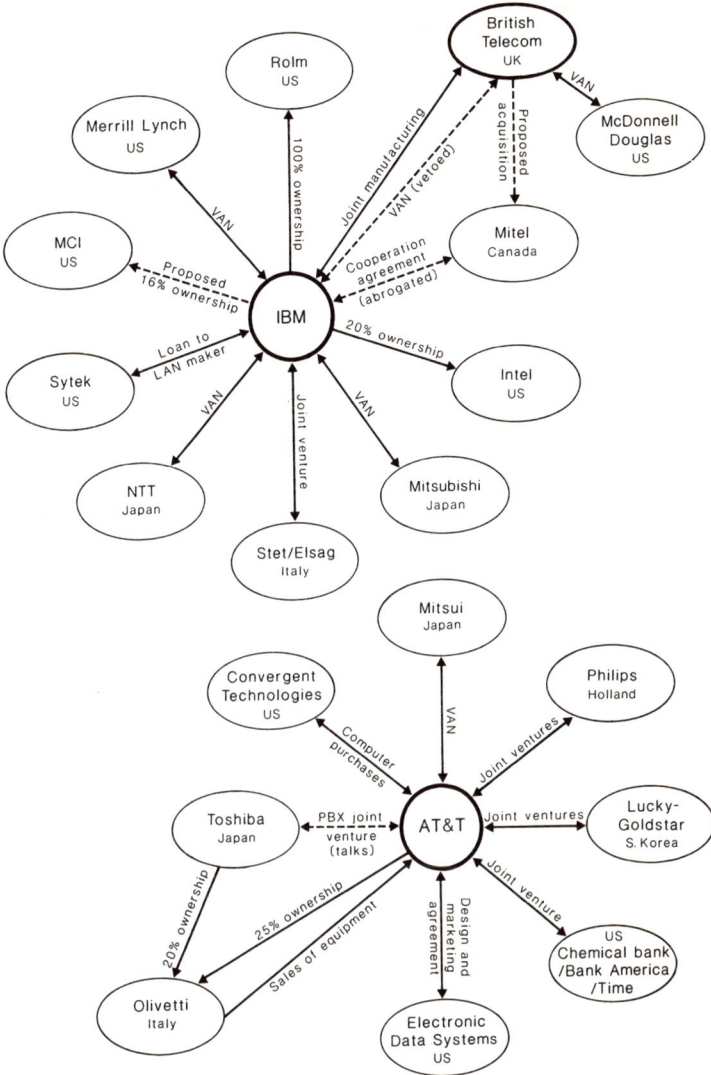

Source: *The Economist,* 23 November 1985.

to a telecommunications administration like BT which is a regulated private sector organisation and to public sector administrations as are found elsewhere in Europe, comes from the major companies in the previously separate fields of telecommunications, computing and information services. As a result of the breakup of the Bell telecommunications monopoly in the United States and the technical advances that have been described, a number of global telecommunciations companies are emerging which are providers of equipment, transmission and information services (Figure 5.4). From the producer side the information economy is big business and a major battle is in progress between the giants that has significant implications for the future development of telecommunications services. Perhaps the most important of these battles concerns standardisation. The value of any network depends on the number of network terminating points that can 'talk' to each other; it is in the interest of the monopoly telecommunications services that they provide interconnect facilities within their own emerging ISDN network. While on the one hand it could be suggested that this increases their monopoly power, it could on the other hand be suggested that under such arrangements small users would be able to communicate with others whatever their equipment. If the battle goes the other way and standards are set by the majors in the industry, a wide range of smaller users could be 'locked out'.

The implications for regional development of this evolving battle probably lie in the relative costs and availability of information services for the small and medium sized businesses on which the development of local economies could depend. In a highly competitive environment access to and use of specialist information will be a key to survival. Unfortunately the evidence that is available suggests that firms in lagging regions, and particularly small and medium sized enterprises, are slow to take up advantages of the potentially distance-shrinking power of telecommunications.

The uptake of services

Even with regard to the traditional services, there is clear evidence of marked regional disparity of uptake within most of the countries of the European Community. This applies to basic telephony (Table 5.4) and to the first business-orientated special

Table 5.4: EEC Nations, summary of regional variations in the number of telephone subscribers (1980 and 1981)

Nation (number of regions)		Region	Telephone subscribers per 100 inhabitants	As % of national average
United Kingdom	highest:	London	42	127
(10)	national average:		33	
	lowest:	Northern Ireland	23	70
Germany	highest	West Berlin	53	156
(18)	national average:		34	
	lowest:	Regensburg	24	71
France	highest:	Paris	40	133
(21)	national average:		30	
	lowest:	Franche Comte Lorraine	23	77
Italy	highest:	Liguria	36	156
(20)	national average:		23	
	lowest:	Calabria	12	52
Netherlands	highest:	Amsterdam	43	126
(13)	national average:		34	
	lowest:	Hengelo	30	88
Denmark	highest:	Sealand/Mon	49	109
(3)	national average:		45	
	lowest:	Mid and N Jutland	41	91
Belgium	highest:	Brussels	36	133
	national average:		27	
	lowest:	Hasselt	19	70
Greece	highest:	Athens Region	35	141
	national average:		25	
	lowest:	Thrace	9	38
Ireland	national average:		21	–
Luxembourg	national average	(1982 end)	36	–

Source: Gillespie *et al.*, 1984.

network, telex (Table 5.5). Considering a more modern service like Prestel, which is particularly suited to the small user, there is evidence of much lower levels of penetration in the Northern region of England as compared to the South East, particularly amongst the smallest establishments (Figure 5.5a).

These differences partly reflect the fact that businesses in the Northern region are more locally orientated — they do not perceive themselves nor do they in fact operate in national and international markets. In spite of the smallness of the local market and the peripheral location of the region, the ratio of

Table 5.5: EEC Nations, summary of regional variations in the number of telex subscribers (1980 or 1981 unless stated)

Nation	Region		Telex subscribers per 100 inhabitants	As % of national average
United Kingdom	highest:	London	0.41	256
	national average:		0.16	
	lowest:	Wales	0.08	50
Germany	highest	Hamburg	0.43	146
	national average:		0.23	
	lowest:	Kiel	0.12	48
Netherlands	highest:	Amsterdam	0.47	204
	national average:		0.23	
	lowest:	Leeuwarden	0.10	57
France	highest:	Ile de France	0.30	188
	national average:		0.16	
	lowest:	Bas Normandie	0.08	50
Italy[a]	highest:	Lombardia	0.14	175
	national average:		0.08	
	lowest:	Basilicata	0.01	13
Greece	highest:	Athens	0.25	166
	national average:		0.15	
	lowest:	Thrace	0.05	33
Belgium	highest:	Brussels	0.56	254
	national average:		0.22	
	lowest:	Libramont	0.06	27
Denmark	national average:		0.20	–
Luxembourg[a]	national average		0.52	–
Ireland	national average:		0.15	–

Note: a. 1982 figures.
Source: Gillespie *et al.*, 1984.

local to international calls in the North is below the national average (Figure 5.5b), and this is notwithstanding the fact that it is possible for firms in the South East to reach nearly a third of the total business telephones in the United Kingdom at a local call rate — compared with only 1 per cent in the major office centre of the Northern region, Newcastle.

IMPLICATIONS FOR REGIONAL DEVELOPMENT

In view of the emergence of the information economy, the

Figure 5.5: North/South differences in telecommunication useage: comparison of the Northern and South East regions. (a) Use of Prestel amongst enterprises of different sizes: (b) Local, trunk and international call ratios

(a)   (b)

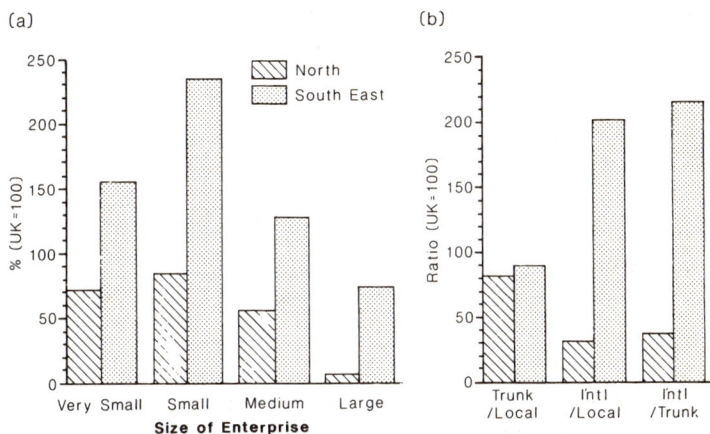

Source: Economist Informatics/CURDS (1985).

patterns of provision and uptake of new services and the way they are regulated have important implications not only for the development of regions but also for the speed with which the economy as a whole is able to make the transition to an information society. The evidence would suggest that in most countries, far from it embracing the economy as a whole, large areas do not seem to be participating fully. Most observers regard telecommunications networks as the 'highways of the future'. As with roads, they are a permissive factor in economic development — that is, a necessary but not sufficient condition. Nevertheless, any shortcomings in the network and the services available in an area will inhibit economic development; but the critical next step is that enterprises make full use of the services that are available. The principal shortcoming in terms of the creation of national markets for information must be the low uptake of services in lagging regions.

Such findings have important implications for both national and local policy. In Britain the government is taking numerous steps to promote, via publicity programmes, the adoption of advanced telecommunications services by businesses. This has involved promotional activities in the regions. What has not been

103

adequately appreciated is that the shift from *awareness* to *adoption* of new technology needs a much fuller demonstration of the relevance of the developments to the user's own environment. While it is the role of the telecommunications administration to market its own services, the full exploitation of the new technology requires the identification of groups of users who have sufficiently common interests to demonstrate the ability of telecommunications to meet their emerging information and communication needs. While there are clearly identifiable national interest groups (such as travel agents), there are also numerous other *local* groups which could operate in a cross-sectoral domain, and it is the exploitation of these domains that could be critical to the advance of the information economy. The chapter concludes by examples of how such opportunities are being exploited in one region.

TELECOMMUNICATIONS STRATEGIES FOR REGIONAL DEVELOPMENT: THE CASE OF THE NORTHERN REGION

We have seen that the region's enterprises — particularly the smaller ones — make comparatively little use of existing telecommunications services. In the future, low uptake is likely to feed back in a much more immediate way than it has done until now into the limited, the late, or the non-provision of new services, which will further hamper the region's ability to participate in the information economy on anything like favourable terms.

On behalf of the region's local authorites and other regional agencies, we have consequently attempted to formulate a strategy to help overcome the problems identified, within — crucially — the context of the broader regional economic development needs of the region (Economist Informatics and CURDS, 1985). Three main elements of a strategy were identified:

(1) To stimulate the uptake of conventional and advanced services by establishing *telecommunications user groups*. A number of possible user groups were proposed, each having a common core of interests — such as a clearly defined sector — and each involving both large and small firms as well as the appropriate agencies. The information and communication needs of these groups would be evaluated by such means as

workshops and company interviews, and assessments would be made of whether advanced telecommunications could be more effectively used to satisfy these needs. The large and more sophisticated users brought into each group would have the purpose of providing 'demonstration platforms' to the smaller and/or less sophisticated users.

(2) To upgrade the region's *skill base* with respect to telecommunications applications, via the training system.

(3) To improve the situation with respect to telecommunications *tariffs*, both by direct action and indirectly by pressurising British Telecom. Regulation severely constrains possibilities of direct action, for example by not permitting the re-sale of lines leased from BT, which could have enabled the provision of long-distance services to small businesses at effectively local call charging rates. With respect to indirect pressure, BT were asked to increase their provision of 'low cost routes' and to increase the size of local call areas, both of which currently serve to disadvantage the region in terms of the cost of using telephony services compared with other regions.

Some elements of this strategy are currently being implemented, thanks to support from the Department of Trade and Industry and, before its abolition, particularly from Tyne & Wear County Council. Together with MARI Advanced Electronics Ltd., a local computer and communications software and system house which has close links with the University, CURDS are engaged on a pilot project to stimulate the application of advanced telecommunications in the region's enterprises, particularly the smaller ones, with a view to fostering the region's economic development potential.

In the first phase of this action research, two sectors of economic activity have been selected — offshore engineering and tourism — and the scope for a telecommunications 'demonstration project' is being investigated for each of them.

Offshore engineering

The North Sea oil boom has created a substantial knock-on effect into the engineering sector. This is not confined to platform fabrication and construction, but extends more widely to encompass a range of specialised engineering products and services. It is estimated that in the North East of England some 300 companies are involved in supplying the offshore oil industry. These opportunities are likely to grow as new oil fields are developed off the Tyne.

Many of the specialist requirements of the oil industry are extremely time sensitive — companies cannot afford to delay production while orders are placed, parts are machined and despatched. Consequently, advanced telecommunications — particularly high-speed data communications — are regarded by the offshore industry as essential. It follows that many of the suppliers and potential suppliers to the offshore industry will be very much better placed in the competition for orders if they are able to communicate electronically with the offshore industry. Our initial objectives will be: first, to establish an 'interest group' of suppliers and potential suppliers to review their existing use of and capability with respect to advanced telecommunications, within the context of the requirements and expectations of the major oil companies and their contractors; and second, to determine whether opportunities exist for regional companies, particularly smaller companies, to make better or more sophisticated use of telecommunications in their attempt to win orders in these very time-sensitive markets. One possibility currently being explored is to establish a computerised 'clearing bank' for orders, which would give a single contact point for the region's companies (thereby avoiding some of the interface problems of inter-enterprise data communication), as well as providing an attractive facility for the offshore industry itself.

Tourism

Information technology is already put to use to facilitate the tourism industry in the North, but only in the process of exporting tourists to other locations. Thus, via videotex services set up for the travel industry, every high street travel agency can provide the potential traveller with information on the cost and availability of flights and package holidays to all parts of the world. The aim of a proposed tourism demonstration project for Tyne & Wear is to apply new technology to encourage *inward* tourism in the area, and hence to contribute to the area's export base and to the creation of jobs in the tourist-serving industries.

The objectives set are very limited: simply to capture more 'business' from those who are, for a variety of reasons, passing through the county area. By encouraging such visitors to spend more time in the area before moving on, and in so doing to spend some money in the county's hotels, restaurants, shops or tourist attractions, it is believed that a significant contribution can be made towards increasing the £80 million per year currently spent by tourists visiting Tyne & Wear.

This is to be achieved by the provision of better information on what the county has to offer at a number of key 'tourist gateways' — such as the airport, the railway station, the motorway service stations, the passenger ferry terminals and the tourist information centres. As a first stage it is intended that an easily accessible computerised information service will be available at 15 such gateway locations in and around the county. The 15 gateway terminals will provide access, via British Telecom lines, to a central computer. As well as providing an easy-to-use, menu-driven system of presenting information in an attractive way on hotels, restaurants, shops, entertainment facilities and tourist attractions, some interactive booking facilities will be available over the network. These booking facilities will grow significantly once the service becomes established and telecommunication links are set up with existing tourist-related information networks (e.g. for car hire), and also when the coverage of gateway terminals is extended to include hotels and other tourist businesses.

In essence, then, what is being proposed is a special-purpose Value Added Network Service for the region. The tourist-industry companies, who would both provide information to and make use of the service, are already displaying a keen interest in the proposed project. Technically the system provides few problems — being at the forefront of technology is certainly not the object of the project. Rather the aim is to make better use of the telecommunciations facilities which are already available in the region, in such a way as to create new 'value added' combinations of users and commercial uses and, in so doing, to help foster regional economic development.

CONCLUSION: THE EUROPEAN PERSPECTIVE

The initiatives that we have described in the North of England have in part been prompted by a concern at the European level with the impact of new information technology on the less-favoured regions of the Community (Gillespie *et al.*, 1984). This concern has led to a new program — STAR (Strategic Telecommunications Action for regional development) — which will provide finance for the extension of digital telecommunciations into the less-favoured regions and also promote the adoption of advanced telecommunication services in these regions (CEC, 1986).

The Community interest in this topic stems from the shift of European industrial policy from a concern with so-called 'sunset' industries — steel, shipbuilding and textiles — to 'sunrise' industries such as computers and telecommunications. The Commission has recognised that Europe is falling behind in these technologies and that positive steps need to be taken to counteract this tendency.

The Commission is concerned not only to promote productive capacity in Europe in high technology industries but also to ensure the maximum uptake of the technologies throughout Europe. It is thus recognised that the maximum economic benefits from new technology will emerge not only from the initial innovations in production but through the widespread diffusion of applications. Nowhere is this more true than in the field of telecommunications, in which the extent of scale economies is clearly a function of the number of users who are attached to the network. The European Commission is therefore trying to foster European markets in particular information services based on telecommunciations, markets which parallel in size those found in the United States (CEC, 1985). There are many legal barriers to European trade in services which are being addressed by the Community and by national governments. But in addition there are specifically regional barriers which take the form of an absence of advanced telecommunications networks in some less favoured regions and a low take-up of telecommunication services in others. In spite of the obvious 'distance shrinking' capacity of telecommunications, it would seem that this form of technological advance is reinforcing existing concentrations of economic activity in the core regions of Europe, creating a new form of regional disparity and preventing the Community from rapidly reaching the necessary scale economies of large information markets.

REFERENCES

Bell, D. (1973) *The coming of post-industrial society*, Basic Books, New York

Clark, D. (1978) 'The spatial impact of telecommunication', *Research Report*, **24**, 'Impacts of telecommunications on planning and transport', Departments of the Environment and Transport, London

Commission of the European Communities (1985) *Work Programme for creating a Common Information Market*, Communication from the Commission to the Council, COM (85) 658 finale, Brussels, November

—— (1986) *Proposal for a Council Regulation (EEC) instituting a Community programme for the development of certain less-favoured regions of the Community by improving access to advanced telecommunications services (STAR programme)*, COM (85) 836 finale, Brussels, January

The Economist Informatics and Centre for Urban and Regional Development Studies (1985), *Availability: cost and use of telecommunications in the Northern Region*, Report to the North of England County Councils Association, Newcastle

Gilliespie, A.E., Goddard, J.B., Robinson, J.F., Smith, I.J. and Thwaites, A.T. (1984) *The effects of new information technology on the less favoured regions of the Community*, Studies Collection, Regional Policy Series No. 23, Commission of the European Communities, Brussels

Goddard, J.B., Gillespie, A.E., Robinson, J.F. and Thwaites, A.T. (1985) 'The impact of new information technology on urban and regional structure in Europe', in Thwaites, A.T. and Oakley, R.P. (eds) *The regional economic impact of technological change*, Frances Pinter, London

Hepworth, M.E., Green, A.E. and Gillespie, A.E. (1986) 'The spatial division of information labour in Great Britain', unpublished paper, Centre for Urban and Regional Development Studies, University of Newcastle, March

Melody, W.M. (1985) 'Implications of the information and communication technologies: the role of policy research', *Policy Studies*, **6**, Policy Studies Institute, London

OECD (1981) *Information Activities, Electronics and Telecommunications Technologies* (Volume 1), ICCP Series, No. 6, OECD, Paris

—— (1985) 'Update of Information Sector Statistics', ICCP Committee Report, OECD, Paris (unpublished)

Porat, M. (1977) 'The Information Economy: definition and measurement', US Department of Commerce, Office of Telecommunciations, *Special Publication* 77–12 (1), Washington, DC

Singlemann, J. (1979) *From agriculture to services*, Sage, Beverly Hills

Smith, I.J. (1979) 'The effect of external takeovers on manufacturing employment change in the Northern Region between 1963 and 1973'; *Regional Studies*, **13**, pp. 421–38

6

Housing Reinvestment and Neighbourhood Revitalisation: Economic Perspectives

Duncan Maclennan

It is self evident that the pattern and scale of housing investment shapes the spatial structure and quality of housing within a city. A great deal of work in urban geography, land economics and economics has drawn attention to the ways in which new construction, especially at the suburban edge, develops and generates feedback effects (movement, succession, etc.) in the rest of the housing stock. However, we have a much less clear understanding of the dynamics of existing neighbourhoods and, in particular, the factors which generate disinvestment and decline or reinvestment and upgrading (see Grigsby, Baratz and Maclennan, 1986).

THEORETICAL ISSUES

The geographical literature on this topic, which has had an important role in keeping the neighbourhood scale as a focus of research and theory, has provided a relatively confused plethora of terminology and 'explanatory' hypotheses. For instance, the specific and clear empirical statements about gentrification, (e.g. Williams, 1976) have come to be supplemented by a vague expansion of the term to cover almost all instances of what could more accurately have been labelled 'upward succession'. As well as cramming an empirical quart into a definitional pint pot, a range of explanations of upward succession are offered, sometimes as if they were different theories. Demographic change, shifts in transport costs, new rehabilitation techniques, rising real house prices (ahead of income), shifts in financier and developer behaviour, as well as reinvestment policies, have all been advanced as explanations, in some times and places, of upward succession. In a recent survey, written from a Marxian standpoint, Smith (1982) essentially indicates that 'gentrification' patterns emerge from the changing pattern of profitable reinvestment opportunities. Such a contention is, of course, consistent with neoclassical or Keynesian models of the operation of urban housing markets. Profits for housing investment, either to developers or to improving owners, arise either from changing balances of demand offers and supply costs at particular locations or, where there are non-price restrictions such as redlining, from the removal of such difficulties. That is, in making a reinvestment decision an owner-user will examine the costs of structure, purchase and upgrading costs against the discounted sum of user benefits plus the resale price of the improved unit. If we are concerned with neighbourhood rather than individual upgrading then we have to establish how supply and demand structures for housing are changing at the neighbourhood scale.

Stated in this way the basic economics of housing reinvestment decisions seem to be quite straightforward, at least at a theoretical level. The real issue is to identify the empirical parameters in supply and demand functions. However, until very recently, housing economics has largely ignored this set of questions. Until the late 1960s, housing economists generally used an aspatial approach in analysing consumer demands for housing. The major focus of research was upon estimating conventional summary parameters of demand functions, such as the income and price elasticity. After 1970, for almost a decade, research then focused around the development and testing of the access-space model of urban residential structure. At a superficial level at least, this move away from spaceless economics appeared to offer some common ground for geographers and economists. Indeed the access-space model came to have a very important effect on the way in which economists and planners theorised the urban housing system.

The access-space model is, however, very limited as a basis for applied economic work. A range of criticisms has been advanced elsewhere (Maclennan, 1982) but a number of points are worth reiterating here. Because the model is concerned with theoretical spatial structure it abstracts a range of housing characteristics apart from size and accessibility of units. Space, or distance from city centre, is treated as a continuous variable and dwelling and neighbourhood characteristics, which may explain up to two-thirds of property values, are abstracted. In addition, households are assumed to have identical preferences and, despite oft-cited and mistaken assertions to the contrary, it is cross-sectional variation in the incidence of constraints (of income and travel time) which shape the results of the model. Given these and many other assumptions, the model predicts complete separation of different income groups and an inevitably suburban location for higher income groups. It is difficult to prove the following assertion, but in my view many city planners, and particularly in North America, came to see such outcomes as likely or normal. In this view of the world the outlook for central city neighbourhoods is always pessimistic.

Almost a decade ago a number of then-younger scholars, such as myself in the UK and Peter Linneman in the USA, pointed out that this view of the world was misleading, and that a more detailed micro-economic analysis of housing demand at the intra-urban scale was required. Urban housing demand studies then evolved in a helpful fashion. Straszheim, for instance, dropped the assumption that the market was unitary and that employment was CBD located (Straszheim, 1975); the implication being that the access-space trade-off became applied to a large number of points within the urban system. Subsequently, in recognition of the complexity of the housing commodity analysts have examined the ways in which economic and social factors influence the demand for specific attributes. These analyses (e.g. Pallakowski, 1982) explore the demand for structural amenity, locational and neighbourhood attributes of dwellings. This growth in interest in an 'expanded' housing commodity has allowed a convergence between 'housing' and 'neighbourhood' economics. The latter area of investigation is well illustrated in Segal's review volume (Segal, 1979); and the recent logit models of neighbourhood choice, most notably by John Quigley (1985), have suggested a sound route for the analysis of neighbourhood choices.

The growing coverage of 'gentrification' studies — despite the inappropriate labelling — and the increasing empirical relevance of housing economics, due to more localised testing and complex commodity specification, indicates yet another area of potential convergence in search of a more general research framework. I have already indicated that a central, and initial, component of such a model is the identification of neighbourhood supply and demand structures. This would facilitate the analysis of choices made at a particular point in time. However, our real analytical and, indeed, policy interest lies in two additional more wide-ranging issues. First, in such discussions we are concerned with how areas change over time in their socio-economic composition and relative prices. Research on these dynamic issues has been almost non-existent; in the UK inter-censal shifts in small-area composition have been our main source of information to date. Second, housing and neighbourhood investment in one set of areas within a city may have spillover effects on other areas or indeed on the urban economy as a whole. Rehabilitation strategies for housing and neighbourhoods, if they are to be effectively advocated and efficiently structured, have to recognise that spillovers exist and that they are impacting upon a dynamic environment.

The context

The paragraphs above indicate the 'niche' of empirical and theoretical work into which this chapter fits. The substance of the chapter is concerned with the rehabilitation of older housing areas in the city of Glasgow over a decade, from 1974 to 1985. For two decades, from 1955–75, Glasgow became a paradigm case of the declining central city in a declining metropolitan region. The economic base of the city is still contracting and population decline is only now reducing to minimal levels, but since 1974 the city has become the locus of a major rehabilitation programme. In a British context, Glasgow is undoubtedly the most extensively renovated older city and in a recent comparative study of 11 countries, only Rotterdam had a reinvestment programme on a comparable scale. Within the broad theoretical framework set out above, this chapter tells the 'Glasgow Story' of change in the last decade. It represents a synthesis of a series of studies undertaken in the City since 1975.

The study uses two main kinds of information. First, three compatible cross-sectional studies of housing choices in the city were undertaken in 1976, 1982 and 1985. This allows us to examine how similar groups of purchasers made different housing and neighbourhood choices over time. Second, from 1974 to the present the Centre for Housing Research has produced a database record, to the nearest 5 metres, of all housing sales and grant-aided reinvestment behaviour in the city. The database makes clear the changing structure of the local housing market from which samples were drawn. The next section of the paper sets out private market perceptions and neighbourhood choices in 1976, a period illustrative of pre-rehabilitation impact. The subsequent sections then outline the major rehabilitation instruments and their impacts. Then the penultimate section indicates how a sample equivalent to the 1976 group made choices in 1985. These comparisons demonstrate the considerable impacts that have stemmed from the style of revitalisation which has been developed in Glasgow.

PRIVATE MARKET CHOICES IN THE PRE-REHABILITATION PHASE

Urban change in Glasgow has seldom been smooth or gradual. From 1860 to 1910 the economic base of the city expanded dramatically with population rising from 400,000 to 800,000. This increase, some of it occurring even before the development of mass transit systems, generated a housing supply response from private landlords. In general, small, low-amenity units were developed in densely packed stone tenements. Residential uses were mixed together with commercial land users on tenement ground floors, and small-scale industrial premises in backcourts and adjacent lots. In this regard Glasgow is more similar to European than to English cities.

Throughout the 1950s, in order to cope with a crudely defined housing shortage, the municipality added new social housing units at the edge of the city. By the early 1960s, the vast municipal engine of housing change had been reoriented to slum clearance. Older, low-amenity private rental and owner occupied dwellings were demolished. Replacement housing was provided at first in peripheral estates and in nearby New Towns and overspill centres and then, after 1960, in central area renewal projects.

By 1974 a more pluralistic approach to housing provision in the city came to be advocated (involving rehabilitation and owner occupation as well as municipal rehousing). However, even at that time local authority new construction was running at around 2,000 units per annum and there was an annual rate of demolition of around 7,700 units from an identified Below Tolerable Standard stock of 75,000 units. At that time there were still

12,000 houses sharing toilets and the first UK deprivation studies highlighted the extreme deprivation of Glasgow's older housing wards.

Thus the period reflected a still continuing process of municipal demolition. The net number of housing units was decreasing rapidly, in spite of a large social housing programme. Central area neighbourhoods were at least half covered in vacant land or compulsorily purchased and vacant dwellings. Private sector investment in housing in the city had been minimal throughout the post-war period. In spite of available land, there were never more than 200 private units built in the city in any year after 1950 and the city never contained more than 10 per cent of new housing starts in the broader metropolitan region. Nor was the existing housing stock apparently being improved. Prior to 1974 no more than 900 improvement grants per year were being used to improve housing quality. In a 1979 sample of 600 houses in the lowest three deciles of the market, half in the ownership of private landlords and half in low-value home-ownership, it was observed that grant aid and significant modernisation had been used in less than 5 per cent of the dwelling units. Prior to 1974 therefore, Glasgow was a city in which net private investment in housing was declining. Central area wards contained elderly and low income populations left behind by social rehousing which resulted in small, low amenity and deteriorating tenements. The neighbourhoods themselves had been fractured and blighted.

Neighbourhood choice in the city, 1976

In the section which follows the policy shifts which began to halt and eventually reverse central area decline are discussed. First, it is useful to set out in more detail an analysis of the neighbourhood choices made in the city by home-buyers in the broad period discussed above. The evidence is drawn from a representative sample of home-buyers in the city in 1976. Some 824 purchasers, a 15 per cent sample for a six-month period of market activity, were interviewed about their housing search processes, area preferences and housing choices, including an analysis of their locational choice influences and satisfactions. Some aspects of this study have been reported elsewhere (Dawson *et al.*, 1982; Maclennan and Wood, 1982; Maclennan

Figure 6.1: Relative house price change by census area, Glasgow, 1972–84

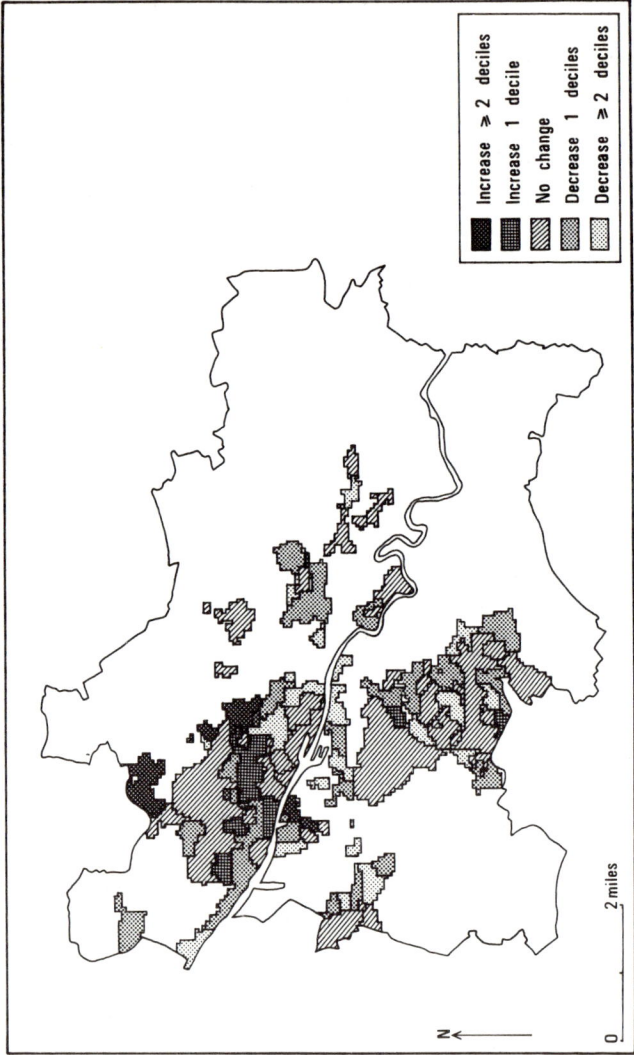

Legend:
- Increase ≥ 2 deciles
- Increase 1 decile
- No change
- Decrease 1 deciles
- Decrease ≥ 2 deciles

Source: Centre for Housing Studies, database.

116

and Munro, 1986; Maclennan and Jones, 1986). Price data are derived from the Register of Sasines and the price database contains all transactions in the city from 1972–84 spatially referenced to the nearest 5 metres.

The map of dwelling prices for Census Areas, Figure 6.1, indicates the spatial pattern of residential opportunities in the city. Low-price housing exists in zones spread throughout the city rather than merely in the 'inner zone'. The underlying pattern of housing and neighbourhood characteristics was revealed in two ways. Data on houses and neighbourhoods for the 824 dwellings were analysed by factor analysis to reveal underlying product groups. The spatial patterning of these groups broadly reflected house type, size and age with neighbourhood and structure types being closely correlated. In consequence, the pattern of product groups available to housing consumers was broadly similar to the residential structure of the city revealed by factor analysis of 1981 census ED data for the city (Figure 6.2). Where there are short-run imbalances in the demand for and supply of units then submarkets may occur, as indicated in Maclennan, Wood and Munro (1986). The detailed pattern of building society lending in the city reveals the absence of formal lending within the bottom two deciles of the market, although it has not been possible to establish that this pattern emerged from a simple redlining process (Maclennan and Jones 1986).

The residents who purchased owner-occupied units ranged from owners moving with substantial assets (up to £40,000 in 1976 prices) and high incomes to low-income large families also moving within the system. First-time buyers (FTBs), albeit with a concentration in price deciles 3–6, were spread across all the price deciles except the most expensive. This pattern indicated clearly that not all FTBs faced affordability problems and that a substantial proportion of purchasers had low incomes and unskilled occupational backgrounds.

In relation to constraints and motivations surrounding purchase there were systematic differences across different price deciles (Maclennan and Wood, 1982). Although the differences shade from decile to decile there appeared to be a significant set of differences between purchasers in the lowest three deciles as opposed to the highest seven. Naturally, economic theory generates the expectation that the lowest income groups will locate in these lowest deciles. And this expectation in relation to consumer's permanent incomes is correct, although current

117

Figure 6.2: Private housing area types, Glasgow, 1981, based on cluster analysis of Census data

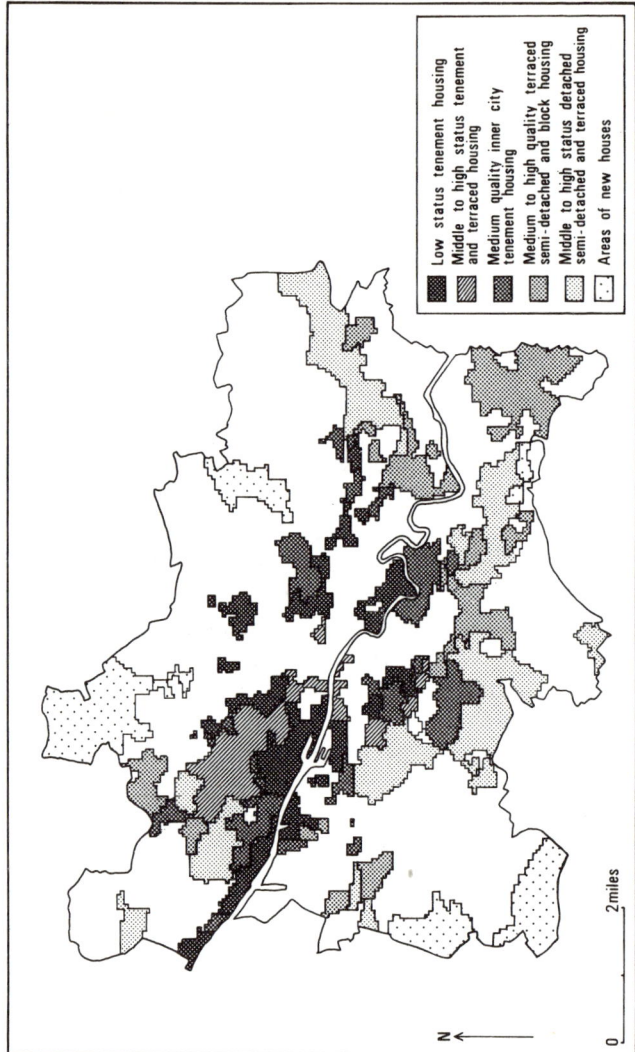

Legend:
- Low status tenement housing
- Middle to high status tenement and terraced housing
- Medium quality inner city tenement housing
- Medium to high quality terraced semi-detached and block housing
- Middle to high status detached semi-detached and terraced housing
- Areas of new houses

N←

0   2miles

Source: Glasgow University Database and 1981 Census

incomes of some FTBs in deciles 3 to 5 were below those of moving households in the lowest three price deciles. Locators in the bottom three deciles contained the bulk of lower income purchasers, but they were also older adult units; more than 70 per cent were continuing movers and the households contained two children, usually of school-age. In examining purchase motives only 10 per cent of the sample stressed asset motives for purchase, almost none had the date of their purchase or move influenced by house price inflation factors. These households had indicated that they had primarily moved to purchase larger units and they had done so by moving small distances. Only 23 per cent of these households expected to trade-up in the market again within the next five years. More than half had considered rental sector opportunities (usually in the social sector) prior to repurchasing.

By contrast, purchasers in deciles, 4, 5 and 6 were predominantly first-time buyers with no children, usually the FTB household included two earners and they had moved into spaces vacated by households trading up within the system. Fewer than 20 per cent had considered rental alternatives and more than half stressed asset motives for purchase. Three-quarters of this group indicated an intention to move upmarket and outwards from the city centre within the next five years. Clearly the market was split between a down-market segment of low-income residents with consumption concerns as opposed to an upper segment in which asset motives and trading-up intentions prevailed. The lower priced segment naturally constituted the houses and neighbourhoods in product groups 1 and 2, that is older smaller tenemental areas of rundown stock. Where more substantial income groups located in the bottom three deciles, around 12 per cent of purchasers therein, they did so without any stated intention to upgrade the housing units. Preferences to minimise housing expenditure rather than intended gentrification appeared to be their key concern.

Patterns of housing market search and bidding behaviour, which were influenced by advice from the main lending agencies, confirmed this market separation with few middle or upper income FTBs examining rental alternatives or locations in product groups 1 and 2. Purchasers not selecting older locations were asked which attributes of these areas they found unattractive and what policy actions should follow. They were also asked to state whether, following policy action, they would consider central locations.

The results of this survey are indicated in Table 6.1, and it indicates the negative view of older neighbourhoods held by upper and middle income households in 1976. Without a change in supply structures it is clear that the older areas of the city would have continued to be associated with low incomes and further decay of the stock would have been probable. Since the number of young households in the metropolitan region, generated from within the city, was increasing (in spite of overall population loss), these areas seemed to have a minimal capacity to attract middle income and younger households.

POLICY AND SUPPLY SIDE CHANGES 1974–1984

During the early 1970s the owner-occupied sector grew at a very slow rate. To some extent, switches of second-hand units from private renting to home ownership offset continuing demolitions, but the rate of new private construction consistently ran below 200 units per year, usually on the suburban edge. Fewer than 100 improvement grants per annum were used in the older stock.

In the late 1960s, as reflected in the 1969 Housing (Scotland) Act, central government recognised that there could be an economic case for housing rehabilitation. From 1969 to 1974 the municipality bought out more than 1,200 rundown units, concentrated in Housing Treatment Areas of 200–300 units, with a view to subsidised rehabilitation. However, although the municipality had extensive housing expertise, it found its mode of operation too centralised and bureaucratic to promote revitalisation with community involvement. In retrospect, a neighbourhood-city revitalisation ethos did not pervade this programme, nor its successors, until well into the 1980s. The 'theory of the problem', perhaps reflecting academic ignorance in this area, has never been well developed.

The inadequacies of policy from 1969–74 have been rectified by large scale programmes in the city implemented under the 1974 Housing (Scotland) Act. The legislation and its impacts are discussed in the technical literature, so only a brief overview is presented here. Houses (and note that the policy is focused upon residences not buildings or neighbourhoods) which are classed as inadequate on any one of 12 factors, including condition as well

Table 6.1: Housing market movers' views on the nature of the five central city wards

	1976 (Before)		1985 (After)	
	Perceived[a,b] problems by non-locators	Dissatisfaction[c] by locators	Problems[b] perceived by non-locators	Dissatisfaction[c] by locators
Area appearance	85	42	50	24
Busy roads	65	51	56	31
Air pollution	52	37	24	18
Housing quality	76	50	42	12
Access to work	36	11	15	9
Violence and crime	75	32	29	11
Schools	43	18	61	19
Parks	56	12	42	11
Community facilities	56	47	54	38
Vandalism	74	28	35	15
Neighbour type	48	15	42	9
Falling property values	71	8	27	5
	N = 824		N = 793	

Notes:

a. Households locating in Glasgow but outside the 5 central wards.

b. Scores in these columns are the proportions noting this area attribute as being a problem in 5 inner wards.

c. Scores are proportion of locators in inner 5 wards citing area attribute as a source of dissatisfaction.

as the absence of amenities, are declared to be Below the Tolerable Standard (BTS). In 1974 it was estimated that there were 74,000 BTS units in Glasgow, almost exclusively in product groups 1 and 2 of Figure 6.2. Where more than 40 per cent of units in an area (which may range in scale from 40 to 400 units) are classed as BTS then the municipality, with the approval of central government, may declare the area to be a Housing Action Area (HAA). The HAA may be for demolition, improvement or a combination of both.

Within an HAA the municipality may adopt a number of strategies to promote upgrading. First, it may initiate market-led strategies wherein owner-occupiers and private landlords use the generally available programme of repair and improvement grants to repair and modernise. HAA status for a neighbourhood has generally been associated with preferential rates of grant (ranging from 75 to 90 per cent of costs, up to some limit). As we shall see below, in the British context, Glasgow has developed a particularly vigorous market-led strategy but not in the bottom two price deciles, where (as was confirmed in 1980 by a retrospective study of modernisation and maintenance by rent controlled landlords and poor, elderly owner-occupiers) there was no modernisation and no uptake of grant aid even when subsidy levels ran at 75 per cent of costs. Further, traditional mainstream housing policies of tax reliefs for owner-occupiers and rent controls had arguably negative effects on older housing quality. The municipality, quite correctly, recognised that a 'buy-out' strategy would be the appropriate route for assisting the poorest households in the worst areas. Recognising its own past incompetence in this process, the municipality, again to an extent distinctive in the UK, turned over HAAs to Housing Associations.

Housing Associations in Britain are financed and monitored by a quango, the Housing Corporation. In Glasgow each association is given three or four Project Areas (which may include ten or more HAAs) usually covering 1,500–2,000 houses. Glasgow's Associations, unlike many in other British cities, therefore have a distinctly local spatial focus. In Glasgow there are now 22 Associations operating in this way and they are, in 1986, almost halfway through their potential improvement stock.

The Associations, usually with a management committee of local residents, identify a set of closes, comprising between 20 and 140 houses, which they wish to improve. Less than 10 per cent of landlords and owner-occupiers, using grant aid, take the opportunity to improve with the Association; on average, 90 per cent will sell to the Association. Rent controlled landlords (with tenants with security of tenure) have opted to sell quickly, and elderly and poor owner-occupiers sell to the Association and receive a capital sum as well as a guarantee that they will be able to rent a dwelling unit improved by the Association. Rehabilitation without displacement is the central concern of the process.

The costs of acquisition and improvement of the tenement flats in question run at around £25,000 per unit with just over 90 per cent of the costs absorbed by the government through Housing Association Grant. The benefits are also important. The changes in property and neighbourhood condition which emerge are considerable (Table 6.2). But the wider spillover effects are also considerable. First, where internal improvement is associated with stone cleaning, then *ceteris paribus* the capital values of properties in adjacent (market sector) blocks have tended to increase by 8 per cent more than anticipated over a two-year period. In fact, since 1981 associated blocks have invariably encountered market-led improvements so the econometric test is too complex to specify (without major *a priori* judgements on the nature of lags and spatial processes in rehabilitation). Second, it could be argued that improvements by Associations generate grant uptake in adjacent areas for there have, since 1981, been high rates of uptake in these locations. However, as is indicated below, the municipality has co-ordinated and targeted aid towards these locations. Third, and again this is discussed below, research indicates that private developers returning to vacant sites in older areas do pick locations adjacent to completed HAA blocks. Private confidence is also restored in that blocks adjacent to HAAs now have 75 per cent building society funding of transactions in older dwellings rather than the 30–40 per cent observed in 1976 (when the Associations were putting their first contracts on site). We also have to note that Association purchases are concentrated in the first two deciles of the house price distribution and, since 1979, they have made almost two-thirds of the purchases in these deciles. The long-run implications of the socialisation of this sector of the market are noted in the concluding section.

From 1976 to 1981 there was a continuing expansion in grant aid, financed by central government but administered by the municipality, to assist market-led improvement. From 1981 to

Table 6.2: Resident perceptions of area quality pre- and post-improvement[a]

	Direction of change of area problem	Area attribute important	Area attribute not important
		Difficulties in organisation of community change	Loss of community spirit
Reduced in scale post-Improvement	Still improving	Derelict houses	Anti-social neighbours
		General poor appearance of area	
		Visual effects of demolition	Similar people moving out
	Deteriorating less rapidly	Derelict land backcourt quality	Provision of indoor recreation
	Deteriorating more rapidly	Vandalism property security	Police services
Increased in scale Post improvement	Deteriorating less rapidly	Non-local traffic in the area	
	Deteriorating more rapidly	General noise level Access to local shops	Noise and dirty factories

Note: a. The basis of the classification is as follows: A problem is deemed to be 'important' if more than 15 per cent of households perceived it to be a problem (either before or after improvement). A reduction in problem 'scale' implies that the percentage of households mentioning this problem as persisting post-improvement is lower than the pre-improvement scale. Whether the status is deteriorating or improving is based on resident perceptions.

1984 grant aid rose dramatically, but has since been curtailed. British academics have often held the view, by focusing on limited evidence from English cities, that improvement and gentrification (however defined) were synonymous. Nationally the recent Distribution of Grant Inquiry produced figures of grant aid in relation to incomes which indicate that inefficient targeting of aid (in relation to income groups) does exist but is by no means the rule. Two studies in Glasgow tend to confirm the DGI findings. Through its area co-ordination of aid, the municipality has ensured that 90 per cent of aid was spent in product groups 1 and 2. Further, area co-ordination and supportive loan finance ensured that the bulk of aid went to existing owners. In aggregate 60 per cent of grant aid went to households with total incomes of less than £10,000 (1984 prices).

The spatial incidence of this programme is indicated in Figure 6.3 and the way in which it reinforces Housing Association 'growth poles' is revealed in Figure 6.4. To date some 40,000 houses have received some assistance in the programmes. When market-led and buy-out strategies are taken together, in the 1980s there has generally been an annual expenditure of around £100m per annum. In very broad terms, since 1974 approximately £1,000m has been spent on improving and repairing older private housing in the city by the public sector, and the programme has generated (directly and indirectly) some 5,000 jobs per year in the local economy.

The third main phase of supply side change has been the development of new private construction since 1980, with units priced between £17,500 and £35,000. Since early 1985 the provision of higher value units and conversions from disused commercial spaces (in the area immediately within the CBD) has become apparent.

Growing confidence in the older neighbourhoods, along with a more supportive view from the local authority, has resulted in a major shift in the volume and pattern of new private construction in the city. From the mid-1970s onwards the annual volume of new private housing construction in Glasgow (against the background of national recession in housing construction) rose from 200 per year to 800 per year by 1979 to more than 1,200 per year since 1982. From 1976 to 1984, there were almost 8,000 new private completions in the city — a sixfold increase in the annual completion rate in comparison with the previous decade. Moreover, within this total the city's share of the regional total rose from 10 to 30 per cent. Also, within the city there has been a marked shift from greenfield to brownfield development. In 1980, only 10 per cent of starts were on brownfield sites, by 1984 this proportion was almost 80 per cent. Approximately half of these dwellings were developed under some form of licensing arrangement with the city council, in an attempt to re-use land which had lain blighted and unused since 1960s slum clearance.

New construction has increasingly located in rundown neighbourhoods and some of it lies close to the fringes of the

Figure 6.3: Improvement grants per 500 metre grid squares, Glasgow 1974–84. Total costs adjusted for inflation to 1983 price levels

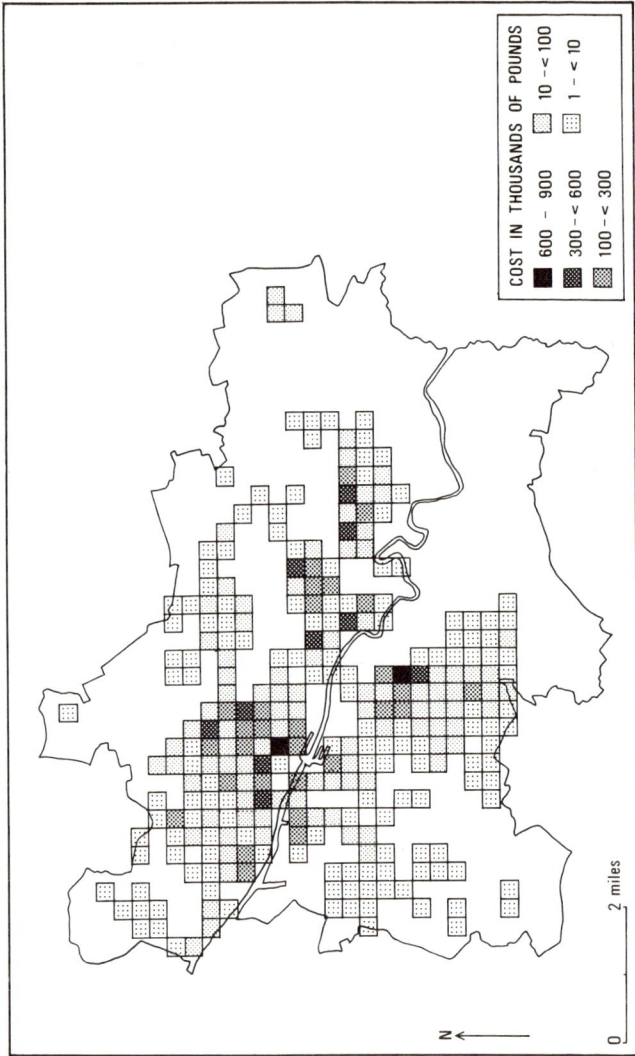

COST IN THOUSANDS OF POUNDS

600 – 900	10 – < 100
300 – < 600	1 – < 10
100 – < 300	

N ←

0   2 miles

Sources: Centre for Housing Studies; Glasgow Housing Department.

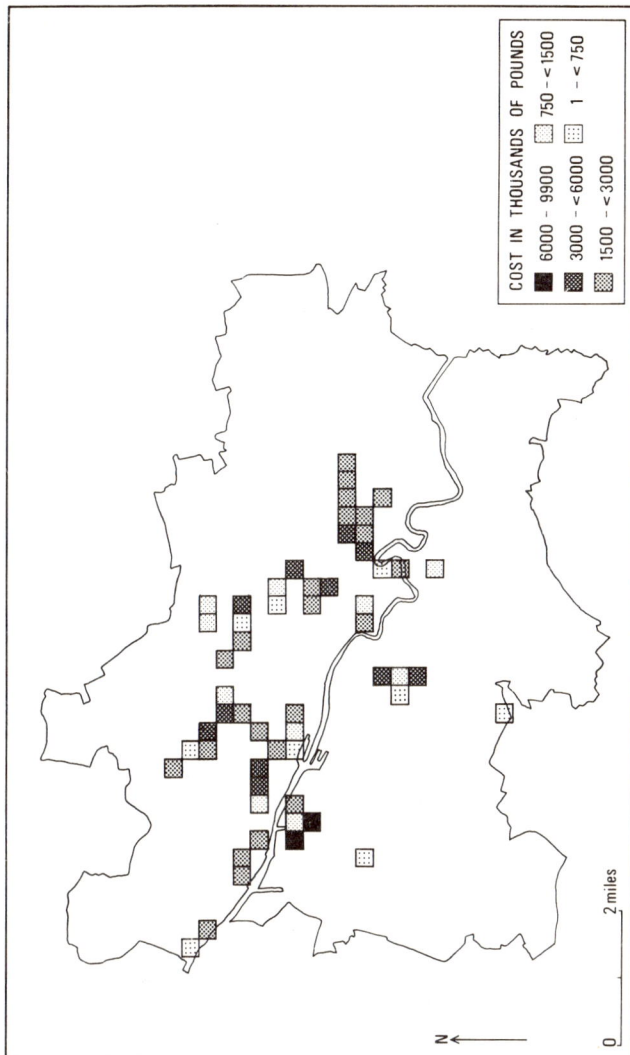

Figure 6.4: Cost of Housing Association areas for improvement per 500 metre grid square, Glasgow 1975–84

COST IN THOUSANDS OF POUNDS

6000 – 9900
3000 – <6000
1500 – <3000
750 – <1500
1 – <750

N

0   2 miles

Sources: Centre for Housing Studies; Glasgow Housing Department.

127

CBD. This raises important questions not only for the city as a whole but for the particular neighbourhoods involved. New construction was able to redevelop vacant sites which were not a feasible option for Housing Associations or the local authority, starved as they were of capital. And, of course, the developments provided a range, style, quality and value of private housing which did not previously exist in these locations. Three-room flats in 4-storey walk-up blocks were the modal form of dwelling produced, and prices ranged in 1985 from £19,500 to £27,500.

Since most of these new private housing developments were located on vacant land, particularly in Product Groups 1 and 2, they considerably boosted neighbourhood reinvestment spending. Adding some 800 units annually at an average of £22,500 implied spending by the private sector of around £175m per annum. This represents a considerable leveraging on the £100m per annum flowing from the municipality and Associations. There is little to suggest that this investment would have occurred without the large-scale and strategically planned effort which the public sector had made from 1974 onwards. In this instance the state, albeit with style, has had to lead the private sector by the hand to a new promised land in older neighbourhoods. To understand this process, and the demand conditions which made it possible, we must consider how Glaswegians changed their image of the city within a decade.

ALTERED IMAGES AND CHANGING PLACES

The dynamics of neighbourhood change need not proceed in a smooth, steady, equilibrium fashion. Some years ago Edwin von Boventer set out an intriguing set of area change models, incorporating bandwagon effects, which have played little part in shaping policy for neighbourhood revitalisation. Strategists in Glasgow, since 1980, have become aware of how one short period of change rapidly creates the preconditions for subsequent change, largely by restoring confidence. Once the process is started it has some cumulative tendencies which eventually reduce the ratio of public to private funding and which, *mea culpa*, progressively render past estimates of cross-sectional demand intentions both outdated and pessimistic.

To bring the substantive section of this chapter to a close I wish to present a survey of consumer choices and attitudes undertaken in 1985 which is structurally identical to the 1976 sample. However, since the choices and attitudes of this group are influenced by the presence of those who relocated in the 1978–84 period into older neighbourhoods, the characteristics of these earlier in-movers are considered first.

Recent research in the city allows us to establish a relatively clear picture of who responded to the new construction effort in older neighbourhoods. In broad terms we can now see that the estimates from the 1976 study (which of course preceded the favourable impacts of rehabilitation) were pessimistic in suggesting that only one-sixth of FTBs would be interested in purchasing within older neighbourhoods.

Sample studies from 1983 suggest that some 70 per cent of 'brownfield' purchasers were FTBs, that is around 550 households. For that period, 2,400 flats were sold in the Greater Glasgow Area in similar price ranges (below £27,750). That is, the new developments attracted around 23 per cent of all FTBs operating in these price ranges of the flat market. Moreover, in relation to the main problems anticipated in such areas, actual residents report a much lower incidence of difficulties. Only one-quarter of households reported crime-related problems, whereas in 1976, 73 percent of FTBs had anticipated such difficulties. The housing quality problem which had discouraged interest from 76 per cent of 1976 FTBs was *de facto* resolved. Area appearance was still a problem for 38 per cent of households, but again this was lower than the 85 per cent of FTBs with negative reactions in 1976, and one-third reported vandalism problems. *Ex post*, the major difficulties reported were the poor appearance and the quality of streets (54 per cent), and the absence of facilities for teenagers (45 per cent). The high score on this factor reflected the fact that around 30 per cent of purchasers were continuing households trading-up from lower-value properties in nearby locations. Around four-fifths of households were satisfied with the housing choices they made.

The purchasers

The nature of purchasers in such locations can be described in more detail since during 1982–3 two household surveys, covering 438 purchasers of 'new initiative' housing, were undertaken by CHR. One survey, for the Scottish Development Agency, was concerned with the GEAR area, and another by Fielder (1986) in conjunction with Glasgow District Council, covered the full range of 'new initiative' housing types and locations throughout the city. Further, Sasines data and a more general survey of purchasers in 1983 provide additional information.

Reflecting the pattern of construction, 70 per cent of sales were made to 1- and 2-person households in central locations. A surprising number of sales was made, as in the GEAR area, to local households with children. The purchasers were predominantly young, with two-thirds below the age of 30. More than four-fifths of the adult population (reflecting a high proportion of two-earner families) were in full-time employment and the unemployment rate was 3 per cent. Compared with the conurbation, city and especially the neighbourhood in which construction took place, the new residents therefore had a favourable employment profile. Regarding their occupation status, one half were 'intermediate and junior' non-manual workers, one-quarter were skilled manual workers but one-sixth were semi-skilled manual workers.

Some 40 per cent of purchasers were new households, predominantly formed by marriage or by a young single adult leaving home for the first time, though around 5 per cent were recently divorced or separated. For the 'new households', almost half had a parental background within Glasgow's public sector housing and taking into account in-moves from New Towns and surrounding municipalities, almost two-thirds of new households had a public sector background. This is an important observation which we consider further below. Around one-third of continuing households were previous home-owners, usually trading up from within the local area, and more than one-fifth transferred from the private rental sector, again usually from within, or near to, the local area. A further important observation was that just over one-third of continuing households transferred from the public to the private sector. This is almost treble the rate of transfer indicated in earlier studies of the city.

Taking new and continuing households together, three-quarters of the purchasers were first-time buyers and this highlights the importance of new construction as a source of owner-occupation growth in the city. A general survey of purchasers in the city (Maclennan and Munro, 1986), indicated that between 1976 and 1983 the income burden of becoming a home-owner (now around 38 per cent of FTB head-of-household income) had increased significantly. Rising real house prices, relatively static real incomes and high real interest rates (reflecting macro-economic policy) were the causes of this change. However, the rising rents and declining quality of rental sector alternatives, even at a time when the asset motives for home-ownership sharply reduced, had resulted in a declining share of purchasers making any consideration of rental sector alternatives. It had become apparent that most households with relatively secure employment had set their face against rental tenures, especially in the public sector. In the survey of 'new initiative' purchasers, only 11 per cent considered rental alternatives, almost exclusively in the public sector. Most households quickly rejected this option, even without applying for a council house.

This set of observations is particularly important as long-term demand will depend not only upon economic change and household formation but upon tenure shift. Thus, for many of this group the alternative to central new construction may not be the higher value neighbourhoods of the West End and the South Side, but instead the public estates of Strathclyde which allocate houses to young households. Thus it has to be noted that even if older Glasgow has been renovated without short-run low income displacement this may, in the long run, only be continued by the destabilisation of post-war council housing in the city and suburbs.

The 'new initiative' residents also had well defined locational choice patterns. Around one-third of purchasers at each location had originated within one mile of the new site and had focused search activity upon that particular area. A further quarter confined their search to the older neighbourhoods around the city centre; thus, more than half of the eventual client group had started with very specific search intentions. The remainder split their search between the rest of inner Glasgow and the surrounding suburbs.

New housing alternatives were preferred because of lower expected maintenance costs (two-thirds), but a further important sub-group (around one-fifth) stressed fixed prices, the avoidance of repeat bidding and the ease of obtaining mortgages with minimal deposits as critically attractive factors. The main factors affecting the choice of a specific neighbourhood were past connections with the location, the presence of friends and relatives in the area and, most importantly, the work and general accessibility of the location selected. The latter factor was particularly stressed by two-earner childless households. All of this suggests that new construction was clearly removing supply side constraints on household choices, both in relation to housing and credit availability in central area neighbourhoods. In many respects, policies in the 1980s are removing policy-induced constraints from the 1960s.

The locational origins of purchasers is also an important consideration. In Table 6.3 the patterns are set out for the 1983 surveys and for the population of movers in 1984. The main observations are that for the majority of schemes, 70 per cent of purchasers originate within Glasgow district. A significant proportion of purchasers, around one-quarter, originate in the rest of Strathclyde, particularly Lanark and Dumbarton. Taken as a whole, however, the sites attracted a relatively modest flow of inter-regional movers. If we examine movement for 1984 in the flat sector for the region as a whole, it can be observed that some 20 per cent of flat purchasers outside Glasgow are inter-regional movers. These purchases are, of course, flats of higher value and quality.

Sasines migration figures for 1984 indicate that higher value conversions within the CBD, in the Merchant City area, have attracted purchasers in a rather different way. The Merchant City has attracted 20 per cent of its clientele from inter-regional movers, and the share of purchasers from Glasgow is barely 50 per cent. Thus the Merchant City, so far, has been particularly effective in 'importing' purchasers from beyond the city. It is also important to note that in the 1976 study, only 10 per cent of first-time buyers in Glasgow (and in the older areas) originated from Strathclyde region. The new initiatives have clearly more than doubled the 'competitiveness' of central Glasgow sites in attracting 'regional' demand for FTB housing and this shift

Table 6.3: Locational origins of 'new initiative' residents

| | Overall study | | GEAR study | |
	New household members	Continuing households	New household members	Continuing households
Local area	35	40	13.7	30.4
Other part of Glasgow	33	33	69.5	57
Rest of Strathclyde	26.5	22 }	17 }	13
Beyond Strathclyde	5	4 }		

reflects broader land-planning policy although it has not yet been adequately considered in the way in which local demand projections are made. It does, however, appear to be a shift in locational choice patterns consistent with consumer preferences.

LOOKING BACK AND COMING BACK

The above discussions of supply adjustments and changing demand patterns clearly illustrate the inadequacy of cross-section snapshots. In this section the results of a survey of 1985 movers in the Glasgow market are compared with the 1976 results. This survey includes respondents choosing units throughout the city and it is not restricted to new or older neighbourhood purchasers. We can, in essence, see how Glaswegians view their city in 1985 by comparison with 1976. It should be noted that the process of change may not yet have terminated, and Glasgow in 1994 may be very different from the city in 1985.

The evidence presented here only broadly summarises some recent research. For a more complete description, and in particular the details of econometric estimation procedures, the reader is referred to Maclennan (1986). The 1985 survey was a one-in-six representative sample of households purchasing units in the city between January and June 1985. In total, 923 households were asked to describe their houses, search procedures, area preferences and housing outlays. The research, as in 1976, focused upon tenure choices, search and locational choice.

The survey data revealed an increased polarisation of tenure preferences since 1976, with in 1985 less than 7 per cent of the sample considering rental alternatives. The consideration was almost entirely restricted to 2-person, young households in manual, unskilled jobs who eventually bought in deciles 2 and 3. In a formal modelling sense, in the British context there appears to be a clear hierarchical choice process, with tenure pre-selected before house-type, neighbourhood and other considerations enter the active decision process. Indeed in 1985, as in 1976, only 5 per cent of the sample actually searched across tenures within a pre-specified set of neighbourhoods. This observation had strengthened in 1985, in spite of the reported fall in asset motives for purchase. By 1985 only 10 per cent of Glaswegians, now spread throughout the price distribution, indicated that asset motives were important in house purchase. It can be hypothesised (although the proposition is not testable with the available data) that the increasing real rents and declining quality of social housing have reinforced tenure separation. The lower inflation rate and the reduced number of bids required before securing a property both reflected the less pressured market conditions of 1985 *vis-à-vis* 1976.

Patterns of spatial search had also changed between 1976 and 1985. In 1976 it was established that after one or two initial searches (usually reflecting undue optimism about individual purchasing power) individuals quickly settled into highly localised search areas after broad housing type had been selected. At this stage, households tended to adjust unit quality or price bid rather than area or unit size (see Maclennan and Wood, 1982). The hierarchy of decisions again prevailed in 1985. However, the extent of areas over which households in a given income range searched had increased markedly and the close association of particular income groups with particular types of neighbourhoods had disappeared.

The preference patterns underlying this search procedure are analysed in more detail below. But the broad structure can be described as follows. Households in the bottom quarter of the income distribution were, as in 1976, largely confined to the bottom 3 deciles of the price distribution. This group, as noted for 1976, would tend not to restrict search to a single sector of the city (radially defined along the old tramway routes), but search across opportunities around the CBD, with the exception of its eastern flank. In 1976 the middle two quarters of the income distribution tended to focus search in Product Groups 2 and 3 and their individual search tended to be sectoral and located north or south of the river. The spatial areas searched were usually contained within a single square mile (62 per cent of this group). The same income groups in 1985, however, had a spatial search pattern which was still largely sectoral, but with search extending from 1976 areas inwards to and around the CBD. For instance, 57 per cent of this group had search areas confined within four square mile areas. Rehabilitation and new construction near the core had greatly expanded the spatial margins within which this group (the bulk of the city's home owners) were now prepared to locate. For the upper quarter of the income distribution search still usually (in 83 per cent of cases) commenced in Product Groups 4 and 5 towards the urban edge of the sector in which the households had been located. This pattern had been even more pronounced in 1976. Now, some 15 per cent of upper income movers included at least one search within three miles of the CBD and, as is indicated below, a significant number located back towards the centre. Hence in less than a decade, albeit with massive reinvestment levels, the associations between income, location and neighbourhood choice had changed significantly.

The basis of the above changes can be explained by examining the purchasing sample in more detail. The shift of higher income groups back towards areas classified in 1976 as Product Groups 1 and 2 reflects the outcome of market processes and policy actions. Return shift could be attributed to either change in demand patterns and or a shift in neighbourhood supply functions. As indicated in the introductory section there is no need to adhere to a single factor explanation of changes in residential spatial structure. Confining our attention initially to demand side factors, the following influences can shape area choices: changes in household incomes; changes in relative prices; changes in transport costs; changes in the demographic structure of the population; and preference shifts. These are discussed in turn.

In the period studied the real income of the purchasing sample had grown by 17 per cent (head of household income deflated by the national inflation rate), although this increase was higher in the upper parts of the income distribution. However, *ceteris paribus* it could have been expected that income growth would probably have generated further decentralisation. Further, the evidence available suggests that after standardising for property quality, the prices of units in deciles 2 and 3 had converged towards the city mean and that lower priced submarkets (defined in relation to a standard bundle of housing attributes) which existed in 1976 had begun to erode by 1979 and were no longer identifiable in 1983. That is, relative price shifts *per se* were not likely to have been the cause of inward movement.

However, shifts in transport costs and demographic-household structure over the decade have been consistent with a growth in demand for smaller and more centrally located units. From the sample studies, the real cost of using the transport modes of the 1976 sample in 1985 would have almost doubled. Further, in 1985, 82 per cent of respondents who worked in the central city reported that it was 'Important' to live near their workplace, compared with 64 per cent in 1976. For those analysts more impressed by revealed behaviour, two-earner childless

135

households in 1985 on average lived 1.5 miles nearer the city centre than their predecessors in 1976. In 1985 more than 80 per cent of this group stressed that near-workplace location was a critical residential location criterion.

The pattern of households in 1985 was markedly different from that observed in 1976. It is useful to divide the sample into groups roughly consistent with life-cycle stages (although we should note that the concept of a 'normal' housing life cycle may not now be a very precise concept). The subdivision divides households in relation to both their constraints (income, capital, etc.) and preferences (space, gardens, access to entertainment, etc.). The patterns observed in Glasgow in 1976 and 1985 are indicated in Table 6.4.

The first point to observe from Table 6.4, is that the two groups regarded as 'normal', and often assumed to correlate precisely with 'new' and 'continuing', that is 'newly married' households and 'moving' households with children, have both fallen in proportional significance. In 1976, these two groups taken together accounted for 78 per cent of the households sampled. By 1985 these groups accounted for 61 per cent. On the other hand there had been a marked increase in the number of single and two-person households through separate processes: first, there were more single first-time buyers; second, there was a marked increase in the number of singles trading up and remaining single; third, the proportion of separated/divorced households had almost doubled; fourth, there was a marked

Table 6.4: Characteristics of purchaser samples 1976 and 1985

	1976	1985
	%	%
First-time buyers	45	38
Moving owners	55	62
New households[a]	42	32
Continuing households	58	68
New 1 person	11	15
New 2 or more persons	34	22
Moving households with children	43	35
Moving 1 and 2 person childless	7	15
Moving adults post child launching	4	10
Moving elderly (>60)	2	6
	N = 824	N = 793

Note: a. New households are defined to be those where all the adults were living at the same address for the first time.

increase in the number of two-person married households who had completed child launching (and this is correlated with the increased number of young single FTBs); and fifth, the proportions of elderly one- and two-person households in the market had increased.

To a significant extent the back-to-the-city behaviour of the first and second of the above groups has already been explained. They were the dominant purchasers in the 'new initiative' housing completed between 1980 and 1983. We have already explained why smaller and more central housing was attractive to them. The other groups — that is the divorced and separated, the post child launchers and elderly — need further discussion as there is no *a priori* reason to expect a back-to-the-city movement on the part of these groups.

Since some of these groups may also be relatively poor we examine here households who purchased units in excess of £18,000, that is the upper 7 deciles of the price distribution. In 1985, as in 1976, poorer households are largely confined to the bottom 3 deciles of the distribution. That is, here we examine households with a range of locational choices.

Split households, due to divorce and separation, generate an increased demand for smaller units. In the 1985 study, where separation produced one or more one-person households, these households indicated an interest in central city living. The reasons given emphasise the work location and recreation alternatives available in the core, plus the correct size mix of new or modernised properties available. *Ex post*, almost 10 per cent of housing units purchased by non FTBs in the older neighbourhoods went to divorced or separated adults. Where divorce left an adult with children there was no expressed interest in a return to more central neighbourhoods. Families with 'launched' children also stressed similar amenities in the core and these individuals had considerable market power. These adult-only households, generally in the age band 45–55, were usually trading down from a house in the 6th to 8th price decile. One-third of such movers examined sites within central areas and 14 per cent actually located in these previously downmarket zones, almost invariably in new units. Those who decided not to purchase in such areas stressed the absence of higher value units (in the price ranges £30,000–£50,000) in these locations as their main motive for locating elsewhere (usually in luxury flats). A surprising revelation of the 1985 survey was that 18 per cent of purchasers in older zones were elderly households. They were essentially seeking modern, small properties near to central city sites.

The evidence cited in the preceding paragraphs stresses our earlier observation that processes of change become cumulative. City housing planners and private housing developers have been quick to recognise how young singles and married couples may initiate neighbourhood diversification. However, once confidence has been restored a much wider range of groups may 'come back' and planning policies are only now beginning to recognise this change.

In both the 1976 and 1985 studies households were asked to identify (on a 5-point scale) the importance of a range of housing and neighbourhood attributes in choosing a housing unit. The aggregate patterns for the two periods show little change, although the 1985 sample put more stress on enhanced internal amenity. Broad perceptions of 'good' and 'bad' options remained fairly constant. Indeed in both years there were more important cross-sectional differences, with singles and FTBs having more urban centre oriented requirements than couples with children. Thus the changing socio-demographic structure of demand rather than any fundamental shift in tastes appears to underpin Glasgow's central area renaissance. An even stronger proposition, with some *prima facie* plausibility, is that supply side changes have merely allowed the expression of locational preferences which had previously been precluded; that is, prior to 1976, policy approaches and developer decisions had partly thwarted locational preferences. Since houses of adequate value and quality did not exist in Product Group 1 and 2 neighbourhoods they were of no interest to median income (and above) households.

The above observations are not a recipe for unbridled optimism about the prospects for the private housing market in central cities in Britain. Few cities have had such an expensive or well co-ordinated approach to neighbourhood housing revitalisation. The Victorian and modern amenities of the areas around the CBD are of a relatively high quality. Importantly, there is a disproportionately small share of coloured minorities within the city and race and private housing issues are relatively unproblematic within the city. Also, Scots, like Europeans, have a long tradition of living in relatively dense, tenemental urban environments. However, the Glasgow experience indicates that the quality of central city areas can be renewed even in the face of sustained decline.

MAJOR CONCLUSIONS

Much of the above discussion has stressed that there is a potential to restore and diversify older, previously decayed neighbourhoods. Naturally the details of policy and potential for action will vary from city to city, but the Glasgow experience seems to offer hope and insights for cities such as Liverpool and Birmingham. The process needs to be resourced generously by central government to create rehabilitation growth poles and a clear area strategy has to be developed. In due course, private developers, invariably prompted by local agencies, will respond to replace public by private funding.

In my view, England will continue to have 1 million unfit houses inhabited by the poor and elderly for as long as market-led strategies lead rehabilitation. In England, the Housing Corporation, preferably operating with the building societies, should be given the resources to plan and implement coherent, area-based, rehabilitation strategies within a decade. And rehabilitation strategy also needs to be closely linked to dwelling replacement, probably by the private sector, on demolition sites. Such a strategy would have a current total cost of around £20 billion, or £2 billion per annum for a decade. Aside from the obvious benefits in relation to housing conditions for the poorest households, such a programme would create 80,000 jobs and generate community action and participative democracy in rundown areas, especially where there are disaffected ethnic minorities. But will we fritter away the prospect of revitalised cities for a 2 pence cut in the standard rate of income tax? Fiscal fiddling will make no sense in the long term if our city cores fall down or, worse, are burned away.

In the academic realm, the Glasgow study makes clear that revitalisation need not be synonymous with displacement and gentrification. Further, it stresses the need for long-term dynamics-oriented research on housing market processes. The present study arose as an accident of timing, job location and researcher preferences. Integrated, dynamic models of residential change need to be developed and tested. The development industry needs to fund substantive research in this field rather than the peripatetic, three-month consultancy reports on housing demand which foul the path to real understanding in this area. Further, although the issue has not been stressed here, there is a pressing need for more scholarly attention to be given to the ways in which we theorise and attempt to measure aspects of housing and neighbourhoods.

ACKNOWLEDGEMENTS

This paper has been based on surveys funded by the Scottish Development Department (1976 and 1980), the Economic and Social Research Council (1983 and 1985) and the Scottish Development Agency (1985). The more general support for this work was provided by the ESRC. I am particularly grateful to Gavin Wood, Colin Jones, Tony O'Sullivan and Moira Munro for shaping my views on this topic.

REFERENCES

Dawson, D. A., Maclennan, D., Wood, G. A., and Jones, C. A. (1982) *The cheaper end of the owner occupied housing market*, Scottish Office, Occasional Paper Series, Edinburgh

Fielder S. (1986) 'Low cost home ownership in Glasgow: widening tenure choice', in Booth, P. and Crook A. (eds) *Low cost home ownership*, Gower, Farnborough

Grigsby, W., Baratz, M. and Maclennan, D. (1986) *Housing and neighbourhood dynamics*, Pergamon Press, Progress in Planning Series (forthcoming)

Maclennan, D. (1982) *Housing economics*, Longman, London

—— (1985) 'Housing rehabilitation policy: an encouraging example', *Policy and Politics*, **13**, pp. 413–29

—— and Jones, C. A. (1986) 'Credit rationing and building society lending', *Urban Studies* (forthcoming)

—— and Munro, M. (1986) 'The development of owner occupation', in Booth, P. and Crook, A. (eds.), *Housing policy under the Tories*, Croom Helm, London

—— and Wood, G. A. (1982) 'Housing search and adjustment', in Clark, W. A. V. (ed.), *Housing market search and mobility*, Croom Helm, London

—— Wood, G. A. and Munro, M. (1986) 'Housing submarkets: evidence from two urban systems', mimeo., University of Glasgow

Pallakowski, H. O. (1982) *Urban housing markets and residential location*, D. C. Heath, Lexington

Quigley, J. M. (1985) 'Consumer choice of dwelling, neighbourhood and public services', *Regional Science and Urban Economics*, **15**, pp. 41–63

Segal, D. (ed.) (1979) *The economics of neighbourhood*, Academic Press, New York

Smith, N. (1982) 'Gentrification and uneven development, *Economic Geography*, **58**, pp. 139–55

Straszheim, M. R. (1975) *An econometric analysis of the urban housing market*, NBER, New York

Williams, P. (1976) 'The role of institutions in the Inner London housing market', *Transactions of the Institute of British Geographers, New Series*, **1**, pp. 72–82

7

The Social Consequences of Housing Design

Alice Coleman

What kind of social structure do we hope for in our residential areas and how far are we achieving it? If we fall short, is the housing itself to blame, and if so, what can be done about it? These are the fundamental questions that were addressed 60 years ago by the creative genius of Le Corbusier and the answers he propounded set the tone for twentieth-century housing in many parts of the world. They have now been re-addressed by the Land Use Research Unit at King's College London — this time on the basis of scientific evidence instead of artistic inspiration — and a completely different set of answers have been adduced.

Le Corbusier regarded the home as a functional machine with three basic roles. First, the inhabitants would use the machine to supply shelter, light, warmth, space and devices to ease existence. Second, the machine would use the inhabitants as units to be processed into a community by throwing them together in open-plan dwellings, multi-dwelling tower blocks, and multi-block estates. Third, even the aesthetics would be machine-like, with all buildings a stark embodiment of their structure and all grounds designed as communal greenery.

Corbusian ideas form a closely argued model, which is convincing as long as it remains untested against reality. Objective testing reveals the enormity of what is left out: the immense diversity of human individuality with a widely differing range of needs. There is the right to privacy with varying needs for solitude; freedom for people to be themselves and not mere cogs in a machine; scope for developing lifestyles that suit them; power to make their unique mark on the home environment, enabling both it and them to be individually recognised by others; and the reciprocal ability to recognise others and develop a mental map of places and personalities in one's surroundings. All these things help to create one's own sense of identity, and without them we entered the era of the 'identity crisis'. They also help to create a sense of community.

INVESTIGATING ENVIRONMENTAL DESIGN

This great gap in understanding means that many of our proud Utopias have been grossly counter-productive, promoting massive social breakdown instead of the social harmony they were designed for. We did not look before we leapt into the fire of the environment produced by blocks of flats. We now need to look, carefully and scientifically, in order to distinguish what is really good or bad in housing design, and this new approach incorporates several important components.

(a)   We need to study a complete range of housing from good to bad, in order to see what kind of design characteristics fade in or fade out as the type of housing worsens.

(b)   We need a measure of goodness or badness that is independent of design, in order to test whether any design features change in harmony with it.

(c)   We need several such measures to test design independently. If they agree with each other they afford stronger evidence than one alone.

(d)   We need to study a large number of buildings in order to avoid accidental results. This is necessary because design does not determine social behaviour. Not everyone who goes to live in a block of flats suddenly becomes a criminal, but the weaker minded may be tempted by the criminal opportunities that the block offers. Some blocks may house weak-minded people while others may not, so we need to study a large number in order to compare the averages for different types of design.

(e)   We need to study all the blocks in an area rather than selecting a sample. This avoids any suspicion that we may, by chance, have picked blocks that happen to agree with the research hypothesis that design can affect the level of social breakdown.

(f)   We need to classify each design into a clear set of values. This is easy for numerical values such as the number of storeys in the block. It is less easy, but nonetheless possible, for non-numerical values. For example, entrance position is classified as 'flush with the street', or 'facing the street but set back', or 'facing into the grounds'.

(g)   Finally, we need impartial methods of analysis that can show whether the research hypothesis is wrong just as clearly as it can show whether it is right.

In accordance with these seven scientific principles, the Land Use Research Unit investigated many design variables and selected 15 to survey in a total of 4,099 blocks of flats in two London boroughs — Southwark and Tower Hamlets — and an out-of-town estate in Oxford. A sixteenth, surveyed in 264 blocks only, has subsequently been added. These 16 variables fall into four groups of four: size variables, circulation variables, entrance variables and characteristics of the grounds and are listed in full in Table 7.1 (Coleman *et al.*, 1985).

Four test measures were chosen as visible evidence of anti-social behaviour readily observable by the survey team, and recorded for all 4,099 blocks as follows.

(a)   Litter inside the entrances or within 3 metres outside them, was noted as either 'none', or 'clean and casual' or 'dirty and decayed'.

(b)   Excrement was noted as either 'present' or 'absent' in the same locations.

(c)   Graffiti were surveyed as 'none', or 'either inside or outside the block', or 'both inside and outside'.

(d)   Vandal damage was recorded as the number of types of target per block. We now check ten target types: fences, sheds, windows, doors, stairs, lifts, refuse facilities, electrical fittings, garages, and building fabric.

Eleven other test measures were added for smaller areas. Figures for numbers of children in care were made available for 1,955 blocks in Southwark, and the Neighbourhood Policing Project Team compiled statistics for nine types of residential crime located in 729 blocks of Southwark's Caster Street Division (Coleman and Brown, 1985). Urine pollution was surveyed in addition to faeces in 1,782 blocks in Tower Hamlets. Altogether there were 15 test measures, which gave considerable scope for

Table 7.1: Harmful design variables and their thresholds

Size variables	Threshold value
Dwellings per block	12
Dwellings per entrance	6
Storeys per block	3
Storeys per dwelling	1
Circulation variables	
Overhead walkways	0
Interconnecting exits[a]	1
Interconnecting lifts and stairs[a]	1
Dwellings per corridor	4
Entrance variables	
Entrance position	Facing the street
Entrance type	Communal only, or individual ground-floor doors fronted by separate front gardens
Doors or open apertures[b]	Doors
Stilts or garages	0
Features of the grounds	
Blocks per site	1
Gates or gaps	1
Play areas	0
Spatial organisation	Semi-public

Notes:

a. Exits and stairs should not interconnect, but fire regulations may require two of each.

b. This is an additional variable tested by C. C. R. Redknap in 624 entrances. For a full explanation of all variables and thresholds, see Coleman *et al.*, 1985.

reinforcing or contradicting our hypothesis of the link between design and social behaviour.

STATISTICAL ANALYSIS

Two methods of analysis have been used: correlation and the drawing of trend lines. Because many of the design variables and test measures are ordinal data, it was not possible to use such parametric methods as Pearson's product-moment correlation or regression. Instead, non-parametric methods were substituted:

Kendall's tau C correlation and trend lines based on percentages for successive values.

The 15 main design variables were correlated with the 15 test measures to yield 225 coefficients. If there is no relationship between the two, we should expect roughly equal numbers of positive and negative results but Table 7.2 shows that the overwhelming majority are positive. We should also expect, purely by chance, about 11 or 12 significant results, of which two or three might be highly significant, but again Table 7.2 shows a

Table 7.2: Comparison of observed and expected coefficients

Type of coefficient	Expected by chance	Observed
Positive	114 or 115	214
Negative	114 or 115	9
Not significant	213 or 214	27
Significant	11 or 12	198
Highly significant	2 or 3	189
Very highly significant	–	170

Figures are the number of coefficients out of the overall total of 225.

Figure 7.1: Slope versus scatter. Line (a) shows a perfect correlation but a weak trend; line (b) shows a weaker correlation, but a more powerful slope to its trend line. The latter is more typical of the results on design disadvantagement

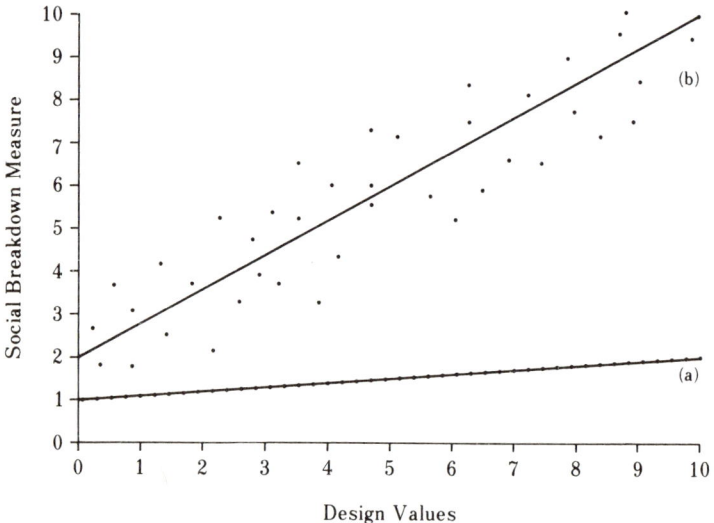

very different picture. The vast majority of associations are significant and 76 per cent are very highly significant. These figures leave no doubt that there is a genuine association between design and social breakdown.

Correlation is not the most informative method of analysis, as it merely measures *consistency* in the variation of two data sets being compared (Figure 7.1). Line (a) shows a case where the strongest possible correlation nevertheless has a low slope, suggesting very little real significance in the relationship as the best designs have almost the same level of social breakdown as the worst. Line (b) shows a much weaker correlation with a wide scatter of points showing that other factors are disturbing the relationship, but in spite of these because the slope of the relationship is steeper the change in design makes a much greater difference to the level of social breakdown. It is this difference that is revealed by trend lines.

Figure 7.2 is a set of trend lines for corridor type. Four classes

Figure 7.2: Anti-social behaviour and corridor design. Six of the 15 test measures (burglary, theft, two types of car crime, criminal damage and juvenile arrest) are not shown separately, but are included in the composite trend for 'crime'.

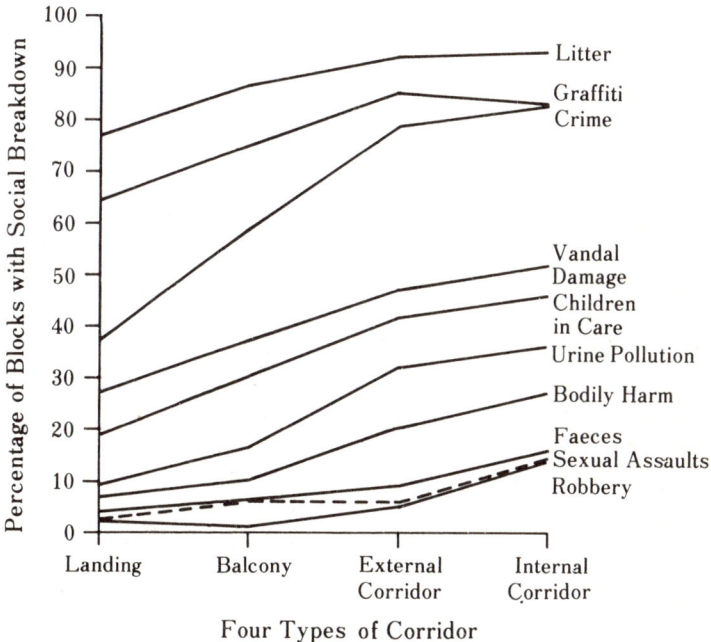

of corridor are marked along the bottom, and the vertical axis is divided into percentages. The various trend lines represent the different test measures and show their percentage frequency in all the blocks with each type of corridor. There is a clear rise in the incidence of each kind of social problem as the design changes from landings to balconies to external corridors and finally internal corridors.

It so happens that the average number of dwellings per block increases in the same direction, so we have to ask whether the rise in the trend lines is merely keeping pace with the increased number of people. This can be checked by comparing the number of crimes per 100 dwellings. Blocks with landings average 10 per hundred per annum, which is bad enough, but those with internal corridors average 17, an increase of over two-thirds. This suggests that it might be possible to reduce crime quite substantially by partitioning long blocks into shorter self-contained sections with landings or balconies instead of long corridors. Oscar Newman, who first discovered the relationships between crime and design (Newman, 1972), showed that design changes can indeed reduce crime rates, but he did not try the effect of shorter corridors because he found only two types, internal and external, which cannot be converted from one to the other.

Corridor-type trend lines show clear differences because there are only four categories, each with a large number of blocks. Some of the design variables are more finely divided, with numerous categories, some of which contain too few blocks to give a representative percentage. In these cases the trend lines are slightly smoothed by plotting running means of three consecutive values. This is not nearly such a gross smoothing as that involved in regression lines, but it seems to be enough. Figure 7.3 shows smoothed trend lines for dwellings per block and dwellings per entrance. The latter shows the effect of partitioning the block into self-contained sections with fewer people per entrance and also, incidentally, fewer people per corridor. This means that the residents in each section can more easily recognise and get to know each other, with the result that social structure improves and anti-social behaviour is reduced. Both sets of trend lines represent the same blocks, but they begin with lower percentages of children in care, vandalism, etc., when classified by internal divisions.

The fluctuations that remain after smoothing seem to reflect

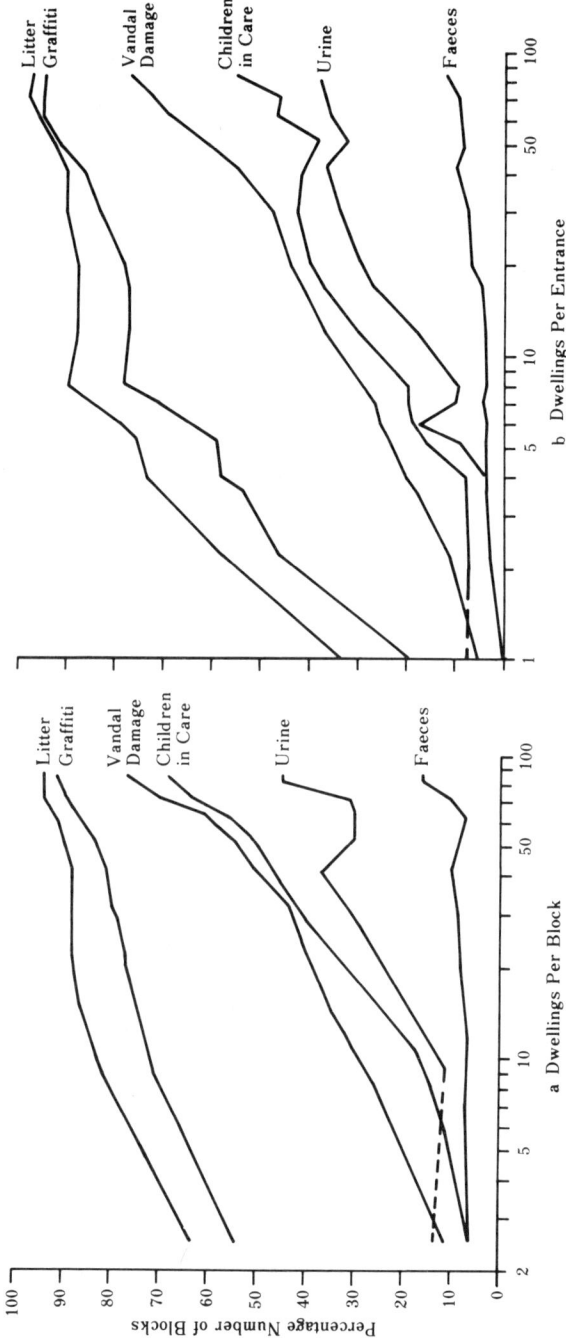

Figure 7.3: Abuse and dwellings density. Trend lines are shown slightly smoothed. (a) Dwellings per block; (b) dwellings per entrance. The effect of more restricted entrances outweighs that of larger blocks to reduce the abuse percentages in the better designs

149

disturbing factors other than the design variable being graphed. This is illustrated by the trend lines for building height (Figure 7.4). Number of storeys is not the worst design variable, but it commands the most public attention because tall towers and slabs are so conspicuous and, as a result, concerted efforts have been made to reduce the number of children living in them. This produces two features in the graph.

First, there is a marked drop in the number of children in care and juvenile arrests in blocks of 12 storeys or more, due to the efforts of social workers to remove problem families. However, while the number of problem families decreases, other kinds of anti-social behaviour go on increasing with building height, suggesting that tall blocks have harmful effects upon ordinary families as well.

Second, most of the trend lines show either a dip or a flattening at five or six storeys. This seems to reflect the fact that families with children are still regarded as not at risk in walk-up blocks without lifts and in the lowest four or five floors in high rise. Their absence or rarity above this level is related to a partial reduction

Figure 7.4: Social breakdown and height of block. Trend lines are shown slightly smoothed. The crime curves mostly show a break of slope at the threshold level of three storeys and thereafter rise more steeply than the six measures of abuse

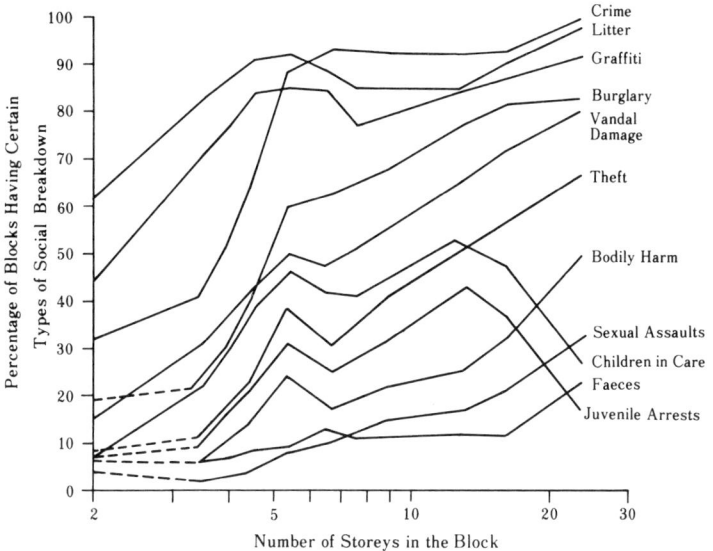

in anti-social behaviour, but even without them the trend lines go on rising. A surer remedy is to take the tops off tall blocks. 'Top-downing', as it is called, has proved highly successful in Liverpool and a few other places where there is a surplus of flats, but elsewhere it is not an easy option because it would exacerbate the housing shortage. Fortunately, many other deleterious variables can be modified without producing this side-effect.

IMPROVING THE PROBLEMS OF DESIGN

What are the best practical ways of improving estates? At present the Department of the Environment finances housing improvement in ways that ignore the social consequences of design and, as a result, public money is being wasted on ineffective schemes. The Land Use Research Unit monitored the first 17 blocks that were supposedly improved in our study area, and found that vandal damage *increased* over two and half times as compared with before the expenditure.

The DoE's Priority Estates Projects (PEP) are based largely on the assumption that bad management is the cause of residential problems (Power, 1982; 1984). Improvement schemes, reported on in PEP's Peptalk series of leaflets, include an estate where rosy claims were made in March 1985 for a highly successful reform of community structure (Zipfel, 1985). Unfortunately, the reformed structure has proved very fragile and in September 1985 the estate rocketed to fame as the scene of the most vicious of modern riots: Broadwater Farm. Management improvement is not enough, and design improvement is increasingly seen as a more constructive alternative.

Design improvement has the advantage of a scientific basis, which permits the specification of precise improvement targets. *Disadvantagement thresholds* pinpoint targets for each design variable and *disadvantagement scores* identify the combination of targets needing to be tackled in any given block.

The threshold is calculated as the worst value of each design variable that still has better-than-chance frequencies of the various forms of abuse. The aim of improvement is to bring each design down to or below its threshold (Table 7.1). Thresholds must be based on a very large number of observations and, once calculated, can be taken as standard.

151

The disadvantagement score, by contrast, is a way of assessing each individual block. A list is made of all the design variables that breach their respective thresholds, and this is used to draw attention to the kinds of remedial action needed. The score is the total number of defective designs, and can range from 0 to 16. The average score for the 4,099 blocks in the study area is a very high 8.1, and it is of interest that council blocks average 9.1 while private blocks have a much better mean of 4.0.

A design improvement scheme aims to reduce the disadvantagement score by as much as possible. In the first five estates we were commissioned to survey, we made recommendations for 71 blocks involving score reductions of the order of six to eight points, and in each case the capital cost proved to be less per dwelling than the standard type of ineffective scheme favoured hitherto. Apart from capital cost, there should also be substantial future savings on repairs and staffing levels, as destructive behaviour declines. These are hopes which need to be taken one scientific stage further. Does design improvement work as well in practice as the evidence predicts? We need properly monitored pilot schemes, and these are beginning to materialise.

Oscar Newman, in the USA, demonstrated that the modification of one or two design variables could bring about a noticeable drop in local crime frequencies. Westminster City Housing Department has successfully removed some overhead walkways, created individual front gardens on wide external corridors, and divided blocks into smaller self-contained sections. In each case there has been an increased sense of privacy and security, demonstrated by the fact that people feel it is safe to leave flower tubs and garden furniture out on their new patios. In Southwark the fencing of individual blocks has greatly reduced litter, vandalism and the sense of fear which formerly resulted in some ground-floor residents boarding up their windows and living in artificial light. A Wandsworth resident reports how the provision of separate front gardens with fences and gates has transformed anonymous hordes of children into polite individuals with a much greater respect for private property.

In all these cases only one or two deleterious designs have been tackled in the same block and, although the results are appreciable, they are not enough; problems still remain. If a simultaneous attempt were made to reduce a block's disadvantagement score by as many points as possible, it might engender really spectacular improvements, and restore true social stability.

Some of our recommendations will shortly be implemented and we shall be in a position to test whether the anticipated social benefits really do accrue. Meanwhile, Liverpool City Council is implementing design improvement schemes which have a great deal in common with our recommendations, and has commissioned us to carry out before-and-after studies of litter, graffiti, vandal damage and excrement in estates where projects were started in June 1985. The theory will be put to the practical test, and the proof of the pudding will be in the quality.

REFERENCES

Coleman, A., Brown, S., Cottle, L., Marshall, P., Redknap, C. and Sex, R. (1985) *Utopia on trial*, Hilary Shipman, London
Coleman, A. and Brown, S. (1985) *Crime and design disadvantagement in blocks of flats*, Report to A2(3) Branch, Metropolitan Police
Le Corbusier (C. E. Jeaneret) (1923) *Vers une architecture*, translated into English by F. Etchells (1974), Architectural Press, London
Liverpool City Council (1985) *Urban regeneration strategy: the total approach*. A set of leaflets on 17 priority housing estates
Newman, O. (1972) *Defensible space*, Macmillan, New York
Power, A. (1982) *Priority Estates Project*, Department of the Environment, London
——— (1984) *Local housing management: a Priority Estates Project*, Department of the Environment, London
Redknap, C. (1983) 'The effect of entrance designs in blocks of flats', unpublished Report to the Nuffield Foundation, Land Use Research Unit, King's College, London
Zipfel, T. (1985) 'Hard Work Transforms a Nightmare Estate', *Peptalk*, March, Department of the Environment, London

8

Land Prices and Land Availability in Inner City Redevelopment

C. D. Adams, A. E. Baum and B. D. MacGregor

The publication, in 1977, of the Inner Area Studies, which revealed that there were extensive areas of vacant urban land in both Liverpool and Birmingham, drew the attention of politicians and the wider public to the scale of land vacancy in British towns and cities. National policies have since placed great emphasis on the re-use of vacant urban land in preference to further development on the urban periphery. A number of subsequent studies, notably by Burrows (1977), Nabarro and Richards (1980), and the Birmingham Inner City Partnership (1982), have helped to assess and classify the extent of land vacancy in most of the conurbations. A common weakness in these studies, however, has been their purely static approach. Most provide no more than an accounting framework for the overall stock of vacant land, within which more detailed information is given on size, distribution and ownership of vacant sites. Few attempt to provide an explanation of the underlying causes of land vacancy or an assessment of the role of vacant land within the development process.

An explanatory model of the development process was produced by Barrett *et al.* in 1978. The model provided a clear description of the sequence of the development process, but did not attempt to explain the inherent causal relationships. A period of vacancy from cessation of previous use to the commencement of development pressure and prospects was not identified as a specifically preparatory stage to the development process. More recent work by Bruton and Gore (1980) and Gore and Nicholson (1983) on publicly-owned vacant land has stressed the transitory nature of land vacancy and placed the period of vacancy firmly within an expanded model of the development process. In this approach, land vacancy can be attributed to specific development constraints, and policies which aim to reduce vacancy will need to eliminate the blockages which result in the development process.

High land prices can be constraints on redevelopment. Some commentators have pointed to the failure of land prices in the inner cities to respond to the apparent excessive supply of land for development. This was mentioned in the Liverpool Inner Area Study (DoE, 1977) and was taken up by Edwards (1977) and Colenutt (1978). Reports were published by the RICS (1977) and the RTPI (1978), but these depended on mainly sketchy or anecdotal evidence.

The role of the public sector as the dominant owner of vacant urban land has been identified by virtually all studies. Several commentators, seeking to explain the resistance of land prices in the inner cities to falling, have pointed to the statutory rules under which public authorities sold and particularly bought land (e.g., Nabarro and Smart, 1978). It was alleged that, under the 'compensation code', public authorities were required to pay an artificially high price for land and that this subsequently set the floor to the market. No detailed empirical work was carried out in support of this hypothesis, although the RTPI report outlined a limited number of cases, often in highly selective locations (RTP1, 1978). More generally the role of the public sector as an important buyer and seller of inner area land can have a similar effect of setting a floor to the market through its influence on private sector valuations and consequent asking prices.

This chapter reports the results of research carried out in Manchester and considers whether established valuation practices operate to prevent inner city land prices from falling, even in areas of apparent oversupply, thereby creating a specific blockage within the development process which delays the re-use of vacant inner city land. In particular the effects of public sector land acquisition are assessed.

THE INNER MANCHESTER RESEARCH

The City of Manchester exhibits many of the classic symptoms of inner city decay. Between 1961 and 1981, manufacturing employment in Manchester fell by 57 per cent, representing a net decline of 91,000 jobs. No noticeable growth was recorded in the service sector to compensate for the steady and seemingly irreversible decline in manufacturing. Average unemployment in Manchester (male and female) now stands at 23 per cent. In the traditional manufacturing area of East Manchester, which specialised in heavy engineering and textiles, the recession has been particularly severe. One quarter of the industrial land in East Manchester, a total of 185 acres (75 hectares), is now lying idle or derelict.

During the past 20 years, a substantial decline has also been recorded in the population of Manchester, from 662,000 in 1961 to 449,000 in 1981. The greatest population loss has occurred in the inner city wards. A massive slum clearance programme removed 83,000 unfit dwellings between 1951 and 1981, most of which were in the Inner Area. Within the city boundaries, 59,000 new local authority houses were provided. Few new private houses were built in the inner city until the early 1980s.

In 1978, when the Inner City Partnership was established, vacant land within Inner Manchester totalled approximately 1,718 acres (695 hectares). By 1984, this figure had been reduced to 1,308 acres (529 hectares), mainly as a result of environmental improvements undertaken by the Partnership. Almost 68 per cent of land vacant in 1984 was in public ownership and a further 12 per cent in mixed public and private ownership. Over half of the land now vacant in Inner Manchester is concentrated in six wards. For these wards, which are situated to the north, east and south-east of the City Centre,[1] detailed information was collected, as part of the research, on every site above half an acre (0.2 hectares) which had been vacant in 1978 or had become vacant in the period 1978–83, irrespective of whether the site has now been brought into use. Evidence was collected, wherever possible, on size, ownership, previous use, duration of vacancy, constraints, planning history and proposed new use. The evidence revealed that, at some time between 1978 and 1983, 384 sites of over half an acre (0.2 hectares) had been vacant. Roughly one-third, or 135 sites covering 388 acres (157 hectares), had been developed or brought into use by the end of 1983, while the remaining 249 sites covering 727 acres (294 hectares) remained vacant.

This initial stage enabled a structured sample to be undertaken of 25 sites which had been developed and 25 sites which remained vacant. Full information was collected on all aspects of ownership and transactions, including owners' intentions, professional valuations, prices asked and paid, market availability and planning status. This made possible a comparative analysis of sites which had passed through the development process and those which appeared to be blocked within the development process.

RECENT TRANSACTIONS IN VACANT LAND

Table 8.1 shows the present ownership (as at February 1984) of the 50 case study sites. The present ownership of developed sites reflects their acquisition by 'development agents' during the study period. As expected, the public sector is the dominant owner of vacant sites. This is not due solely to historic ownership.[2] Three of the vacant sites owned by the City Council and the one owned by the County Council have all been acquired since 1981. In each case, the Local Authority has specifically acquired derelict land or premises for reclamation purposes and with the intended aim of subsequent disposal to the private sector. In this way, local authorities play a major role in recycling land in the inner city.

All developed sites and nine of the vacant sites changed ownership during the study period. In some cases, where for instance a site had been acquired in parcels, more than one transaction per site is recorded. Altogether 46 transactions are recorded, of which 35 are in sites now developed and 11 in sites still vacant. Although the number of transactions recorded in the case studies is low, related evidence[3] suggests that the case studies cover approximately half of all transactions in vacant land in the six wards during the period 1978–83. The evidence shows

Table 8.1: Present ownership of case study sites

Owner	Sites now developed	Sites still vacant
City Council	–	16
County Council	–	1
British Rail	–	1
Other public	1	–
Housing associations	8	–
Companies (excluding residential developers)	13	7
Residential developers	3	–
TOTAL	25	25

Table 8.2: Transactions in case study sites by vendor and purchaser

Vendor	Sites still vacant				Sites now developed						Total
	City Council	County Council	Company[a]	Total	Other Public	Housing Associations	Company[a]	Company[b]	Company[c]	Total	
Public Sector											
City Council	–	–	–	–	1	4	11	3	2	21	21
County Council	–	–	–	–	–	–	–	–	–	–	–
British Rail	–	–	1	1	–	–	–	–	–	–	1
Gas/Electricity Boards	1	–	–	1	–	–	–	–	–	–	1
Other Public	–	1	–	1	–	–	–	–	–	–	1
Housing Associations	–	–	–	–	–	–	–	–	–	–	–
Private sector											
Company	5	–	–	5	–	–	1	4	2	7	12
Charity/Trust	–	–	–	–	–	4	–	1	–	5	5
Private individual[d]	3	–	–	3	–	2	–	–	–	2	5
Total	9	1	1	11	1	10	12	8	4	35	46

Notes:
a. Company purchasing to construct unit for owner-occupation.
b. Development company purchasing to construct standard industrial/warehouse units.
c. Development company purchasing to construct new dwellings.
d. Includes three slum clearance sites acquired by City Council under Compulsory Purchase Order.

Table 8.3: Frequency distribution of recorded transactions in development land by sub-sector, 1978–80 and 1981–83

Price/Premium per acre	Land for industrial and warehousing		Land for commercial purposes		Land for housing association		Land for private residential development	
	1978–80	1981–83	1978–80	1981–83	1978–80	1981–83	1978–80	1981–83
£20,000 or under	1	1				1		
£20,001–£30,000	4	4			1	4		
£30,001–£40,000		2				3		
£40,001–£50,000	1	1	1		1			1
£50,001–£60,000	1	1						2
£60,001–£70,000		2		2				
£70,001–£80,000		1	2					1
£80,001–£90,000				2				
£90,001–£100,000								
Over £100,000	2		1					
Total	9	12	4	4	2	8	–	4

that the number of transactions in the inner city land market each year is small, that the role of the public sector, particularly in the supply of land, is substantial and that mean prices can easily be distorted by abnormal transactions.

Table 8.2 shows the distribution of transactions between vendors and purchasers. It can be seen that the City Council is the most important vendor of sites for development, while companies are the dominant vendor of sites still vacant. This reflects the activity of local authorities in buying up redundant industrial land and premises for reclamation, referred to previously. Among the purchasers of development sites, companies acquiring for owner-occupation took the greater share, closely followed by housing associations and developers of speculative industrial or warehousing units. Private residential developers take fewer sites than housing associations, although it is small sites in which the latter are more active.

The frequency distribution of the prices, premiums and capitalised ground rents[4] achieved in 43 out of the 46 transactions is shown in Table 8.3. The three sites acquired by the City Council under slum clearance procedures are excluded since compensation cannot strictly be assessed on a 'per acre' basis. The table is subdivided into two development periods and four development sub-sectors. The two development periods are 1978–80, when the market[5] showed some signs of growth, and 1981–3, a period of stagnation and even of decline.[6] The four development sub-sectors are:

(i) *Sub-sector for land for industrial and warehousing purposes*. These sites lie mainly to the east and the south-east of the City Centre. In the period 1978–80, development companies purchasing land for the construction of speculative industrial units were the dominant class of purchaser. In the period 1981–3, the City Council, purchasing decaying industrial premises for reclamation, took a major role among purchasers.

(ii) *Sub-sector for land for commercial purposes*. This sub-sector is concentrated to the north and north-east of the City Centre, in the traditional wholesaling area, and is now dominated by 'cash and carry' developments and discount retail warehouses. The sub-sector can be regarded as 'spillover' from the City Centre. Land for car showrooms can also be included in this sub-sector.

(iii) *Sub-sector for land for Housing Association purposes*.

160

Generally, Housing Association activity is concentrated on the smaller residential sites, some of which are located in areas where the demand for private residential units is low.

(iv) *Sub-sector for land for private residential development.* The City Council's 'Build for Sale' programme,[7] under which sites owned by the City Council have been released for private development, led the way for private residential developers to enter the inner city. Subsequently land has also come on the market from private sources. The case studies include sites bought from both types of vendor.

Table 8.4 shows the price ranges recorded[8] and the mean and median values for each sub-sector. It is surprising to find that the prices paid in the small number of transactions recorded is so wide. Nevertheless, each inner city site is likely to have its own individual site difficulties or site advantages. The wide range of prices is felt to be explained more by variations in site characteristics than by volatile price fluctuations. Under these circumstances the median is probably a better measure of the 'average' than the mean but, without further evidence, only limited conclusions can be drawn. It was therefore decided to

Table 8.4: Range of recorded transactions in development land by sub-sector, 1978–80 and 1981–83

	£ per acre	
	1978–80	1981–83
Land for industrial development		
Number of transactions recorded	9	12
Mean	52,250	41,000
Median	37,750	38,750
Range	12,500–106,750	9,500–73,000
Land for commercial development		
Number of transactions recorded	4	4
Mean	89,000	76,750
Median	77,500	77,250
Range	54,500–146,500	63,000–89,500
Land for Housing Association development		
Number of transactions recorded	2	8
Mean	34,500	27,500
Median	34,500	30,000
Range	20,000–49,000	11,250–37,250
Land for private residential development		
Number of transactions recorded	0	4
Mean		57,250
Median		54,000
Range		50,000–71,500

interview a number of senior valuers in both the public and private sectors in order to discover their view of current (February 1984) land prices in the study area.

As a result, it is possible to compare the recorded data with the experience of practicing valuers for two out of the four sub-sectors. An assessment of the price range and the mean and median values in each sub-sector is now made.

Industrial and warehousing sub-sector

A greater number of transactions is recorded in the later period, mainly reflecting local authority activity in buying up redundant industrial land and premises for reclamation. Although the mean price of industrial land shows a noticeable fall between the two periods, public sector intervention appears to have helped stabilise the median at around £38,000 per acre. Nevertheless, this is towards the upper end of the range of £25,000 to £40,000 per acre for industrial land within which most of the valuers interviewed appeared to work.

Commercial sub-sector

Apart from the substantially higher prices clearly paid for commercial land, the small number of transactions makes it difficult to draw any firm conclusions on price movement. A figure of around £77,000 per acre for commercial land in inner Manchester is indicated by the closeness of the mean and median in the later period.

Housing Association sub-sector

Traditionally, Housing Associations have paid lower prices for sites than private developers. This may be due to the absence of competing demand in certain locations or it may result from the influential role of the District Valuer in determining prices paid by Housing Associations. In the later period, greater activity was recorded, but both the mean and the median fell. A number of transactions in this period were connected with the diversification of Housing Association activity into shared ownership and similar schemes. This brought Housing Associations into competition with private residential developers for the medium-sized and more attractive sites, and in these cases higher than average prices were generally paid.

Private residential sub-sector

No transactions were recorded within the earlier period and only four within the later period. Both the mean and the median are above the range of £40,000 to £50,000 per acre for residential land within which the interviewed valuers appeared to work. This may be because of the small number of sites which could have been 'prime' and thus atypical. It could also be that valuers are slow to adjust to upward trends in the market. A further explanation is the 'novelty' of the 'Build for Sale' programme and the competition among volume builders entering the inner area for the first time. The evidence does however confirm that, in the later period, land for residential development in inner Manchester commanded a higher price than land for industrial development. This was probably due to an increase in residential land prices caused by greater interest in inner city development among the volume housebuilders.

In general the comparison between mean and median figures and the 'normal' range of prices used by valuers suggests caution in interpretation of the results. Explanations can be offered for these differences, but it is also possible that a small number of sites produces abnormal results. Such a problem is unsurmountable in a study of this nature.

MARKET AVAILABILITY OF VACANT LAND

An attempt was then made to assess whether the 25 vacant sites, all of which from a planning point of view were considered potentially available for development, were in fact on the market. The results, in Table 8.5, show that 32 per cent of the case study sites were, for one reason or another, held off the market, a further 48 per cent were available for sale or under offer, and the remaining 20 per cent had all been sold in 1983.

The known asking price for sites on the market or under offer, for industrial or residential development, are shown in Table 8.6.

Table 8.5: Market status of 25 vacant sites

Status	Present owner City Council	County Council	British Rail	Private	Total
1. Sites sold in 1983					
(a) for reclamation	3	1	–	–	
(b) for other use	–	–	–	1	
					5
2. Sites under offer	2	–	–	–	
					2
3. Sites on the market					
(a) known asking price	5	–	–	4	
(b) offers invited	–	–	1	–	
					10
4. Sites off the market					
(a) awaiting clarification of permissible uses/developable area	2	–	–	1	
(b) awaiting release under Build for Sale programme	1	–	–	–	
(c) awaiting physical infrastructural work	2	–	–	–	
(d) in temporary use	1	–	–	1	
					8
Total	16	1	1	7	25

Ground rents sought are capitalised on the bases set out in Note d. One site, where industrial land and buildings were offered together at £425,000, was excluded from the analysis. The median prices achieved during the period 1981–3 are also included in Table 8.6. All the asking prices shown were determined from the advice of professional valuers.

Asking prices for residential land were all below the median of sale prices for private residential land, though all but one of the four was within the range given by valuers. However, all were above the median for Housing Association development. It may be that the comparison with private residential land reflects the poorer quality of sites now available, although discussions with valuers suggested that previous prices paid were considered to have been too high due to the novelty of the 'Build for Sale' programme. The unusual circumstances of these sales and other factors influencing Housing Association purchases make it

Table 8.6: Known asking prices for vacant case study sites on the market or under offer

Land for industrial development		
Case study	Asking price	
Number	£ per acre	Valuer
39	£30,000–35,000	Local private valuer
Median	**38,750**	
31	48,750	CEVO[a]
29	54,000	CEVO
33[b]	60,000	CEVO
30	70,250	CEVO
Land for residential development		
Case study	Asking price	
Number	£ per acre	Valuer
Median, housing association development	**30,000**	
50[c]	36,000	Non-local private valuer
49[d]	40,000	Local private valuer
43[c]	46,250	CEVO
47[c]	50,000	CEVO
Median, private development[e]	**54,000**	

Notes:

a. City Estates and Valuation Officer.

b. Site 33 may be offered for industrial or commercial development, depending on the planning permission which can be obtained.

c. Sites 50, 43 and 47 are of a size and location suitable for private residential development.

d. Site 43 is under offer to a housing association and is probably too small for private residential development.

e. See text for an explanation of why the median for housing association development is lower than the median for private residential development.

difficult to draw conclusions on asking prices in this sector.

Four out of the five asking prices in the industrial sector are above the previously quoted range of £25,000 to £40,000, and indeed also above the observed median for sites which have sold in the period 1981–3. In some cases the difference is substantial. Each of these sites is being offered for sale by the City Council. Whether the sites have particularly attractive characteristics or whether the asking prices are inflated is difficult to determine.

Asking prices may, of course, be regarded as the vendor's initial bargaining position and substantial downward revisions may be necessary before a price is finally agreed. Nevertheless, the high prices which are asked, at least initially, suggest that, in

165

certain cases, vendors may be slow to accept evidence of low demand for and excess supply of inner city land and may therefore be reluctant to revise prices downwards. The final section of the chapter considers, in detail, four aspects of this in the light of evidence collected in the case studies.

FOUR HYPOTHESES

We can consider four hypotheses to explain the apparent rigidity of inner city land prices.

Hypothesis I. That conventional valuation practices maintain high land prices

The most commonly used methods to value vacant inner city land are the comparative and the residual methods. The comparative method (direct capital comparison) is predicated on the assumption that the sale prices of similar properties to the subject can be used as the basis of an estimate of the market value of that subject. Adjustments may be made for differences in location, the transaction date, structural quality, lease terms, age, quality of covenant (occupier or leaseholder), size, shape and facilities, but the accuracy of such a valuation — which is extremely difficult to gauge, and therefore to question — depends upon choosing properties which are as similar as possible. Physical differences are usually dealt with quite easily by relating value to the cost of changing the subject to match its paired equivalent. Differences in location and the transaction date do, however, lead to considerable adjustment problems. Value is peculiarly sensitive to changes in location; and values change over time. Consequently, a paucity of transactions in a particular location will tempt the valuer to use comparable evidence which is either outdated or from non-comparable locations.

When valuing vacant land, however, a more reliable method should in principle be the residual method, which is based on a sound rationale. The value of land is the value of the most likely development to be completed upon that land less the costs of construction and service provision, and less the developer's profit.

The developers who were interviewed all considered the value of land to be a residual and approached it as the final stage of a development appraisal. Generally, this produced a low value for inner city land. Developers would only use a comparative to check whether it was worth bidding for land. By contrast, all the valuers interviewed admitted a reliance on the comparative method, even where it produced a value unsupportable by the residual method. Since the comparative method depends on comparison with sales which have taken place previously, it generally produces a higher value in a declining market than the residual method. For instance, a price of £40,000 per acre is being asked for site 49. This is based on a similar figure achieved in 1981 for the nearby site 25, although evidence from property market reports and from local valuers pointed to a distinct drop in activity in the intervening period.

Since developers, as bidders for inner city land, assess value as present-day potential, and sellers, advised by professional valuers, base value on prices paid previously, the discrepancy between a residual valuation and a comparative valuation can be quite marked. For instance, in the case of site 38, now owned by the City Council, a comparative valuation by the City Estates and Valuation Officer produced a figure of £40,000 per acre, while a residual valuation by a prospective developer produced a figure of £20,000 per acre. It may be that prices paid in the past when times were better generates the hope or, indeed, the expectation among vendors that at least the same level of prices can be achieved in the future. In cases where the variation is not so great the valuer may be tempted to 'construct' a residual valuation in support of his original comparative.

There are two reasons why the comparative method may overvalue land in the inner city. First, since relatively few trans-actions take place in inner city land in any one year, fully comparable and recent evidence for valuation purposes may be hard to find. For instance, in six valuations of Housing Association case study sites made on behalf of the vendor, it was found that in four sites only one 'comparable' was available and, in the other two, three comparables were used. In some cases, compar-ables were drawn a distance of three or four miles from the subject site, occasionally from the outer suburbs. The profes-sional valuer is left with a daunting task of adjusting the compar-ables for distance, location and size, irrespective of any change in market conditions.

Second, this may be compounded if information on the few

167

transactions which do take place is not fully exchanged. Certain valuers in the private sector, for instance, allege that the City Estates and Valuation Officer is 'out of touch'. The four industrial sites on offer above the median achieved in the period 1981–3 are all owned and being marketed by the City Council. The asking prices range from 25 per cent to over 80 per cent above the median. Whether or not the City Estates and Valuation Officer or indeed any other valuer is out of touch, the valuer with the best access to information is able to pick and choose among comparables to establish the most advantageous bargaining position for his client. Where valuers act for the vendor, as most do, this involves searching through the records to find the highest possible comparable. Of course, the initial asking price may be substantially reduced during negotiations and what Nabarro and Smart (1978) call 'an amicable bargain' struck, but the whole process is one which tends to support previous levels of value, even in a declining economy. The auction is not an accepted means of sale, although it has recently been used by the British Rail Property Board. So far, auction sales within inner Manchester have been too few to draw any firm conclusion.

The concern of the Royal Institute of Chartered Surveyors (1977) that the comparative method could be open to criticism 'if, in a falling market, insufficient regard was paid to trends in values indicated by the evidence and if too much regard was paid to levels of values pertaining in the past when better times prevailed', is supported by the empirical work in Manchester. The comparative method of valuation appears unable to cope with few transactions or with a declining economy, both of which are evident in Manchester. Instead, the comparative method is felt to underpin existing values, even when no longer justified by the level of demand. The first hypothesis appears, therefore, to be supported by the empirical evidence on which we have been able to draw.

Hypothesis II. That the prices paid by public authorities on acquisition in the open market raise vendor's expectations and set a floor below which open market prices will not fall

This hypothesis requires evidence on three counts: first, that a significant[9] number of transactions in the open market consist of acquisitions by public bodies by agreement; second, that the public bodies pay higher figures in general than would be paid by a private buyer, or are believed to do so; and third, that this encourages vendors to hold out for a public sector acquisition or alternatively for a private purchaser willing to match the public sector prices.

Four of the case study sites (sites 35, 37, 38 and 48), all within the East Manchester wards of Beswick and Clayton, Bradford and Miles Platting, were acquired by the Local Authority by agreement between 1981 and 1983. All were large sites and the total area acquired was slightly over 46 acres (18.5 hectares). From more general information obtained on all transactions in the study area during the period, it would appear that these four large sites may account for over half of all development land sold in the three East Manchester wards between 1981 and 1983. It is clear that public sector activity has been significant and that the first requirement of the hypothesis is satisfied.

Clearly the dominant role of the local authorities as purchasers of development land in East Manchester during the period 1981–3 would be likely to be the main influence upon any measure of average prices. It is therefore considered that the period of marketing and the presence or absence of alternative bidders could provide the basis for a more objective evaluation of the impact of local authority acquisition. This is shown in Table 8.7. It is evident that two of the large sites (sites 38 and 48), which had been on the market for over a year without alternative bidders, were bought by the City Council at prices ranging from £24,000

Table 8.7: Marketing periods and alternative bidders for case studies 35, 37, 38 and 48

Site no.	Purchaser	Price £ per acre	Marketing period	Alternative bidders
35	County Council	70,000 ⎫	5 months	One (property devel-
35	County Council	50,000 ⎭		opment co.)
35	County Council	40,000		
37	City Council	30,000	2 months	Tenders invited — 30 received
38	City Council	55,000	12 months	None
38	City Council	37,500	12 months	None
38	City Council	27,000	12 months	None
38	City Council	25,000	12 months	None
48	City Council	24,000	3 years	None

per acre to £33,000 per acre. (The part of site 38 acquired for £55,000 per acre included three existing industrial buildings, two of which were outdated and in poor condition. It was later decided to demolish all the buildings on the site in order to facilitate comprehensive redevelopment. Consequently, some element of the price paid for this part of site 38 may be explained by the presence of buildings at the time of purchase or by possible marriage value, but how much is open to dispute.)

During this period, the City Estates and Valuation Officer was under pressure from local politicians who themselves were under pressure from central government to spend additional Urban Programme (financed 75 per cent by central government) and Derelict Land (financed 100 per cent by central government) monies before the end of the financial year. If the money is not spent, then under present rules it is not available in the following year.

If the City Council had been prepared to wait, markedly lower prices may have been agreed for sites 38 and 48. However, the Council was more interested in removing the scars of industrial dereliction than waiting until the vendors came to terms with a more realistic valuation of their redundant premises. A Compulsory Purchase Order would have involved an unacceptable delay in acquisition and, even if it were confirmed, compensation assessed under the statutory rules on a comparable basis with the previously existing level of values may not have produced any saving on the figure agreed in negotiations. This could be one of the indirect effects of the compensation code, mentioned briefly under hypothesis III, which is worthy of further investigation.

Since 1978 local authorities have not been required to obtain District Valuer approval before seeking loan sanction. Department of the Environment approval is still necessary before a Derelict Land Grant or Urban Programme funding can be obtained. Whether the prices paid by the City Council in these instances were excessive is a matter for debate. Nevertheless, the prices paid by the Council for sites 38 and 48 (and, indeed, for other sites in the locality not included in the case studies) in the absence of competing interest, created a widespread view among the private sector valuers interviewed that the City Council was prepared to pay too highly for vacant inner city land. This widespread view satisfies the second requirement of the hypothesis. The third and final requirement concerns the wider impact of public sector agreement by acquisition.

No valuer stated that his client was holding on to vacant land waiting for the City Council to acquire it at an excessive price. The chain of causation is probably more subtle. Since there is scant market activity in industrial land in East Manchester, valuation by the comparative method (see hypothesis I) is dependent on relatively few transactions. The major sales of land which have taken place to the City Council appear as the best evidence of open market prices paid by a willing buyer to a willing seller. As a result, prices paid by the City Council tend to set or more likely maintain the perceived level of values, despite this no longer being justified by the lower level of demand.

Evidence for this is provided by two of the case studies (sites 39 and 50) in private ownership and on the market. Site 39 is adjacent to site 48 (previously acquired by the City Council), and has been marketed at £30,000–£35,000 per acre for two years without success. Site 50 is close to site 38 (previously acquired by the City Council), and has been marketed for 18 months, although the asking price has been reduced from £60,000 per acre to £36,000 per acre. In both cases, the nearest comparable sale has been the site sold to the City Council.

However, it should be added that there is no conclusive evidence of private sector asking prices being in excess of average prices, and *no* evidence that they are above public sector asking prices.

It is apparent that in East Manchester the local authority acted to acquire redundant and unwanted industrial premises, often with high conversion costs, which might otherwise have been left to decay for several years to come. Acquisition prices appear to reflect less the absence of alternative bidders and more the level of values which prevailed when times were better. Evidence from Manchester therefore confirms the view of Edwards and Lovatt (1980) that 'the presence of public authorities as buyers of last resort may help to support the market'. In the short term at least, intervention by the public sector which, however unwittingly, prevents market prices from falling, appears to be reinforced by the undue importance attached to such transactions in subsequent comparative valuations. The length of time during which public intervention may maintain perceived values is unclear. Further investigation is needed into the relationship likely to exist between the period of marketing, vendors' expectations and any downward price revisions.

Hypothesis III. That the statutory rules of valuation within the Compensation Codes produce a higher sum paid in compensation on compulsory acquisition than would be achieved in an open market sale. This raises vendors' expectations and sets a floor below which prices in the open market do not fall

As already noted, earlier commentators have linked the high price of inner city land to the statutory rules of valuation embodied in the land compensation codes. In Inner Manchester, it is apparent that the great waves of compulsory acquisitions in the 1960s and early 1970s are now ended. Slum clearance programmes are mainly complete; road schemes are largely halted. Many of the case studies passed into public ownership at that earlier time. The City Council does not allow the cost of prior compulsory purchase to influence its view of the resale value of land. It is therefore unlikely that compensation settlements of 10 or 15 years ago would have much effect on today's market. There is no discernible belief in Manchester that compulsory acquisition will return as a major feature of the inner city redevelopment process in the immediate future.

The lack of evidence during a period of little compulsory acquisition therefore means that hypothesis III remains unproven. At any different time, or in a different locality, there may well be a direct link between the statutory rules of valuation and land prices. Nevertheless, the prospect of paying high sums in compensation may encourage local authorities to reach voluntary settlements which exceed market prices but fall below the level of compensation assessed under the statutory rules. (Acquisition by voluntary agreement is considered in the next sub-section.) Further, the compensation code may deter local authorities, in the current financial climate, from pursuing worthwhile schemes which may involve compulsory purchase. Edwards (1977) suggests, for instance, that 'when a site becomes obsolete for the industry using it, (the compensation codes prevent) a local authority from buying at a lower price rather than one which reflects the more lucrative potential use'. It was not possible during the study to assess the indirect effects of the compensation code, but it is considered a subject worthy of more detailed investigation.

Hypothesis IV. That the cost of converting problematic sites in the inner city into readily developable land is high and is not reflected in reduced land prices

This hypothesis was suggested by the RTPI Working Party on Land Values and Planning in Inner Areas (1978):

> Once an authority has bought a site it may still have heavy costs to bear before it is capable of development. It is common in many inner areas for a century or more of industrial exploitation of land to have left behind major impediments which are costly to remove. In other cases, the ground is chemically contaminated by previous uses. Often the infrastructure of main services and roads is obsolete and needs replacement. For these reasons, an authority may have very substantial costs to pay over and above the acquisition costs, before it owns a useful piece of land.

Although conversion costs can undoubtedly be extremely high, evidence from the case studies suggests that this is not necessarily so. For site 35, reclamation costs have worked out at £8,000 per acre; for site 38, they average £17,000 per acre; for site 37, the scrap value of redundant plant within the power station is expected to pay for its demolition.

Table 8.8 provides details of six case study sites where the purchaser had incurred substantial reclamation or conversion costs. The sites involved a total of 11 transactions. It can be seen that in 7 out of the 11 transactions the price paid for the land alone fell below the appropriate median. However, when conversion costs are added to acquisition costs total costs exceed the median in 9 out of the 11 cases. Indeed, in these cases, the amount by which the median is exceeded range from 8 to 86 per cent. This would suggest that acquisition costs make some allowance for site difficulties, but a difference that is far from adequate.

It is felt that the failure of acquisition costs to take full account of site difficulties can again be attributed to the comparative method of valuation. The comparative method places most weight on the general level of values thought to pertain in a district, rather than the potential of any one site. In the inner city, the general level of values may be hard to discern and, since many sites experience various kinds of difficulties, the potential

173

Table 8.8: Conversion costs and land prices

Site difficulty		Land cost	Cost of work £ per acre	Total cost	Difference between Land cost and appropriate median %	Total cost and appropriate median %
16	Poor ground conditions	11,250	11,750	23,000	− 62.5	− 23.3
21	Rubble, services, foundations	22,750	17,000	39,750	− 24	+ 32.5
25	Service road	57,000	10,000	67,000	+ 5.5	+ 24
35	Reclamation	70,000	8,000	78,000	− 15	− 5
	works	50,000	8,000	58,000	+ 29	+ 50
		40,000	8,000	48,000	+ 3	+ 24
38	Reclamation	55,000	17,000	72,000	− 42	+ 86
	works	37,500	17,000	54,000	− 5	+ 39
		27,500	17,000	44,500	− 30	+ 15
		25,000	17,000	42,000	− 35	+ 8
48	Reclamation works	24,000	19,000	43,000	− 38	+ 11

of each can be unique. Where site difficulties are identified prior to purchase, a comparative valuation may be reduced in part, but not in total, compensation (case studies 16 and 21). It is felt that the payment of Derelict Land Grant at 100 per cent (for instance, on sites 35, 38 and 48) provides no incentive for purchasers to ensure that the cost of land acquisition fully reflects the cost of reclamation and the eventual site value.

In certain cases, a comparative valuation of land subject to site difficulties may encourage the owner to take an overoptimistic view of the site value. For instance, British Rail has been seeking an industrial value for site 34, which is mainly a tip where settlement is likely to take several years.

As Gore and Nicholson (1983) point out: 'Physical constraints do not necessarily *prevent* development, as they can normally be expressed in terms of extra preparation or construction costs'. Although extra preparation or construction costs need not necessarily be high, there is evidence from the case studies to suggest that these costs are not fully reflected in land prices and this offers support, in part, to the fourth hypothesis. If this is the case, it puts redevelopment in the inner city at a further comparative disadvantage.

CONCLUSIONS

Transactions do take place in vacant land in the inner city, but they are few in number and the range of prices paid is substantial. The public sector is involved in most transactions either as buyer or seller. Since the size, location and particularly the physical condition of each vacant site endow every transaction with individual characteristics, it becomes extremely difficult for the valuer to generalise a particular level of prices from a recent set of transactions. Indeed, many would contest whether an inner city land 'market' exists at all, in the pure sense of the term.[10] The professional valuer faced with the client's request for valuation does his or her best to apply the method of comparative valuation, in spite of the inherent and apparently irresolvable practical difficulties.

In such instances, valuation by the comparative method places undue emphasis on the most favourable recent transaction. This is because the general level of prices is hard to discern and no single transaction can be considered typical. Acquisition by the public sector in the open market may compound this habit and delay a reduction in inner city land prices. Further, the costs of converting problematic sites seem to be inadequately taken into account in valuations.

As a result, asking prices for vacant land on the market are often substantially in excess of median prices actually achieved in recent transactions. Land prices in inner cities are therefore revised downwards only slowly and reluctantly in response to lack of demand or excess supply. This creates a blockage in the development process and prolongs the period of vacancy.

ACKNOWLEDGEMENT

The research was funded jointly by the Economic and Social Research Council and the Royal Institution of Chartered Surveyors. It was carried out between October 1983 and July 1984 in the Department of Land Management and Development, University of Reading.

NOTES

1. The East Manchester wards were in the City Council wards of Bradford, Beswick and Clayton and the Miles Platting Sector of Central ward.

2. In this chapter, historic ownership is defined to include any land acquired prior to the commencement of the study period (1978).

3. Records in the City Planning Department reveal only 92 transactions in the 384 sites over half an acre, known to have been vacant at some time between 1978 and 1983.

4. Ground rents have been capitalised at yields of between 8 per cent and 12 per cent on the advice of the City Estates and Valuation Officer. Generally, industrials are capitalised at 9.25 per cent and commercials at 8.25 per cent.

5. In this chapter, the term 'market' is used in the colloquial sense rather than the strict economic sense.

6. Wider property market reports, confirmed by interviews with local valuers, pointed to a distinct slackening in the Manchester property market during 1980–1.

7. Under the City Council's 'Build for Sale' Programme, private developers are invited to compete for sites by tender. The tender must specify the number and type of the proposed dwellings, the selling prices and the proportion of the selling price (usually 12 per cent) which the Council will eventually recoup as the price of the land. The winning developer is granted a licence to enter upon the land and construct the dwellings as agreed. Marketing is the responsibility of the developer but certain categories of prospective purchasers (for instance, first-time buyers) have priority. The land is conveyed directly by the Council to the eventual purchaser and, at this stage, the Council recoups the given proportion of the sale price as the price of the land. No working capital need, therefore, be tied up by the developer in land acquisition costs.

8. All prices are rounded to the nearest £250.

9. In this context, significant means a sufficient number to induce a general belief that public acquisition of any one parcel of land by agreement might take place in the immediate future.

10. Not only are there relatively few transactions in inner city land but the product is by no means homogeneous. Buyers and sellers do not possess 'perfect knowledge' and significant externalities or spill-overs exist. Finally, prices do not adjust rapidly to eliminate surpluses or deficits.

REFERENCES

Barrett, S., Stewart, M. and Underwood, J. (1978) 'The land market and development process', *Occasional Paper*, No. 2, School for Advanced Urban Studies, University of Bristol

Birmingham Inner City Partnership (1982) *Vacant land in the core area.* Birmingham

Bruton, M. J. and Gore, A. (1980) *Vacant urban land in South Wales,*

Final Report to LAW and Prince of Wales Committee, UWIST, Cardiff

Burrows, J. W. (1977) 'Vacant urban land and its planning implications', unpublished M. Phil. thesis, University College, London

—— (1978) 'Vacant urban land: a continuing crisis', *The Planner*, **64**, pp. 7–9

Colenutt, R. (1978) 'Are inner city land values a problem?' *Architects Journal*, **168**, pp. 20–1

Department of the Environment (1977) *Change or decay: Liverpool Inner Area Study Final Report*, HMSO, London

Edwards, M. (1977) 'Vagaries of the inner city land market,' *Architects Journal,* **165**, pp. 206–7

—— and Lovatt, D. (1980) 'Understanding urban land values: a review', SSRC Inner Cities in Context, *Working Paper*, 1, Bartlett School of Architecture and Planning, University College, London

Gore, A. and Nicholson, D. J. (1983) *Frameworks for the analysis of public sector land ownership and development*, Conference Paper, Land Policies for the 1980s, Oxford

MacGregor, B. D., Baum, A. E., Adams, C. D., Fleming, S. C. and Peterson, J. (1985) '*Land availability for inner city development*', Final Research Report to ESRC, Department of Land Management and Development, University of Reading

Nabarro, R. and Richards, D. (1980) *Wasteland*, a Thames Television Report, Methuen, London

—— and Smart, G. (1978) 'High cost and low value in urban land', *Built Environment*, **4**, pp. 229–36

Royal Institution of Chartered Surveyors (1977) *Inner city regeneration — a report of some aspects of inner city problems.* RICS, London

Royal Town Planning Institute (1978) *Land values and planning in the inner areas*, Final Report of Working Party, RTPI, London

9

The Development Plan: Vision or Vacuum?

Derek Lyddon

The original title which was suggested for this chapter was 'Do Planners have a Role to Play?' Since I am a practising physical planner (having worked in a local authority and New Towns before joining central government) I have no doubt that we have a role to play; indeed a key role, and perhaps thereby an impossible burden. For without the particular skills and experience which the town and country planner can contribute to both public sector departments and private sector developers, few research results could be translated into action. Conversely, of course, some of the city problems about which there is justifiable concern may have been caused by the action or inaction of the city planner, and the politician or developer client he serves.

So I have no doubt the planner has a role — he is in the thick of it — and taking this as my sub-title I would wish to concentrate on how he operates that role; what instruments or tools does he use or need; and equally what new skills does he require. The short answer, which figures in my main title, is 'the Development Plan': the land use Development Plan drawn up under the statutory planning system and the associated Economic Development Plan. With both, there can be purpose and vision; without either, there will be uncertainty and a vacuum.

I want to set the scene by defining the purpose of planning and the characteristics of the British Statutory System and then to look at the various roles which local authorities are adopting towards city planning and management. Against this background I attempt to assess the joint contributions of economic and physical development planning; planning for work and planning for land.

178

WHAT SORT OF PLANNING AND DEVELOPMENT?

The terms planning and planner are used in many contexts. Often they are used as 'aerosol' descriptions, sprayed on anything that has gone wrong. When planning works it goes unnoticed as the natural order of things or as the market being allowed to operate. There are many sorts of planning, from family through to fiscal. So we need to be clear what we are talking about. Essentially, we are dealing with change: understanding change, promoting it, controlling it. It has been said that any person or organisation faced with the future and the change it might bring can adopt one of three attitudes: predict and prepare for it; make it happen; wait and see. Planning is predicting and preparing; making *arrangements* for future changes. In the case of what is termed the British land use planning system embodied in legislation — the Statutory System — we are concerned with *making* arrangements for future changes in the use of land and buildings; and *securing* those arrangements.

This system has been in operation since 1947 and in spite of many political, economic and social changes since then it has attracted a remarkable political and public consensus on its fundamental elements. All governments since 1947 in seeking to adjust the system, whether to capture changes in land value for the benefit of the community, or to release constraints on change required by the 'market', have declared that it is not their intention to dismantle the system. There is often silence, however, about what the essential elements of this system are. I suggest that there are five:

(1) The definition, in legislation, of the type of change which is to be the subject of the arrangements: termed 'Development'.
(2) The statutory duty on a local authority to make arrangements, in a Development Plan.
(3) The legal requirement to obtain consent from the authority before development is carried out.
(4) The right of appeal to central government against the decision of the authority.
(5) The power for central government to intervene in any decision on a Plan or an application for consent.

I have been attempting to raise discussion on these five elements

179

or 'pillars of planning' at various national and international occasions over the last 18 months. Internationally I have found general agreement that some definition of this sort is required and that my suggestions provide the basic structure which each country has incorporated in legislation, or is striving to achieve.

The main areas of debate have been whether the right to be consulted or to participate, and the power to capture the increase in land value for the community arising from development, should specifically be part of a statutory planning system or of wider legislation. Generally, however, in discussion with colleagues from other European countries, I have found that there has been some sympathy with my attempt to define the basic statutory requirements of a planning system in any country; while at the same time describing to a wider audience one of the roles of the town and country planner.

Discussion in Britain, however, has led immediately to arguments concerning the merits of the system, rather than whether the definition is right. The response to my paper to the Town and Country Planning Summer School was, according to one commentator, 'disappointing — not because the paper provoked disagreement but because there seemed to be an almost universal failure to understand and acknowledge the importance of the theme' (Robinson 1985). It appeared that I was attaching too much importance to an 'arbitrary, statutory, and administrative definition of planning'. One of the discussion groups at the Summer School seemed to come to the conclusion that there was nothing wrong with the definition of the system, only that all the pillars were rotten.

This experience has led me to the conclusion that it is worth continuing to attempt to be clear about what we mean when we refer to 'the statutory planning system' so that any necessary adjustments or parallel systems can be considered in the context of the whole structure. Are there any basic elements or pillars missing from my analysis? For example, there is a statutory requirement to give adequate publicity to, and to consider any representations on, various aspects of the Development Plan. It can be claimed that this should be seen as an additional fundamental component of the system, and unique to it. It can also be argued that greater emphasis should be placed on the links between the various elements, particularly between the Development Plan which has been the subject of publicity, representation or participation, and subsequent development control consents. Individuals and those with a stake in the area need to be assured that the Plan gives them some guarantee about the nature of future changes, and what may happen next door. For them, this is an essential connection, but there are wider more fundamental links that bind the whole structure together, which, although often taken for granted, are at the very root of the discussion I touch on in this chapter.

LOCAL AUTHORITY ROLES

This system, however defined, provides only one of the 'predicting and preparing' instruments operated by planners for a local authority; that is through Development Plans and Development Control. There are of course many other such instruments available to a local authority; for example dealing with arrangements for roads, housing and education, but they are not Statutory Systems in the same way — fundamentally because they are not interfering with the rights of individuals to change the use of that property, or protecting individual property values and environmental quality from a devaluing change of use next door.

This Statutory Planning System is not by itself an instrument for implementing change; for making it happen. It was not designed for this; indeed it could not be. A statutory *duty* to carry out change or to construct development of any type is scarcely conceivable because there is a wide variety of people or interests who want to change the use of land or buildings; that is 'Developers' ranging from the individual householder or business, through corporate bodies in both public and private sectors to government departments. It is the planner's job to advise any of them, and in that sense implementation is the prime business of the planner; but it is not the role of the statutory system.

It is necessary, therefore, as far as the corporate body which is a local authority is concerned, to distinguish clearly between two roles: as a Development Planning Authority, acting uniquely under Town and Country Planning Acts; and as a Development Executive Authority acting as one among many other types of developer. Until recently these two roles have proved sufficient for adequate city management. First post-war reconstruction, then population and economic growth gave a very clear need both to plan and allocate land resources and to build roads, services, houses and schools, all in response to evident demand and agreed purpose.

As Professor Donnison has noted, a service-orientated style of urban government was formed — functional, specialist, professional and centralised (Donnison, 1983). These professional traditions and administrative strategies enabled local government to achieve so much during the post-war years. In the last ten years however, with the collapse in the economies of many of our older industrial cities, the position has changed fundamentally. The two roles are no longer sufficient. City planning and management 'for growth' has had to be switched as it were to planning and management 'for decline'; an impossible brief and a traumatic experience. Even when translated as 'a constructive approach to the contraction of the city' (Checkland, 1976) this has proved difficult for local authority members and citizens to accept.

Hence two new roles have emerged. First, from urban government by the city fathers, there has been a change to municipal marketing by civic entrepreneurs: to a city advertising that it is 'miles better'. To the 'worst first' of national policy embodied in the urban aid for deprived areas, has been added the lever of public money to invest in private success. The comprehensive redevelopment area has been supplanted by the enterprise zone.

Second, Donnison has noted three closely related themes which have emerged in the responses of many cities to the new circumstances:

> They are *economically orientated* — more concerned than hitherto with people's opportunities for work and for increasing their incomes both in the formal and the informal economies. They are *community based* more concerned than hitherto to respond to people's perceptions of their own problems and to support whatever initiatives local groups may take in tackling these problems. And they are *area focused* — more concerned than hitherto with the needs of everyone, in a particular neighbourhood or quarter of the city, and with the contributions which all the services operating there can make to improve living conditions and enlarge opportunities in the area (Donnison 1983).

Hence from predicting and preparing, by means of plans and infrastructure developments, there has been a new search for ways in which 'to make it happen'. In operating both of these new roles local authorities have used as their instrument Local Economic Initiatives, based very often on an Economic Development Plan drawn up by an Economic Development Officer. This has arisen beside and, in staffing terms, very often in competition with, the Statutory Development Plan and Control.

LOCAL ECONOMIC DEVELOPMENT

It is therefore necessary to look more closely at the characteristics of Economic Development Initiatives and then at the purpose of physical Development Planning. Innovations and initiatives in the field of local economic development have multiplied since 1981, creating a major new planning and development scene which is highly varied and can only be summarised briefly here, using a number of selected examples.

The Planning Exchange has, since 1981, run a Local Economic Development Information Service (LEDIS). It now has 192 sheets on individual initiatives, 26 subject overviews, and 19 notes about research in progress. A selection of the overview titles provides some idea of the scope: Enterprise Workshops, Community Business Development, Science Parks, Enterprise Trusts, Industrial Improvement Areas, Local Authority Companies, and company information services.

The Policy Studies Institute, the Institute of Local Government Studies, and the Economic and Social Science Research Council are all engaged in research into various aspects of economic development dealing with both policy and operational aspects, which is being disseminated quickly into practice.

As many as 90 per cent of authorities claim some involvement in promoting economic development. A study by the Policy Studies Institute found that out of the 242 authorities in England and Wales surveyed, over 80 per cent provided sites and premises and/or supported business development, and nearly 50 offered direct financial assistance to industry and commerce (Burton, 1985).

In 1984 the Association of District Councils updated a survey carried out in 1982 and found that, out of 249 District Councils, only 11 per cent did not undertake any economic development work (Association of District Councils 1984). For the purpose of analysis the activities of the authorities were grouped under the headings resource/finance commitment, promotion/information, and general support. Between 1982 and 1984 there were much greater levels of involvement in making grants and loans. There was a clear increase in providing premises, but a significant decrease in providing sites.

Expenditure by local authorities directly on economic development is now very considerable. The PSI study found that 161 authorities had a combined capital budget of £145 million, and 171 authorities a combined revenue budget of £75 million. Nineteen per cent had revenue budgets over £0.5 million per year, and 8 authorities spent £2 million (Burton, 1985). These figures compare with budgets of £424 million for regional assistance provided by central government, £97 million for the Scottish Development Agency, and £43 million for the Welsh Development Agency.

A wide variety of organisational forms have been adopted by local authorities, from one person appointed to handle business enquiries as part only of the job, to economic development departments with a staff of over 50 people. It is common for an economic development unit to have been set up in a Planning Department. Typical features include one point of contact for all business enquiries, short lines of communication between economic development staff, Council members and senior officers in other parts of the Council, and the scope to act effectively and to use initiative. Some authorities have set up separate bodies at a distance from the local authority for special purposes, for example taking equity investment in local companies or providing business advice.

'Economic Development Officers' now have their own job title and description. Over 70 per cent are drawn from a public sector background, many previously employed in planning jobs, just over 30 per cent have been working in this field for over six years. Courses for these officers have been arranged by the Local Government Training Board in conjunction with the Manpower Services Commission and opportunities are being presented for planners to develop entirely new roles.

This theme is followed up in a Royal Town Planning Institute Working Party report which explains how a more explicitly people-based approach might be developed, and identifies six broad policy fields: economic structuring, job creation, the quality of employment and equal opportunities, permanent unemployment, local control and influence, and skill development (RTPI, 1985). The Chairman of the Working Party notes that

> In expanding these six policy fields, the Working Party raises questions on four 'organisational fields': Are there different administrative levels or different organisational structures by which different types of policy should be pursued? How can policy and implementation be properly integrated? What sorts of criteria should be used to allocate resources and evaluate projects? Perhaps most fundamental of all, what are the constraints upon local action and how should these change in future? (Howl, 1985).

A valuable paper by Derrick Johnstone of the Planning Exchange highlights some key topics and stresses the need: for an organisational framework appropriate to what the local authority is trying to achieve; for overcoming constraining attitudes within the local authority; for training in the technical skills required by Economic Development Officers and others; for work in partnership with other organisations; and for monitoring and review activities. Linking all this together is the need for a strategic view to guide the implementation related to identified local needs and opportunities, so that each form of support can reinforce the other (Johnstone, 1985).

One way of getting an insight into such a strategic view is to look at the Economic Development Plan No 4 produced by Glasgow District Council in December 1984. This document contains a review of existing economic policies and their effectiveness and puts forward refinements and new suggestions, where necessary revised in the light of changed circumstances. Its main purpose is to detail how the Council's policies can be implemented, but at the same time it provides a context for the activities of other agencies. The plan outlines the state of the economy then reviews the Council's objectives under 14 topics. Each topic chapter deals with the current corporate policy, the context, progress and effectiveness of the policies, suggested action for 1985/6, and the resources required. The chapters deal with industrial promotion, business support, financial assistance to local industry, community businesses, office development, and retail employment. Another section deals with industry and the environment, land and premises. Support for the unemployed, training, and job creation are also covered together with tourism and area initiatives.

THE PHYSICAL DEVELOPMENT PLAN

How then do these economic and social initiatives culminating in an Economic Development Plan relate to the Statutory and Physical Development Plan? Since a certain professional polarity seems to be emerging between the two, I would like to return to the Physical Plan and consider it in greater detail.

As we have seen, economic initiatives are concerned essentially with making more efficient and effective use of the resources embodied in companies and organisations, in property and premises, in people and their skills, and in an information network that links them all together. The economic plan or strategy is concerned with identifying the best opportunities for the use of these resources and in resolving competing claims.

Similarly, physical planning is concerned with the efficient and effective use of the resources embodied in land, buildings and the built environment. Plans and policies are concerned with the resolution of the competing claims for those resources, and identifying the opportunities for their most appropriate use. As growth and expansion have dropped away, the competition and conflict have become more fierce and more economically significant; the opportunities and priorities more difficult to identify.

Both types of planning — of resource allocation and claim mechanism — need to be seen as interrelated and reinforcing one another. The Royal Commission on Local Government in Scotland (Wheatley, 1969) reporting in 1969 saw this clearly when it noted that:

It has become customary in the past, with regard to economic and land use planning, to distinguish these 2 types of planning sharply from one another and to regard the first as the product of central government alone. We do not consider that such a differentiation can usefully be maintained any longer in the context of local government. It is within the ambit of local government rather than of central government that land use and economic aims have the greatest impact on one another. Physical planning lacks means and purpose unless it has regard to economic objectives. Economic planning is ineffectual unless it is translated into physical terms, and unless it has regard to values such as amenity and recreational need (Paragraph 197).

We do not claim that all will be plain sailing. The activities of strategic planning outlined constitute a very far reaching function indeed. They involve the local authority in setting overall economic and social objectives for its area, and in considering what are the main projects and policies through which these objectives should be achieved. This implies an interest not just in plans for local authority services, but also in the plans of private industry and Government Agencies which cannot in the nature of things be subject to local authority control (Paragraph 206).

To illustrate some of these relationships in the products of physical planning, I would like to turn to our experience in Scotland over the last ten years, following the reorganisation of local government based on the Wheatley Commission Report and the adoption of adjustments to the planning system. The latter, in particular, divided the Development Plan into two parts: the Structure Plan dealing with general policies for development and redevelopment; and the Local Plan with more specific locations for land uses or activities. To these two levels of physical planning a third has been added in the form of National Guidelines. With an evolving series of National Planning Guidelines, with nearly complete coverage of up-to-date Structure Plans, and with half of the country covered by Local Plans, there is evidence to show how the physical aspect of planning can both reveal and reinforce economic initiatives.

The Guidelines deal with nationally significant land resources and have for example recently identified potential for individual high-quality sites for high-technology firms.

Structure Plans have made a major contribution to establishing a coherent urban structure and settlement pattern, and to the location of development and redevelopment, and hence to priorities for land use and land release. They have therefore provided a foundation for the priorities and programmes of local authorities, and for the area initiatives of government agencies.

They have demonstrated their potential to deal with land supply and demand over a wider market area than a single district can handle, to sort out competing claims, and to resolve conflicts.

Local Plans have provided the only vehicle for citizens, small businesses and developers, and all those with a stake in the area to consider the form and the potential of sites in local areas. There is evidence to show that a Local Plan in place provides an immediate background against which area initiatives, economic developments, other forms of enterprise or investment, can be assessed and the investment obtained. There is also evidence to show that Local Plans, with up-to-date policies, can reduce conflict.

During the period, the overall level of planning activity has remained high. The average number of planning applications received per annum was 36,600, or 180 every working day; 93 per cent of these were approved. About 1 per cent of all planning applications were the subject of appeal against refusal; 0.3 per cent were in the main employment sectors (in 1983, 117 applications of which 88 were for retail development) leading to about 0.2 per cent being refused. The total output of the construction industry in Scotland in the last five years, which gives a measure of investment in the environment, has risen slightly to a current total of some £2,000 million.

There is an awareness on all sides of the need for better measures of the performance of the planning system in terms of efficiency and effectiveness. The indicators we do have show the scope for improvement at all levels: a better understanding of what is appropriate at each level, more readable plans, a clearer identification of development opportunities and priorities, and a more purposeful resolution of uncertainty wherever possible. Above all, further work is required to achieve a better fit between the social, physical and economic objectives and planning for our cities.

With the two new roles for city management that I have mentioned — promotion and marketing on the one hand, and area based and community focused on the other — the need to establish the structure of the city and the image or identity of place has returned. Before reinvesting human and financial resources in a site in the city the community and the developer want to know what is going to happen across the road, or to the road, and to the site behind. There is a need to know how it all fits together.

Physical planning thus has a major contribution to make to the restoration of confidence in the city. Glasgow itself provides some appropriate examples of the return of this confidence which has been achieved by economic and physical planning working together. Strathclyde in conjunction with Glasgow District Council and the Scottish Development Agency, and aided by the University, has drawn up an Integrated Development Operation report, which identifies the priorities for the economic and physical regeneration of the city, in part as a basis for a claim on European funds. The Economic Development Plan for the city, which has already been mentioned, exists alongside the citywide physical plan; both originating from the Planning Department. Consultants from Glasgow and Strathclyde Universities, who were engaged to review progress on the Glasgow Eastern Area Renewal Project, identified the need for a spatial strategy and this has been supplied by reviewing and combining the Local Plans for the area. Among the several other examples to be seen in the city, none is perhaps more symptomatic than the study drawn up for the centre of Glasgow by McKinsey on the one hand and Gordon Cullen on the other. No better example could be found of market analysts working in conjunction with civic designers.

CONCLUSIONS

I hope I have been able to illustrate the system, instruments and essential characteristics of economic and physical planning. It is a volatile mix between a well-tried system and new-found action. Much is being achieved; but more needs to be done to understand the impact of change on our cities, and to create new instruments for implementing and integrating economic, social and physical adjustments. This will require a federation of skills in practice, an increase in understanding by research, and the transfer of experience by education. In each there is a particular contribution which the planner can make. It is a role which is directed at spatial relationships and the connections between investment opportunities; which communicates form arising from function, and identity of place; which follows up the science of analysis by the craft of negotiated synthesis.

REFERENCES

Association of District Councils (1984) 'Economic development by district councils', *Best Practice Paper*, **6** (Revised), ADC, London

Burton, Tony (1985) *Local authorities and economic development*, Planning Exchange, Glasgow

Checkland, S. G. (1976) *The Upas tree: Glasgow 1875–1975*, University of Glasgow Press, Glasgow

Donnison, D. V. (1983) *Urban policies: a new approach*, London

Howl, David (1985) 'A "people based" approach to local economic planning', *The Planner*, **7**

Johnstone, D. (1985) 'Effective economic development', *Occasional Paper*, **19**, The Planning Exchange, Glasgow

Robinson, A. (1985) 'R.I.G. in context', *The Planner*, **7**

Royal Town Planning Institute (1985) 'How effective is local economic planning? A consultation document', *First Report*, Economic and Employment Working Party, RTPI, London

Wheatley (1969) 'Royal Commission on Local Government in Scotland', *Report*, Cmnd. 4150, HMSO, London

10

Counter-urbanisation and the Rural Periphery: Some Evidence from North Devon

D. J. Grafton and N. Bolton

Since 1970, the population geography of Britain has undergone a profound change, during a sustained period of minimal natural growth. The results of the 1981 Census showed that the fastest growing areas of the country were mainly remote rural regions, whilst those declining most rapidly were the largest cities and conurbations. Between 1971–81 all British cities over 250,000 in size lost population, with the exception of Plymouth. In some cases this population loss was very large, such as Glasgow (15 per cent) London (10 per cent) Liverpool (16 per cent) and Manchester (17 per cent) (Robert and Randolph, 1983). At the same time, counties such as Cornwall, Somerset, Norfolk, Powys and the Highlands and Islands region all grew by more than 10 per cent (Champion, 1981), representing a clear reversal of traditional population trends.

Britain's experience of this population turnround is not unique. Rather, all Western industrialised countries have undergone similar demographic changes over the last two decades, with a population redistribution away from the metropolitan areas, to rural and remote rural regions (Vining and Pallone, 1982). The term 'counter-urbanisation' (Berry, 1979) has been coined to explain this process of population decentralisation and population deconcentration.

The basic patterns of counter-urbanisation within the UK have been well described at the regional and sub-regional scales (Champion, 1981; Robert and Randolph, 1983). Although detailed work also exists at the intra-urban scale on population and employment losses, relatively little attention has been paid to local-scale patterns of population and employment growth in the rural periphery. This is surprising given the widespread and unexpected turnround of population trends in remote rural areas revealed by the 1981 census (Cloke, 1985). It is the intention of this chapter to provide information on recent demographic, social and economic change with reference to a remote rural area in Devon. Such changes will be interpreted with reference to current theories of counter-urbanisation.

STUDY AREA

Although South West England is conventionally regarded as a peripheral region (Manners *et al.*, 1981), it is one of the fastest growing regions of the country with a population increase of 7 per cent between 1971 and 1981. Within the region, Devon has shown an identical growth rate over the same decade, and parts of the county, especially the remoter north-west, have experienced population gains for the first time in many decades (Devon County Council, 1983).

Since it is our intention to focus on a remote rural area that demonstrated a recent reversal of depopulation, a locality was required which exhibited a high degree of rurality and remoteness in 1971; that had a history of depopulation prior to 1971; and, ideally, that was not affected to any great degree by boundary changes through time. Given these criteria, North Devon seemed a particularly promising study area. This part of the county has traditionally been recognised as suffering from problems of rural depopulation and remoteness (SWEPC, 1967; Devon County Council, 1979). D'Abbs, (1974) makes the important point that, although the remoter rural zones experienced widespread depopulation in the 1960s, it was continued growth rather than decline that characterised the largest urban settlements (such as Barnstaple and Bideford) and their contiguous Rural Districts (Figures 10.1 and 10.2). Spooner (1972) reinforces this point with reference to rapid industrial growth in Barnstaple during the 1960s, in part attributable to UK regional policy. For the remoter parishes, however a comparison of Figure 10.1 and Figure 10.2 reveals a striking turnround in population trends.

Given these intra-regional contrasts in employment and population trends, it was decided to concentrate on the old (pre-1974) Rural District of South Molton. Unlike the 'non-rural' Districts around Barnstaple, this area was classified by Cloke

Figure 10.1: Parish population change in North Devon, 1961–71

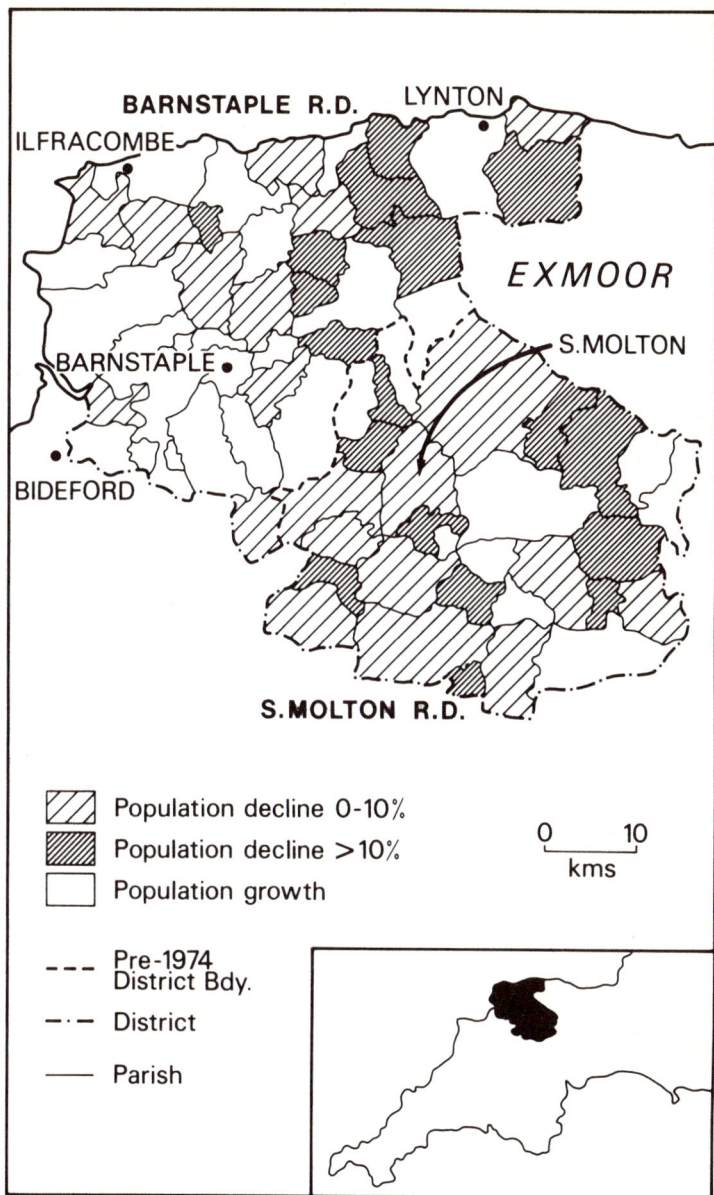

BARNSTAPLE R.D.   LYNTON

ILFRACOMBE

EXMOOR

S. MOLTON

BARNSTAPLE

BIDEFORD

S. MOLTON R.D.

Population decline 0-10%

Population decline >10%

Population growth

0   10
kms

Pre-1974
District Bdy.

District

Parish

Figure 10.2: Parish population change in North Devon, 1971–81

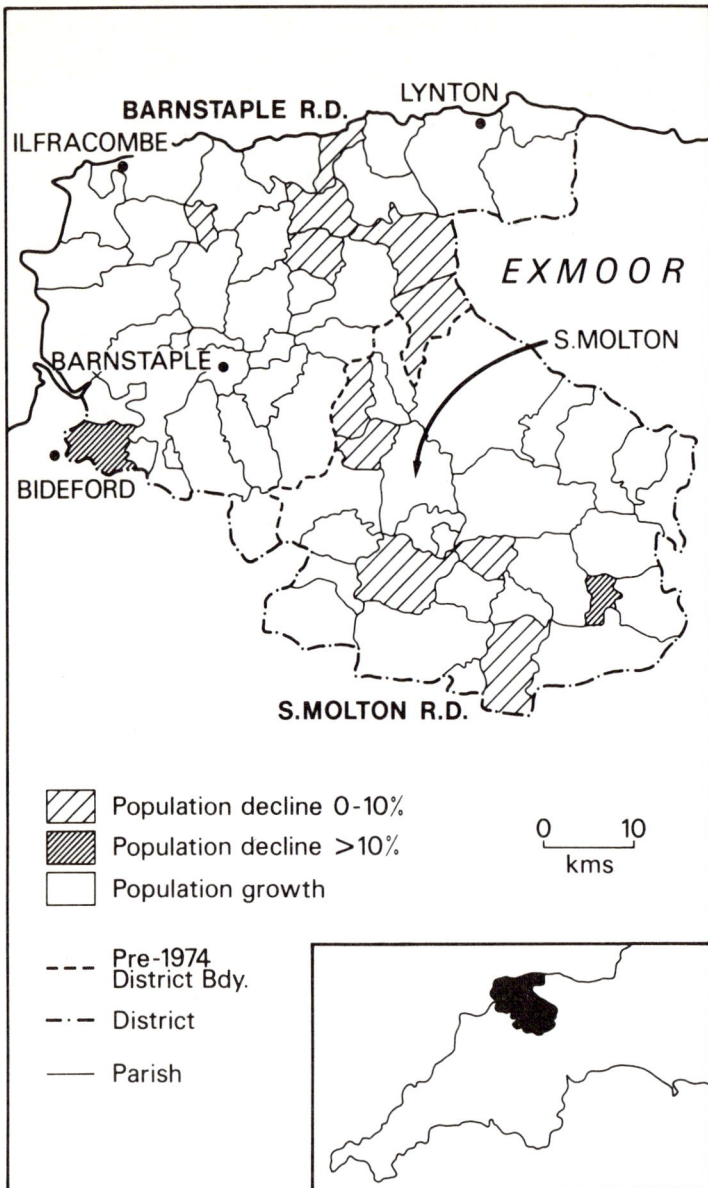

(1977) as 'extreme rural' using 1971 Census data, and was in the most remote quartile of all English Rural Districts in an analysis by Grafton (1981). Only two very minor boundary changes occurred in South Molton RD between 1901 and 1971, greatly facilitating inter-censal comparisons. Following local government reorganisation in 1974, the old Rural District became part of the much larger North Devon District and therefore no published 1981 District figures are available for the pre-1974 administrative area. However, the sub-division of the new North Devon District into wards, for which unpublished Small Area Statistics are available, was made in such a way as to allow the old South Molton RD to be rebuilt precisely by amalgamating six wards. It is therefore possible to provide a comparable spatial framework for a complete time span from 1901 to 1981. Clearly, though, great care must be taken in interpreting changes through time, especially when using the 10 per cent sample Census data, in view of both the Barnardisation procedures applied and the small base population involved (Rhind, 1983).

South Molton Rural District is an area of mixed arable, cattle and sheep farming that is characterised by a rolling topography and a diverse settlement pattern. The largest settlement is the market town of South Molton (population 3,611 in 1981), but more typically the population is low-density and highly scattered. This dispersed settlement form is best seen on the marginal upland fringe, especially on the flanks of Exmoor in the north-east.

POPULATION CHANGE: TEMPORAL AND SPATIAL DIMENSIONS

An examination of population change at the parish level within the pre-1974 South Molton Rural District reveals a number of important trends. These are summarised in Table 10.1 for the decades 1951–81. While the period 1961–71 witnessed a slowing of population decline, it is clearly in the 1970s that the full impact of population resurgence may be seen. It is of interest to note that population growth between 1971 and 1981 was not restricted to a small number of large settlements, as may have been suggested *a priori*, and as appears to have been the case in the 1960s. Rather, these later gains were widespread in a range of different

Table 10.1: Population change by parish, South Molton Rural District, 1951–81

	1951–61	1961–71	1971–81
Population change (abs.)	−1041	−93	+1790
Population change (%)	−9	−1	+16
No. of parishes increasing in population	2	9	24
No. of parishes decreasing in population	27	20	5

Note: The 1981 population figure is calculated on the same basis as that for 1971, i.e. population present on Census night.
Source: Census.

settlement types and locations across the District. For several of the smaller parishes, 1971–81 was the first decade of growth this century.

Although these changes in trend are important, and can produce very large percentage increases in parishes with a small base population, the largest *absolute* gains are to be found in the larger settlements. Indeed, the four most populous parishes — South Molton, North Molton, Chulmleigh and Witheridge — together account for three-quarters of the total population growth in the District. Given the settlement policy operated by Devon County Council, which leans heavily on the concept of key settlements, the growth of South Molton as a designated Area Centre, and Chulmleigh and Witheridge as Selected Local Centres, may in part be explained by policy considerations. It is more difficult to understand the level of new growth outside these settlements, particularly when one considers that, given a reduction in average household size of 0.13, the rate of increase in the number of private households is greater than the rate of population growth (21 per cent compared with 16 per cent for the District as a whole).

Figure 10.3 illustrates parish population trends for the decades 1961–71 compared with 1971–81, following Woodruffe's (1976) classification system. Of the growth parishes between 1971 and 1981, by far the largest number (17) are in the 'reversed depopulation' category. Some major settlements fall into this group, such as South Molton itself, but interestingly a number of other extremely remote parishes are included, such as Twitchen, located on the Exmoor fringe. This parish grew by 34 per cent between 1971 and 1981 yet had a population at the start of the decade of just 67. There is no clear relationship between parish

Figure 10.3: Parish population trends in South Molton District, 1961–81

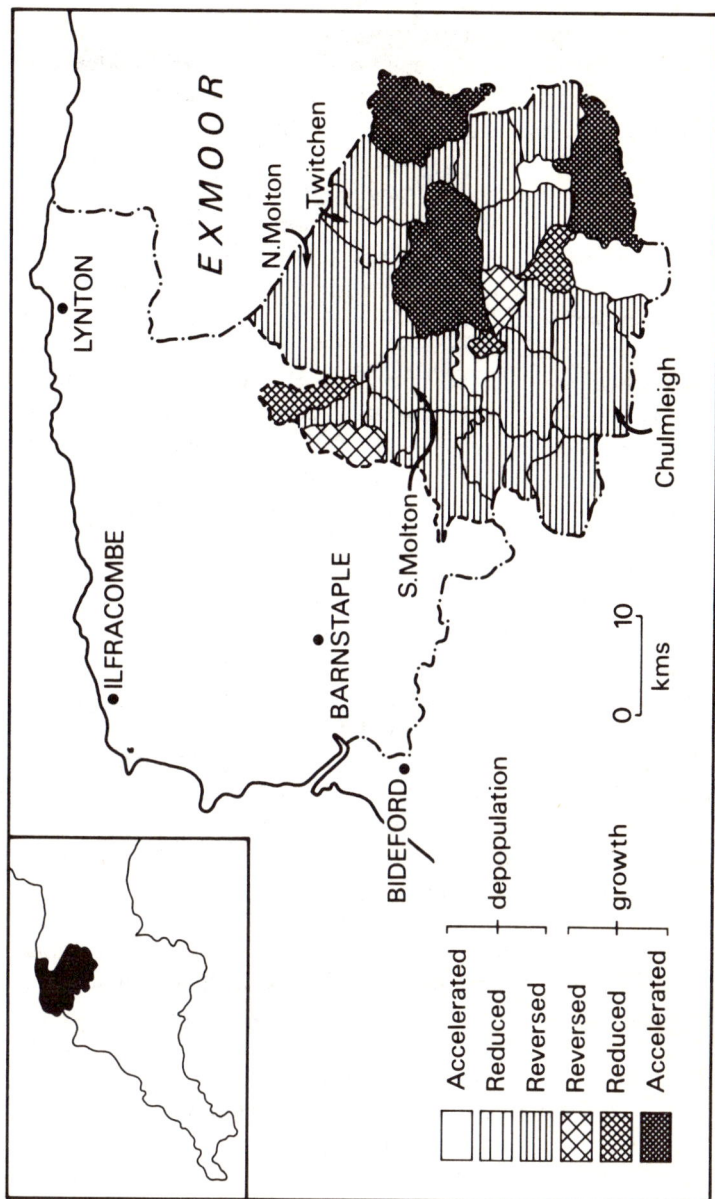

197

population size and population change, nor is there a link between settlement pattern and population change, so widespread has been the repopulation of this area.

The small number of declining parishes (five) makes generalisation about decline difficult, but there is some evidence to suggest that it tends to be found in parishes which are small, remote, and characterised by a highly dispersed settlement pattern. Most of these parishes have had a very long history of depopulation, unbroken throughout this century.

The evidence presented here may appear to suggest that there has been a clear break with traditional patterns of decline. Before making such an assertion, however, it is necessary to establish that long-term trends have indeed been broken: it is perfectly possible that the trends shown by the 1961–81 comparison may also be found in earlier decades this century. Rural population change may previously have oscillated between a decade of decline and a decade of growth, with the latest figures merely representing one phase of this cycle. Clearly, data are needed which will allow a longer-term perspective on these trends.

By plotting parish population change in South Molton RD from 1901 to 1981 it is evident from Figure 10.4 that for the smaller parishes the 1971–81 changes do indeed represent a remarkably clear break with traditional trends. The 'reverse tick' effect is surprisingly widespread, occurring to some extent in the 1960s, but most clearly apparent in the 1970s. This seems compelling evidence for the 'clean-break' hypothesis at the local scale. The continued growth of the larger parishes is not unexpected, especially in view of the rural settlement policies for this area, discussed earlier.

While these spatial and temporal trends are of interest in themselves, it is important to recognise that such changes are essentially a response to pressures both internal and external to the rural area itself. Small-area census data allow an assessment to be made of some emerging social and economic forces that have accompanied the population turnround in this area. By examining socio-economic change between 1971 and 1981 at the local scale, some light may be shed on competing theories of counter-urbanisation as they impinge upon the rural periphery.

Figure 10.4: Parish population trends in South Molton District, 1901–81

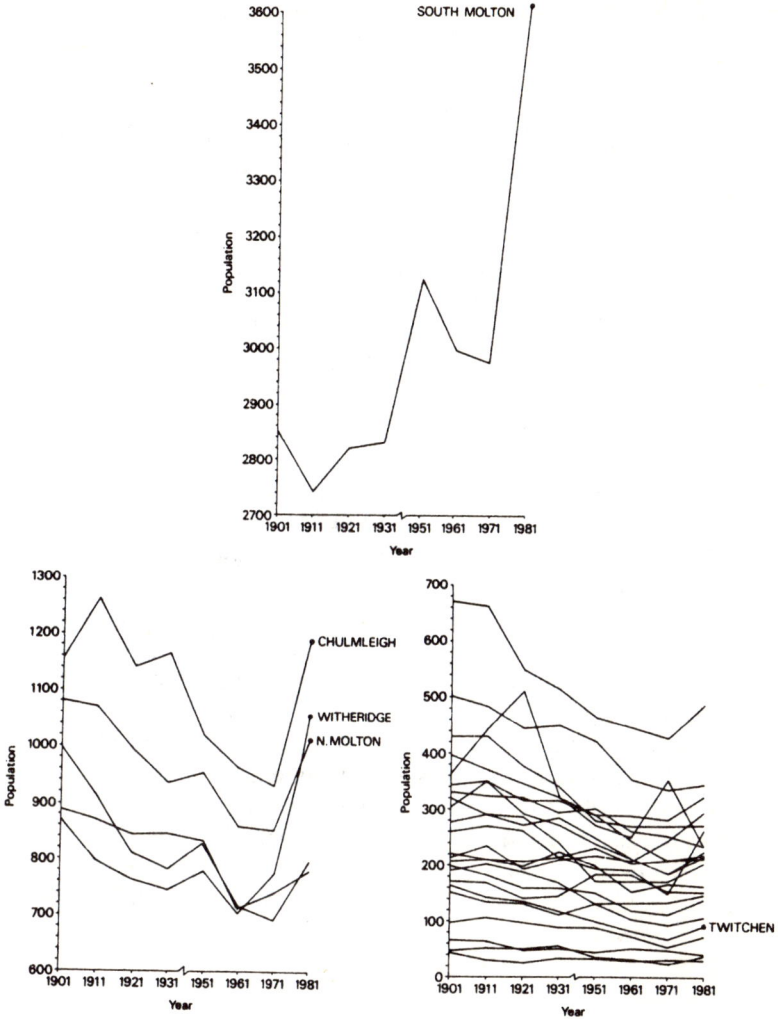

THEORIES OF COUNTER-URBANISATION

It is intended that only the briefest overview of this topic will be given here. Following Fielding (1982) and Moseley (1984), the counter-urbanisation debate polarises around theories which advocate voluntarist explanations and those which adopt economic determinist positions. Under the former, the repopulation of the rural periphery is due essentially to persons exercising individual choice in seeking a more attractive remote rural environment and voting with their feet in order to achieve it. The free market supposedly adjusts to these changes in preference, and the housing and labour markets respond accordingly. Attractive though this idea may be, it is clear that very few groups in society are able to exercise free choice in locational decision-making. Fielding and Moseley both suggest that in the UK those with such freedom would include the very wealthy, those with job skills in high demand, the retired and possibly also the unemployed.

The non-voluntarist hypotheses stress the importance of those forces operating in society as a whole which determine spatial and temporal patterns of economic and demographic change. It is argued that economic changes cause population change and that the behaviour of firms under advanced capitalism has led to a re-evaluation of the attractiveness of the rural periphery as a location for branch plant manufacturing industry. Massey (1979, 1984) has suggested that such areas now offer considerable advantages to the multi-plant firm in respect of low wage levels (especially amongst women) and weak unionisation. Some of the key elements in these ideas may be tested with reference to small-area census data and it is possible therefore to make an assessment of the relative importance of voluntarist as opposed to non-voluntarist explanations of the population turnround in the South Molton District.

Voluntarist explanations

An obvious starting point in attempting to explain population growth in the rural periphery is to consider the relative contribution made by the elderly. Law and Warnes (1976) note the popularity of Devon as a retirement area, and the voluntarist school would identify the elderly as a major group whose residential location decisions are relatively unconstrained and who may therefore (income permitting) be increasingly attracted to a rural environment such as the South Molton District. 1981 Census figures reveal that 23 per cent of the resident population of the District were of retirement age. Although above the national average (18 per cent), this proportion is the same as that of Devon as a whole, and has only increased by 1 per cent since 1971 (Table 10.2). There seems little evidence here to suggest that retirement migration is the main cause of population growth in the District. The absolute number of elderly persons has certainly increased, and in some parishes can account for a third of the total population, but these trends have in general been balanced by an increase in the absolute numbers of those in younger age groups, with persons of working age equally well represented.

Three further groups within the voluntarist approach may be identified. First, it has been suggested that the migration of the unemployed may be causing population growth in the rural periphery. Census and unemployment data show no evidence for this in the South Molton District, although the position in some nearby seaside resorts may be markedly different. The District has a lower level of unemployment than in Devon as a whole (5 per cent compared with 15 per cent for Devon): a relative position that has not altered since 1971.

A second group of voluntarist migrants to the rural periphery are those seeking a self-sufficient, back-to-the-land type of lifestyle based on small farm units. Certainly such farms do exist in the District, particularly on the poorer uplands, but Census data would suggest that the size and growth of this group is larger in the public imagination than in reality. By taking an admittedly imperfect estimate based on those recorded by the Census as self-employed farmers, it would seem that this group registered a decrease in number of 30 per cent between 1971 and 1981. Self-

Table 10.2: Age structure 1971–81, South Molton District

| | 1971 | | 1981 | |
	%	Nos.	%	Nos.
Over pensionable age	22	2,438	23	2,680
Under 16	20	2,216	20	2,576
15-pensionable age	58	64,264	57	7,614

Source: Census.

employed farmers now number 540, representing only 10 per cent of all those economically active within the District.

Another facet of the alternative lifestyle theory suggests a third potential migrant group associated with the increasing trend towards early retirement and associated 'golden handshakes'. This, it might be argued, has encouraged new small-firm formation in the rural periphery as the early retirees invest in their own businesses in a more congenial physical environment than the metropolis (Dean *et al*. 1984). The evidence from the District, however, is that self-employment levels have in fact fallen between 1971 and 1981 by 1 per cent, casting doubt on this factor as a major explanation of the population turnround. Even when this form of new business does arise, evidence from Cornwall (Perry, 1979) would suggest that employment creation is low and that such firms operate in a satisficing rather than profit/employment maximising manner.

From the discussion above, it should be clear that voluntarist explanations of the population turnround in South Molton District are at best a partial answer. Of greater significance are the employment-led non-voluntarist reasons and it is to these that attention will now turn.

Non-voluntarist explanations

The data shown in Table 10.3 illustrate the principal changes in employment structure between 1971 and 1981. These figures suggest that a radical restructuring of the local economy took place during the 1970s. Overall, employment increased by 15 per cent, due mainly to a remarkable increase in manufacturing industry in both absolute and percentage terms. This reflected

Table 10.3: Employment change in South Molton District, 1971–81

Industry of Employed Persons	1971 Nos.	1981 Nos.	1971–81 Nos.	Change (%)
Agriculture	1,510	1,390	−120	−9
Manufacturing	310	890	+580	+287
Services	2,210	2,410	+200	+9
Others	550	560	+10	+2
Total	4,580	5,250	+670	+15

Source: Census, 10 per cent sample.

both increasing commuting to the industrial estates at Barnstaple and Bideford and the growth of indigenous local small industries in the larger settlements within the District. Regional or sub-regional analyses (e.g. Fothergill and Gudgin, 1982; Keeble, 1980) obscure the important point that employment in manufacturing industry is not necessarily restricted to the major urban areas of the remoter regions, but may be diffused widely throughout the rural periphery.

Although employment in agriculture showed a loss of 9 per cent, this may also, in a sense, be a factor contributing to net employment *growth*, since such a decline is considerably less than that recorded in previous decades. D'Abbs (1974), for example, notes that employment in the primary sector fell by 48 per cent in just five years between 1966 and 1971. This leads to an interesting question of whether it is the *presence* of new employment that is crucial or if it is the *absence* of massive losses of agricultural labour that is of greater importance. It is certainly the case that industrial employment in North Devon grew more rapidly in both absolute and percentage terms in the 1960s than the 1970s, but this growth was masked by a massive decline in agricultural labour. A note of caution is necessary, therefore, in that the net increase in employment in South Molton District is not, as may appear at first sight, due solely to gains in the manufacturing sector. This is an extremely important point, since attempts to explain employment and population growth may concentrate more profitably on why agriculture is not declining rapidly rather than focusing on an illusory turnround in manufacturing trends.

The service sector is the main employment source and continued to show modest growth throughout the 1970s, with the major elements being employment in distribution and catering, and in public sector services. This latter group has more than doubled, a trend also evidenced by Cooke (1981) in Wales. Other employment sources are principally in construction and showed modest growth.

The gender differences associated with this new employment structure are likely to be marked (Massey, 1984). Table 10.4 indicates that the fastest rates of employment growth have been in female rather than male occupations, with part-time female employment increasing by almost one-half during the 1970s. These trends lend some support to Massey's hypothesis, but it must be noted that the bulk of female employment is not in

Table 10.4: Employment change by gender, South Molton District, 1971–81

	1971	1981	1971–81 Nos.	Change (%)
Females — full time	940	1,043	+103	+11
Females — part time	400	807	+407	+202
Total females	1,340	1,850	+510	+38
Total males	3,086	3,400	+314	+10

Source: Census, 10 per cent sample.

manufacturing (25 per cent) but in the service sector (66 per cent). Unfortunately, detailed figures on employment type by gender are not available in the 1971 Census, precluding inter-censal comparisons of manufacturing employment for females.

The social class composition of South Molton District shows changes which are parallel, both in their nature and their timing, to the economic changes in the area. Data for 1951, 1971 and 1981 are shown in Table 10.5. The 1981 figures reveal a very high proportion of persons in the highest social classes with a corresponding under-representation of those in classes IV and V. The essentially middle-class nature of the area has, perhaps surprisingly, not altered radically since 1971. Certainly there has been a small increase in the representation of social classes I and II at the expense of the lowest social groups, but the major social class shifts took place in the period 1951–71 at a time of rapid employment growth in manufacturing industry and equally fast decline in agriculture. The evidence from South Molton District would suggest that counter-urbanisation defined in terms of the population turnround does not necessarily imply a sudden new influx of an adventitious middle-class population. Rather, it would seem that the reversal of depopulation occurred ten years or more after rapid social class changes had occurred. It is important to stress that the social, economic and demographic trends that characterise counter-urbanisation need not occur simultaneously, as seems implicitly assumed in much of the current literature.

Table 10.5: Social class change in South Molton District, 1951–81

Social class	1951 (%)	1971 (%)	1981 (%)
I and II	35	47	50
III(N) and III(M)	30	32	34
IV and V	35	21	16

Source: Census, 10 per cent sample.

IMPLICATIONS FOR THEORIES OF COUNTER-URBANISATION

Attempting to link these patterns to the literature explaining the turnround is not an easy task. The evidence presented here suggests that, while voluntarist reasons are extremely limited in explaining the urban-rural shift, they cannot be dismissed completely. Of greater significance, however, are the non-voluntarist explanations of the population turnround which have been demonstrated by examining economic and employment changes in the South Molton RD.

In relating this work to the extensive literature on counter-urbanisation two points of caution need to be made. First, the duality between voluntarist and non-voluntarist explanations is a false and unhelpful dichotomy. In seeking a single overriding causal process, the literature has generally masked the complex set of reasons which combine and inter-relate to initiate change in a remote rural area. Only by examining both voluntarist and non-voluntarist migration and their relations between and to each other can a fuller understanding of the process of counter-urbanisation be gained. The second note of caution is that the literature generally assumes the locality plays a merely passive role. Socio-economic change in rural environments has often been explained by the *impact* of a middle-class adventitious sector of the population in the case of voluntarist explanations, and by the spin-off *effects* of broader structural changes occurring in the UK space economy, in the case of non-voluntarist explanations.

The recent revival in locality studies has attempted to re-instate the importance of local uniqueness (Cooke, 1983; Gilligan, 1984). Massey (1983) writes:

Local changes and characteristics are not just some simple

'reflection' of broader processes: local areas are not lost in passive receipt of changes handed down from some higher national level. The vast variety of conditions already existing at the local level also affects how these processes themselves operate.

With the exception of Cloke (1985), there has been surprisingly little in the counter-urbanisation literature which examines local conditions that are likely to influence the *nature* of social and economic changes occurring in the rural periphery. A crucial element here is the role played by the state, at a variety of levels, which can be argued to determine the provision and development of industry and housing in a particular area.

One view of the state's role at the regional level has been described by Fielding (1982) in terms of the pluralist state intervention model. Here the state is seen as relatively autonomous and responsive to political pressures in a pluralist manner. It is argued that population growth in the rural periphery is due to employment generation caused by state regional policy formulated in response to the wishes of the electorate both locally and nationally. As Fielding correctly points out, such a view has several critical weaknesses, not least of which is the assumption that the interests of the state and the interests of capital may be readily dissociated.

An alternative interpretation of the role of the state in the planning process is that proposed by Cooke (1983). He stresses that, far from the state being an autonomous, pluralist agent: 'The planning system is important in bringing together land and labour in ways which are constructive for capital (as a general rule)'. It is in this light that we should be alive to the impact of non-regional policies that nevertheless have a regional impact. Apart from the manufacturing sector, these would include agricultural policies favouring high productivity and larger farms, and state service provision such as defence, health and education. Local planning policies may also be viewed from this perspective. First, policies that allow only small-scale employment growth in rural settlements may act in the interests of capital through the development of a local monopoly on labour supply and a continued fragmentation — both sectoral and spatial — of the labour force. Structure Plan policies favouring small industries in key settlements (Devon County Council, 1979) provide a clear example of this. Second, development control policies which seek to protect on environmental grounds the more attractive settlements of the area have facilitated the gentrification of several villages within the study area (for example North Molton and Chulmleigh). Third, the direct intervention of the state in housing provision has a profound impact on the social composition of the locality. In South Molton District, traditionally a low-spending authority, council house construction has almost ceased, following small-scale development in the 1960s and 1970s almost exclusively in South Molton village itself. At the same time, planning permissions have been granted principally for new owner-occupied semi-detached or detached properties in response to developer pressure. Inevitably, the sum of these trends has been to shift the property market in favour of the new middle classes.

The legacy of Devon's settlement policy can clearly be seen in the distinction between those settlements that were designated within the settlement hierarchy and those that were not. During the 1960s and 1970s small-scale council housing developments took place exclusively in the designated settlements of the area, and predominantly in South Molton itself. Since 1980 council house construction has almost ceased. Despite these attempts to provide housing for those with few resources, the bulk of new housing in the key settlements has taken the form of owner-occupied semi-detached and detached estate development. Approximately 700 such dwellings were built in the key settlements (including South Molton) between 1971 and 1981, with North Molton and Chittlehampton attracting substantial 'key worker' housing. Outside these settlements, housing development has been restricted to infilling and to a few individual owner-occupied semi-detached or detached properties. The property market in many of these non-designated parishes has also clearly moved in favour of the new middle classes. Nowhere is this more clear than in the parishes on the main Barnstaple-Exeter axis, such as Chittlehamholt and Kings Nympton. These parishes show clear signs of gentrification, in part due to strict development control policies which seek to protect the more attractive villages on environmental grounds.

Thus in terms of housing and industrial provision, the local state rarely works as the pluralist state intervention model indicates. Research carried out recently in Devon (Richmond, 1985) shows that the local state rarely recognised local housing needs. Rather, established guidelines are followed which have a profound effect on the social composition of the locality. Moreover it appears that important differences in housing and industrial supply do exist within South Molton RD itself. These must be examined if a fuller understanding of the counter-urbanisation process is to be gained.

CONCLUSION

The interaction between state policies and developers' interests in determining the scale and nature of housing and employment *supply* is of crucial importance, since it is ultimately the nature of *provision* that will determine the kind of counter-urbanisation experienced by a locality. It has been the intention of this chapter to illustrate the importance of local conditions in shaping counter-urbanisation trends. It could be argued that in the counter-urbanisation literature to date, too much emphasis has been placed on the development of all-embracing demand-side theories (which assume the locality plays a passive role) with too little consideration of the supply-side influences within specific localities. These provide a particular surface that both pre-modifies and is in turn modified by counter-urbanisation processes. Clearly, further local-scale work is needed to develop this perspective in the rural periphery: what has been demonstrated here is the impact of a set of macro social, economic and demographic processes that are fundamentally restructuring the character of a formerly remote rural locale.

REFERENCES

Berry, B. (1979) *Urbanization and counter-urbanization*, Urban Affairs Annual Reviews, **11**, Sage, New York

Champion, A. G. (1981) 'Counterurbanisation and rural rejuvenation in rural Britain: an evaluation of population trends since 1971', *Seminar Paper*, 38, Dept. of Geography, University of Newcastle Upon Tyne

Cloke, P. J. (1977) 'An index of rurality for England and Wales', *Regional Studies* **11**, pp. 31–45

—— (1979) *Key settlements in rural areas*, Methuen, London

—— (1985) 'Counterurbanisation: a rural perspective', *Geography*, **70**, pp. 13–23

Cooke, P. (1981) 'Tertiarisation and socio-spatial differentiation in Wales', *Geoforum* **12**, pp. 319–30

—— (1983) *Theories of planning and spatial development*, Hutchinson, London

D'Abbs (1974) *North Devon 1966–74: aspects of social and economic change*, Community Council of Devon, Exeter

Dean, K., Brown, B., Perry, R. and Shaw, D. (1984) 'The conceptualisation of counterurbanisation', *Area* **16**, pp. 9–16

Devon County Council (1979) *County Structure Plan*, Devon County Council, Exeter

—— (1983) *County Structure Plan: First Alteration 1981 Data Base*, Devon County Council, Exeter

Fielding, A. J. (1982) 'Counterurbanisation in Western Europe', *Progress in Planning*, **17**

Fothergill, S. and Gudgin, G. (1982) *Unequal growth: urban and regional employment change in the UK*, Heinemann, London

Gilligan, J. H. (1984) 'The rural labour process: a case study of a Cornish town', in Bradley, T. and Lowe, P. (eds.), *Locality & rurality*, Geo-Books, Norwich

Grafton, D. J. (1981) 'Geography and planning in remote rural areas', Unpublished Ph.D. thesis, University of Southampton

Keeble, D. (1980) 'Industrial decline, regional policy and the urban-rural manufacturing shift in the United Kingdom', *Environment and Planning*, A, **12**, pp. 945–62

Law, C. M. and Warnes, A. M. (1976) 'The changing geography of the elderly in England and Wales', *Transactions, Institute of British Geographers, N.S.*,**1**, pp. 453–71

Manners, G., Keeble, D., Rodgers, B. and Warren, K. (1981) *Regional development in Britain*, 2nd ed., Wiley, London

Massey, D. (1979) 'In what sense a regional problem?', *Regional Studies*, **13**, pp. 233–43

—— (1983) 'Industrial restructuring as class restructuring: production decentralisation and local uniqueness' *Regional Studies*, **17**, pp. 73–90

Massey, D. B. (1984) *Spatial divisions of labour*, Macmillan, London

Moseley, M. J. (1984) 'The revival of rural areas in advanced economies: a review of some causes and consequences', *Geoforum*, **15**, pp. 447–56

Perry, R. (1979) *A summary of studies of the Cornish economy carried out 1974–78*, Cornwall Industrial Development Association

Richmond, P. (1985) 'Housing associations in rural areas', *South West Papers in Geography*, No 7, Plymouth Polytechnic, College of St Mark & St John and Exeter University, Department of Geography

Robert, S. and Randolph, W. G. (1983) 'Beyond decentralisation: the evolution of population distribution in Great Britain 1961–81', *Geoforum*. **14**, pp. 75–102

Rhind, D. (1983) *A census user's handbook*, Methuen, London

South West Economic Planning Council (1967) *A region with a future*, SWEPC

Spooner, D. J. (1972) 'Industrial movement and the rural periphery: the case of Devon and Cornwall', *Regional Studies*, **6**, pp. 197–215

Vining, D. R. and Pallone, R. (1982) 'Migration between core and peripheral regions: a description and tentative explanation of the pattern of 22 countries', *Geoforum*, **13**, pp. 339–410

Woodruffe, B. J. (1976) *Rural settlement policies and plans*, Oxford University Press, Oxford

11

The Policy Framework

Brian Robson

Where then do we go from here? What would an effective urban policy begin to look like? The authors of the preceding chapters have made a variety of specific suggestions which would form elements of such a policy. Amongst them, I would emphasise: the importance of achieving greater co-ordination — both across agencies and across the spatial scales of local, urban and regional; the need for regional impact assessments of mainstream spending and for the establishment of English regional agencies which could both co-ordinate development and add political muscle to attempts to compensate for regional inequity; the recognition of the role that infrastructural investment can play in leading the development process; and the importance of developing more effective targeting of resources to the people most in need. There are many other policy implications which flow from the details of the preceding chapters. However, I wish to stress the importance of an overarching urban policy, not of isolated programmes. Rather than formulate a check list of desirable innovations, let me spell out three of the lineaments of such a policy.

COMBATING POVERTY

The ESRC research, of which Chapters 3, 4 and 5 are part, shows that the economic policy for our urban areas is too important to be left to the short-term adversarial nature of our political system. It is vital that we develop a sensitive, long-term a-political approach aimed at establishing the basis for a stable and law-abiding society. It is highly unlikely that this could be achieved until we face the need to redistribute wealth through a combined tax and social security system or a basic income support scheme which will go hand in hand with an acceptance that a regular paid job is not the measure of a man's — or woman's — worth. The danger for our cities lies in the fact that not only has the gulf deepened between the haves and have-nots, but also that the serious and much-needed attempt to bring us into the world of enterprise and competition has been enveloped by the selfish indolence of a century of inbred anti-industrialism. This has produced an appalling stalemate since 'comfortable Britain' prefers not to rock its own very well-cushioned boat. The business world has prospered: finance, banking and insurance still offer affluence to our brightest young people; the 'clean' industries of tourism and technology take many more. For those who fear the uncertainty of the business world there has been the security of state employment in professions at central or local level: professionals have flourished, particularly those like the doctors and lawyers who can secure both public and private payment. Few of *us* are trapped in any of the miserable run-down inner or outer city areas: even those who work in the more nitty-gritty world of the caring professions tend to live at some distance from their clients, understandably but undesirably. Few of such jobs have been open to the 'uncomfortable' other-world of the urban deprived. Development schemes have largely bypassed the poor in the absence of the more effective targeting of resources for which I argued earlier. The tensions of our society like those of Victorian Britain show themselves in unrest and violence. The lessons are plain: Scarman, in his report on the Brixton disorders (Home Office, 1981), quoted President Johnson's introduction to the US report of the National Advisory Commission on Civil Disorders in 1968:

> The only genuine long-range solution for what has happened lies in an attack — mounted at every level — upon the conditions that breed despair and ignorance. All of us know what those conditions are: ignorance, discrimination, slums, poverty, disease, not enough jobs. We should attack these conditions — not because we are frightened by conflict but because we are fired by conscience. We should attack them because there is simply no other way to achieve a decent and orderly society . . .

And that attack has to be something in which we all believe and are willing to participate in. One way of changing inbred attitudes would be a full-scale involvement of young people in the work of regenerating the run-down parts of our cities and in helping the less fortunate in our society. All young people between the ages of 16 and 25 should be expected to participate in such a city service, no matter what their abilities or background. It would do no harm to the supposed academic 'high-flier' to spend a year or 18 months in such activity. The educational treadmill that took so many of us through from 5 to 21 can produce blinkered beings who, fearing the world outside, despise those who do not share their sheltered existence. The idea of education as being a life-long possibility to be dropped in and out of at will is one that needs further development and funding. Such a scheme might go some way both to shaking loose the ordered rigidity of our current educational escalator — an escalator which offers benefits to those who are on it, but few ways back on for those who have once stepped or been pushed off. It might also go some way towards removing the stigma associated with MSC schemes whose unpopularity — manufactured by the purist left — derives from the sense that they are for those who cannot succeed in the 'real' world of proper jobs. It might also further that sense of concern, which materialism has so eroded, for the plight of those in the underbelly of our collapsing cities. Mao-Tse Tung may have gone to extremes when he ordered all academics and teachers to take a turn in the factories and on the farm, but it is that sort of mobility and flexibility we should be looking towards. We need to mix unpopular compulsion with a revivifying sense of central purpose.

DECENTRALISED CONTROL

Such a compulsory scheme also addresses a second vital element of the policy for which we should aim: the need to combat the sense of alienation which stems from the lack of control which the 'uncomfortable' can exert over their own life chances. The unsatisfactory 'top-down' solutions offered by central and local government alike have only emphasised the threadbare short-term nature of urban policy. We need once again to start from the point that 'people are living there'. This has been a vital ingredient of the success of small-scale localised involvement of

213

Housing Associations in refurbishment schemes. The success of many small-scale initiatives has restored hope and pride to the people responsible, whether it be a co-operative self-build, a priority estate project, a Saturday school, a victim support scheme, a neighbourhood watch or a small business. These are not of course solutions, but they bring to an otherwise alienated population an important degree of local control over their own day-to-day circumstances. Targeted to the disadvantaged, among whom the black and Asian populations are so significant a part, such schemes can be used as forms of positive discrimination which can recreate the sense of involvement of local people on which social stability so critically depends.

Community policing is a case in point. Whether such 'community' policing was or was not used in Handsworth — whether or not Broadwater Farm was a Priority Estate Project — is immaterial to the outbreaks of violence in both areas since the real point is that community policing can only succeed, as Margaret Simey rightly says, in 'a stable and law-abiding society'. Writing after the 1981 riots in a fascinating collection of essays (Simey, 1984), she comments:

> Without that [stable and law-abiding society, community policing] is no longer a viable proposition. Nostalgic yearnings after village policemen will get us nowhere in the 1980s. Nor can we acquiesce in the imposition of order by force after the demonstration on our own doorsteps of the disastrous consequences which flow from such a policy. The onus is inescapably on us to see that the police are only asked to undertake that which is within their capacity; the rest is for us to do. It was our failure as a society to set about the conditions in the inner cities which led to the breakdown of social order in the 1980s. Let us not be found wanting twice. The responsibility is ours, and it is one which we cannot delegate to the police.

Developing a degree of local control through more effective decentralisation of a range of local activities is one prerequisite to removing the alienation which has sapped the spirit from local communities in inner areas. We are equally unlikely to develop entrepreneurial enterprise unless the locus of its control is also shifted more firmly to a local level (so that decisions about investment risks can reflect the views of local industrialists and so that local communities and local and regional authorities are given scope to play a more central role in the determination of their economic circumstances). At a national level, the impulse is always to distinguish and compartmentalise the dimensions of social and economic change, not least in the remits of national government departments. Only rarely is a more effective regional integration between agencies achieved. Were regional agencies to be extended to England, it would be important that they were complemented by local small-scale councils with genuinely devolved powers and responsibilities — at the level of estates or neighbourhoods. The more decentralised the structure, the more realistic does such integration become.

NATIONAL WILL

The final, and the most overarching, point is the need for us to agree priorities in policy. While there will always be competing claims from different ministries of central government and therefore a hierarchy of calls on limited national resources, the most effective and efficient use of those resources can only come from policies which do not cancel out one another's effects. Only if there is a national will to tackle the problem of our collapsing cities could such consistency be achieved. Without a genuinely new determination to become the people we so often claim we are, our cities will survive, but only in the horrifying scenario of divided ghettoes that I suggested in my introductory essay. Is that what we really want? President Kennedy, in instigating the American Urban Program, said: 'We will neglect our cities to our peril. For in neglecting them we neglect the nation.' How much more true is that of us in our urban-dominated islands?

REFERENCES

Home Office (1981) *The Brixton disorders 10–12 April 1981*, Report of an Enquiry by the Rt. Hon. The Lord Scarman, Cmnd. 8427, HMSO, London

Simey, M. (1984) 'Partnership policing', in Benyon, J. (ed.), *Scarman and after*, Pergamon Press, Oxford, pp. 135–42

Contributors

David Adams lectures in the Department of Town Planning at the University of Manchester

A. E. Baum is Reader in Valuation at the City University, London

Martin Boddy lectures at the School for Advanced Urban Studies at the University of Bristol

N. Bolton lectures in Geography at Plymouth Polytechnic

Paul Cheshire lectures in the Department of Economics at the University of Reading

Alice Coleman is Director of the Land Use Research Unit at King's College London

Andrew Gillespie is a Research Associate at the Centre for Urban and Regional Development Studies at the University of Newcastle

John Goddard is Professor of Geography and Director of the Centre for Urban and Regional Development Studies at the University of Newcastle

David Grafton lectures in Geography at Plymouth Polytechnic

Bill Lever is Professor in the Department of Social and Economic Research at the University of Glasgow

Derek Lyddon was formerly Chief Planner at the Scottish Office in Edinburgh

Bryan MacGregor lectures in the Department of Planning at the University of Glasgow

Duncan Maclennan is Director of the Centre for Housing Studies at the University of Glasgow

Brian Robson is Professor of Geography and Head of Department at the University of Manchester

Index

Adams, C.D. 4, 14, 216
aerospace industry 68–72
 see also Bristol
anti-urbanism 7

Baratz, M. 110
Barrett, S. 154
Baum, A.E. 4, 14, 216
Bell, D. 40
Berry, B.J.L. 191
Boddy, M.J. 3, 15, 16, 17, 69, 75, 81, 216
Bologna 30–1, 32
Bolton, N. 5, 11, 216
Bradford, M.G. 12
Bristol, general 3–4, 12, 16, 18, 60–1
 aero space industry 68–72
 defence jobs 77
 defence expenditure 72–3
 industrial structure 61–2
 unemployment 60
British Association 2, 5, 6
Brown, S. 144
Bruton, M. 154
Buck, N. 16
Bull, D. 44
Burridge, P. 24
Burrows, J.W. 154
Burton, J.W. 183, 184

Carbonaro, G. 32
Champion, A.G. 191
Checkland, S.G. 182
Cheshire, P.C. 3, 11, 24, 28, 32, 216
city service 213
Cloke, P.J. 192, 206
Coleman, A. 4, 13, 144, 216
Colenutt, R. 155
Cooke, P. 203, 205, 206
counter-urbanisation, definition 191, 200
 explanations 200–4

 see also decentralisation, migration, population change
Crawford, P. 14

d'Abbs 192, 203
Danson, M. 46
Dawson, D.A. 115
deadweight 48, 54
Dean, K. 202
decentralisation of population 26
decentralisation of control 213–15
defence expenditure 72–5, 79–80
 and economic growth 81
 see also Bristol
Department of the Environment 28–9, 45, 151
Derelict Land Grant 170, 174
Devon, study context 192–5
 elderly migrants 200–1
 gender change in labour force 203–4
 migration components 200–2
 planning policies 206–7
 population turnaround 195–8
 social class change 204
Diamond D.R. 48
disadvantagement scores 151–2
disadvantagement threshold 151
displacement 49
Donnison, D. 182
Dunne, J.P. 77, 80

Economic and Social Research Council 3, 15, 211
economic development and local authorities 183–6
 see also Glasgow, Bristol, telecommunications
Edwards, M. 155, 171, 172
Enterprise Allowance Scheme 54